DISNEY, PIXAR, AND THE HIDDEN MESSAGES OF CHILDREN'S FILMS

DISNEY, PIXAR, AND THE HIDDEN MESSAGES OF CHILDREN'S FILMS

M. Keith Booker

PRAEGER
An Imprint of ABC-CLIO, LLC

A B C ☕ C L I O

Santa Barbara, California • Denver, Colorado • Oxford, England

Library of Congress Cataloging-in-Publication Data
Booker, M. Keith.
    Disney, Pixar, and the hidden messages of children's films / M. Keith Booker.
        p. cm.
    Includes filmography.
    Includes bibliographical references and index.
    ISBN 978-0-313-37672-6 (hard copy : alk. paper) — ISBN 978-0-313-37673-3
(ebook) 1. Children's films—United States—History and criticism. 2. Animated
films—United States—History and criticism. 3. Children's films—Political aspects.
4. Motion pictures and children. 5. Walt Disney Company. 6. Pixar (Firm) I. Title.
    PN1995.9.C45B56   2009
    791.43′75083—dc22   2009029420

ISBN: 978-0-313-37672-6
EISBN: 978-0-313-37673-3

14   13   12   11   10   1   2   3   4   5

This book is also available on the World Wide Web as an eBook.
Visit www.abc-clio.com for details.

Praeger
An Imprint of ABC-CLIO, LLC

ABC-CLIO, LLC
130 Cremona Drive, P.O. Box 1911
Santa Barbara, California 93116-1911

This book is printed on acid-free paper (∞)

Manufactured in the United States of America

For Benjamin, Skylor, and Adam

Contents

Personal Prologue

Conservative commentators have, in recent years, gained considerable attention with their claims that America's youth are being corrupted by television and, especially, film. Employing a fairly standard conservative rewriting of history, such commentators have constructed a nostalgic (and mostly fictional) narrative of cultural history that describes the prominence of violence and sexuality in contemporary American popular culture as a decline from earlier days in which popular culture was dominated by more wholesome images. As with most nostalgic narratives, this one constructs a past that never really existed. In point of fact, there has been considerable suspicion about the possible negative influence of film in particular on America's children (and on America as a whole) ever since the inception of the film industry at the beginning of the twentieth century.

As Robert Sklar points out in *Movie-Made America*, his important cultural history of American film, the movies emerged as an important force in American culture "from the bottom up, receiving their principal support from the lowest and most invisible classes in American society" (3). Further, Sklar points out that the American film industry emerged during a crucial turning point in American history, as the explosive growth of consumer capitalism at the turn of the century led to a radical restructuring of American society and in particular the rapid growth of an urban working class that included unprecedented numbers of immigrant workers, newly arrived (mostly from Europe) to feed the ever-expanding demands of burgeoning American capitalism for more (and, preferably, cheaper) labor. The growth of this new class of American workers understandably led to considerable tensions and anxieties; even as these new workers provided the principal fuel for the growth of what we now think of as the American way of life, they were at the time widely regarded as a dangerous threat to established American values.

Given that movies were intimately associated in the American consciousness with this new immigrant working class, it should come as no surprise that there was considerable anxiety about the cultural influence of movies as well. Indeed, for many years it was widely felt that movies were inappropriate fare for children altogether. By the 1930s, however, the film industry was becoming more firmly established as a part of American culture, and children were becoming a more and more important part of the market for that industry. This phenomenon, while reflecting a greater acceptance of film as a cultural form in American society, only served to increase anxieties about the possible negative impact of film on American children. In response, Hollywood began producing films that were overtly designed as wholesome fare suitable for the entire family, with the Disney company emerging in the decade as the leader in the production of movies designed principally for children.

Indeed, as Nicholas Sammond points out, Disney profited substantially from public concerns that movies were bad for children by producing movies specifically designed and marketed as alternatives that were good for children. Meanwhile, social scientists began to undertake studies designed to determine the effects of movies on America's youth. One of the most prominent of these undertakings was a study supported by the Payne Fund of New York City beginning in the spring of 1929, based on the assumption that movies have a powerful and direct influence on young audiences—and that this influence was likely to be negative. The Payne studies involved a large network of psychologists, sociologists, and educational specialists, who studied the supposed effects of movies on America's youth for four years, producing a number of research reports as well as summaries intended for popular audiences.

One of the latter was Henry James Forman's 1934 *Our Movie Made Children*, the title of which provided the inspiration for Sklar's title—ironically so, given Sklar's much more positive vision of film as a cultural phenomenon. For Forman, movies have tremendous educational potential, but one that was not being effectively utilized for the public good. Indeed, Forman argues that the current organization of the film industry (sometimes dominated, he hints with what may be thinly disguised anti-Semitism, by "questionable characters") was "extremely likely to create a haphazard, promiscuous and undesirable national consciousness" (140). For Forman (employing what came to be known as the "hypodermic needle" model of communication), the minds of children begin as "unmarked slates," subsequently to be written upon by the movies, often in morally deplorable ways. Indeed, the tone of moral outrage in Forman's writing is clear, as, upon close examination, is the association of movie-made immorality with immigrants and Jews.

A more moderate public volume produced by the Payne studies was Edgar Dale's *How to Appreciate Motion Pictures: A Manual of Motion-Picture Criticism Prepared for High-School Students* (1938), though this volume involves the same assumption that movies can have a powerful formative influence on young minds. Aimed, as the title notes, at high-school students, Dale's study purports to provide practical advice to that audience on what films to watch and what to look for in those films, thus preparing them to resist the most deleterious effects of movie-watching. Among other things, Dale's vocabulary is avowedly consumerist, putting a great deal of emphasis on "shopping" for films that are appropriate for teenagers. But Dale also puts considerable emphasis on education, arguing that high schools should teach classes in film appreciation so that their students can learn to be better consumers of films. Indeed, Dale's own book seems designed partly to serve as a textbook for such classes. Along these lines, Dale even envisions the possible establishment of government-sponsored schools to train artists to work in the motion-picture industry. Finally, Dale describes his "ideal motion-picture studio," designed not to make profits but to make movies that meet the needs of the people, dominated by artists who seek to make good pictures simply for the satisfaction of producing good work. Casting a haughty and dismissive glance at the glitz and glitter of Hollywood (and, incidentally, making positive comments about the less commercialized film industry of the Soviet Union), Dale concludes by imagining that these film artists of the future will "look with amused contempt on those so-called artists who obtain their satisfactions in the vulgar display of expensive cars, Hollywood villas, and all such glittering trappings" (230).

The complaints of both Forman and Dale foreshadow quite directly the more recent concerns of commentators such as Medved about the possible negative impact of the film industry on America's children. I think, however, that there is an inherent contempt for movies (i.e., an inherent assumption that the effects of movies on kids will be bad) built into many critiques of the film industry and its effects on children. Moreover, it seems to me that the more recent right-wing attacks on the effects of media on children may be informed by a subtle contempt for children as well.[1] These attacks seem to begin with the assumption (unsupported by actual data) that our children have become horrors; there must, therefore, be some reason for this sad state, with popular culture ranking as one of the prime suspects. For my part, I love movies, my kids love movies, and, by and large, I'm happy that my kids love movies, especially given some of the alternative entertainments that are available today. On the other hand, as a parent as well as a film critic, I naturally have concerns about the effects of film (and most other things) on my children, though I suspect that the perspective of my concerns differs from that of Forman, Dale, and Medved. In particular, I share very little of the right-wing concern that movies will teach my kids to be immoral. I don't even worry very much about the liberal concern that the movies will teach my kids to be sexist or racist: I'm pretty sure I can overcome those possibilities (though sexism is more subtly ingrained in American culture than is racism, I think, and therefore harder to surmount). What I really worry about is that movies might teach my kids the mainstream American values of capitalism, such as valuing competition with others more than cooperation, or valuing money more than people.

Among other things, this means that I typically have to read American children's films against the grain, because these films do generally reinforce, at least on the surface, the mainstream values of American capitalism. Moreover, pressure to adhere to certain preconceived norms of acceptability, especially from the Right, means that American children's films are often oppressively banal. The right-wing critique of American media is generally couched in almost entirely negative terms, as declarations of what should *not* appear in children's films, rather than of what *should* appear in such films (other than occasionally vague nods toward "family values"). All too often, this attitude results in the removal of so much material that there is very little left with any real bite to it. The result, for Bazalgette and Staples, is tepid fare that hardly matches up to our society's "much vaunted concern for children and the sanctity of childhood," which should cause us to devote considerable resources to the production of a far richer and more varied body of children's films than currently emanates from the "low-risk, high-yield philosophy" of the children's culture industry (108).

I am, among other things, a professional academic film scholar, and, yes, I should admit up front that I am an unrepentant leftist egghead intellectual. But I am also a dad, and I've come to understand that the complexities and responsibilities associated with being a parent to kids who watch movies need to be dealt with by all parents, eggheads or not, and of whatever political persuasion. I hope I have some special experience to share in this sense, because I'm a professional film critic, but also because I've been a dad for such a long time, including sharing the childhood of my first son *before* I became a film scholar and bona fide egghead intellectual. Some of my fondest memories of times spent with my sons involve viewing movies with them; even if I haven't necessarily always enjoyed the particular movies they've enjoyed, I've always taken pleasure in their enjoyment.

My eldest son, Adam, was born in 1980; my adopted son, Skylor, was born in 1999, though I didn't meet him until 2002, and didn't live with him until the middle of 2003. My youngest son, Benjamin, was born in 2005. So I've had an especially long and varied tour of the world of kids' movies, or at least of movies watched by kids—especially if you consider my own experience as a child, which began around 1958 with the first movie I clearly recall seeing in a theater, a Saturday morning showing of *Queen of Outer Space* (1958), starring Zsa Zsa Gabor, of all people. A dreadful film I now realize, but it must have made quite an impression, and I was so amazed by the spectacle of the big screen that I still remember it, even if I remember very little about the film itself. I have loved science fiction film ever since (and written extensively about it), though I hope my tastes have improved.

Most of my childhood film viewing (whether in theaters or on that new TV thing our family first acquired in 1957) was dominated by the products of the Disney corporation, with films such as the *Davy Crockett* sequence, *Old Yeller* (1957), *Swiss Family Robinson* (1960), and *The Absent-Minded Professor* (1961) engraving themselves indelibly on my consciousness. Looking back, I'm a bit surprised to realize that there are absolutely no animated films in my memory of things that made an impression on me in my childhood, but that might be because Disney issued only one animated feature during my early formative years (1959's *Sleeping Beauty*), and, given the Southern working-class milieu in which I grew up, I (and my parents) probably dismissed that one as being for girls. My own lack of attachment to animated films may provide part of the explanation for the fact that, as Adam was growing up, I never really tried to steer him toward such films. Then again, the 1980s, like the late 1950s, were a relatively dull decade for such films.

When Adam was born, Walt Disney had been dead for fourteen years and the movie studio he founded had been in a slump (especially in animation) ever since, while no other studio had picked up the slack. Disney's business fortunes began to turn around soon after Michael Eisner took the helm of the company in 1984, but it was not until the release of *The Little Mermaid* in 1989 that Walt Disney Pictures began to recover some of the aura of their glory days in movie animation. Consequently, it may be no surprise that, as with my own childhood, none of the movies I remember from Adam's early childhood were animated. I also made no effort to seek out Disney films for him, having become aware of the controversy over the racism, sexism, and imperialism that seemed to be the primary stuff of which these films were made, at least according to some critics. I'm not quite sure, looking back, how clearly I thought about it at the time, but it seems to me in retrospect that I was also especially suspicious of any films that were overtly marketed as children's films, on the premise that they were specifically designed to manipulate young minds and therefore were probably unsuitable viewing for any child whose father wanted him to grow up to challenge received ideas and think for himself. That was a mistake on my part. Children's films may potentially affect children in negative ways, but they have a great potential to reach them in positive ways as well, especially with appropriate parental guidance. And, in any case, children growing up in America will be confronted by a barrage of media all their lives, so it is probably a good idea to learn media-coping skills early on.

In any case, most of the films I watched with Adam weren't really children's films at all, even when he was quite young. Adam started watching movies at age three, just after I got my first VCR (and just as I was involved in my first divorce, which meant that Adam and I had a lot of time together, just the two of us). I myself wasn't a very sophisticated viewer of films at that time; I certainly wasn't a professional student of them as I am now. That was during my first professional incarnation as a research scientist/engineer at the Oak Ridge National Laboratory. To qualify for that position I had a fair amount of technical training and some innate facility with mathematics, but I really had very little of what I would later come to regard as a more important kind of education, education in the humanities. (Most scientists, engineers, doctors, lawyers, and other highly trained and respected professionals—usually thought of as highly educated— similarly lack much in the way of education outside their specific fields, which may be part of the problem with our society today.)

The first movie three-year-old Adam fell in love with was the original *Star Wars* (1977). Maybe I steered him toward science fiction because I was a scientist. Maybe it was that Zsa Zsa Gabor film. Maybe it had something to do with the fact that I had been an avid reader of science fiction since age ten (when I discovered the novels of Andre Norton in my public school library, soon to transition to the hard stuff, like Isaac Asimov and Robert A. Heinlein). Or maybe it was just an accident, because *Star Wars* was broadcast on television just as Adam was getting old enough to watch movies (and just after I had gotten that VCR, so that I could tape it for him). Having seen virtually no television or movies before, Adam was mesmerized by the film, which he clearly regarded as a sort of miracle, even on grainy home-recorded video. Using the then-magical rewind feature, we must have watched the big light-saber fight between Darth Vader and Obi-Wan Kenobi hundreds of times. Ditto for the scene in the giant trash compactor on the Death Star in which most of the heroes are nearly pancaked along with the day's refuse. Back then, in 1983, I saw *Star Wars* as innocent, rollicking, high-adventure entertainment. I've subsequently come to see it as more troubling, but it isn't really a children's film and so is not quite within the purview of my concerns in this book, even if it nicely illustrates the difficulty of drawing a boundary between what qualifies as a children's film and what doesn't.

I should say at this point that I am relatively little troubled by the question of defining just what constitutes a "children's film," though

that question (and allied concerns, such as making distinctions
between children's films and family films) is obviously relevant to
my project in this book. However, rather than attempt a theoretical
definition of the subject matter of this book, I have instead pursued a
pragmatic definition. For me, children's films are largely defined simply as the films that have interested me primarily as potential viewing
matter for my sons. I have also focused almost exclusively on American films as the films that have been most accessible (culturally and
linguistically) to my boys.[2]

The other films Adam enjoyed as a youngster were similarly problematic in terms of their status as children's films, and, looking back,
I'm not sure I can entirely remember my criteria in selecting films for
him to see. My theory then was that he could watch anything he
wanted as long as he watched it with me and as long as we talked
about it together, though of course I greatly influenced his choices by
taping things specifically for him.

The other films he loved in the 1980s (all viewed repeatedly on
homemade videotapes) included Joe Dante's *Gremlins* (1984), which
I guess could qualify as a children's film (or at least a member of that
allied and equally poorly defined species, the family film), though it
would have to be characterized as a children's horror film, which already raises all sorts of questions. And was it really appropriate for a
children's film to feature a scene in which a fuzzy little critter, however vicious, dramatically explodes from being cooked in a micro-
wave oven? (That is the moment both Adam and I remember most
from our original viewings of the film.) *Gremlins*, incidentally, was
produced by Steven Spielberg's Amblin Entertainment, with Spielberg as executive producer. It followed soon after Spielberg's *E.T. the
Extra-Terrestrial* (1982), with which it had much in common, *Grem-
lin*'s cuddly Gizmo joining E.T. as cute creatures misunderstood by
most humans over twenty or so.

Released so closely after *E.T.*, *Gremlins* also announced the arrival
of Spielberg/Amblin as a major player in the children's film business,
even as Disney was struggling to keep its feet. Among other things,
Gremlins was immediately followed by two other genre-bending kids'
films from Amblin that Adam and I also enjoyed. *The Goonies* (1985)
is an action-adventure flick geared toward children, while *Harry and
the Hendersons* (1987) returns to the formula of the benevolent
would-be monster who has to be saved from a suspicious (and

potentially deadly) public. Another genre-crossing favorite was Disney cast-off Tim Burton's *Pee-wee's Big Adventure* (1985), a postmodern satire masquerading as a children's film. I think Adam and I finished off that first VCR endlessly replaying the scene in which the truck driver Large Marge's eyes bulge comically out of her head, frightening the bejesus out of poor Pee-wee. And then there was John Carpenter's *Big Trouble in Little China* (1986), perhaps Adam's favorite film of the whole decade. I never quite understood the appeal of this one, but Adam may have had better judgment than I: the film has stood the test of time and gained something of a cult following (though not primarily among seven- and eight-year-olds, I suspect). There were others Adam liked that I didn't quite take to, such as the three *Karate Kid* movies that appeared in the 1980s.

And then there was Arnold. Anything Arnold, including bloodbath extravanganzas such as *Commando* (1985), which I still regret letting him watch. Not sure what I was thinking on that one, other than some vague reaction against the lunkheads who blame all of the world's ills on the contaminating effects of television and movies on young minds. But *The Terminator* (1984) was definitely worth watching, and Adam and I have enjoyed the subsequent *Terminator* films together as well, not to mention the campy science fiction media satire *The Running Man* (1987) and the underrated *Total Recall* (1990). *Total Recall* will always stand as the first film Adam and I saw in a theater in Fayetteville, Arkansas, when we were in town as a still-single father and son looking for housing in the summer prior to the beginning of my second professional incarnation, this time as an English professor at the University of Arkansas.

Looking back, I realize (though I didn't realize it then) that the 1980s constituted a particularly interesting climate in which to be watching children's films. If nothing else, the weakness of Disney during the decade opened the door for other players (led by Spielberg) to enter the market. This was the decade in which children's film for the first time became market-driven (quickly leading to much greater box-office success for children's films), as filmmakers scrambled to give children what they wanted, as opposed to earlier decades, in which the Disney company, with a stranglehold on the children's film market, basically gave children what Walt wanted. In short, while Disney had in some (and only some) ways stood as a bulwark against the total commodification of children's film, by the 1980s this commodification was virtually complete. Of course, this reduction of works of art to the status of commodities is, for leading theorists of postmodernism such as Fredric Jameson, one of the crucial markers of postmodern art. The increasingly postmodern tendencies of Hollywood film[3] came to bear on children's film in the 1980s in other ways as well, most obviously the tendency to ignore traditional genre boundaries and to mix multiple genres within a single film. In retrospect, it is clear that this phenomenon led to the production of much more interesting and diverse children's films, a phenomenon that has continued over the past two decades, under the leadership of DreamWorks and Pixar.

Incidentally, I might point out that, having received a doctorate in English, I was now much better educated than when I had been a mere government scientist, but I was still not necessarily a sophisticated viewer of film, having studied literature in graduate school and having written my doctoral dissertation on the fiction of James Joyce. On the other hand, by 1991 I was remarried—to a Yugoslav woman who said that she fell in love with me largely because I was the first American man she had met who could actually understand sophisticated movies. Maybe that was part of what inspired me to begin to study movies more seriously, but, alas, Adam was by this time approaching the terrible teens and it was too late for my newfound expertise, gained through the 1990s, to be of much use in helping him negotiate the formative film viewing of his tender young years.

Flash forward to 2003, when Skylor and his mom moved in with me, the Yugoslav woman having departed via another divorce three years earlier. So I suddenly watched far fewer European films and far more kids' films, though I must confess that I had seen the first Pixar film, *Toy Story* (1995), on my own with no kids around, just because I was fascinated by the technology of a completely computer-generated film. In 2003, four-year-old Skylor already had a significant amount of film-viewing experience in which I had played no part, but we subsequently became great movie buddies. It was my first experience viewing movies and television with a young child in the era of easily available video on DVD, a whole different world. Adam and I had watched mostly whatever I could tape from HBO; Skylor and I have had access to virtually every film ever made, though Disney films have still sometimes been a little problematic thanks to their business model, which still involves the periodic removal of their major films from distribution on video, presumably to pump up the market when they are rereleased a few years later for a new batch of kids. (Amazon.com largely solves that problem, of course, with copies of most out-of-print DVDs easily available via their marketplace vendors.)

Skylor also came along after the focus of my professional research had begun to shift toward film and television, so there was the advantage that I knew and understood much more about how films and television programs work. But there was the disadvantage that I had to watch so many things for work that much of what we watched together was part of my research, rather than selected specifically by me as appropriate for him. For example, when Skylor came into my household, I was furiously at work on a book about science fiction television that required me to watch hundreds of hours of everything from *The Twilight Zone* to *Farscape* and *Stargate SG-1*. That took up so much time that most of our initial experience in mutual viewing was of television he didn't enjoy (though there were occasional moments and characters that he liked, such as the shape-shifter Odo from *Star Trek: Deep Space Nine*, who for some reason really captured his imagination). We also watched a sprinkling of movies, which was largely a sort of nostalgia trip for me as I attempted to introduce him to many of the films I had watched earlier with Adam. By and large, he wasn't impressed, though he did take some pleasure in *Pee-wee's Big Adventure,* and he was already a *Star Wars* fan. I quickly discovered that, for kids of his generation, the real *Star Wars* is the prequel trilogy, while the original trilogy seems quaint and outdated.

I moved almost immediately from work on the science fiction television book (which came out in 2004 with the simple and straightforward title *Science Fiction Television*) to work on a book about science fiction film (which would come out in 2006 as *Alternate Americas: Science Fiction Film and American Culture*). So, in the process of working on that book, Skylor and I saw lots of science fiction films, most of which he again found a bit boring. Both *Alien* (1979) and *Blade Runner* (1982) were far too slow and plodding, for example. He did enjoy some films that were peripheral parts of my research, such as *Enemy Mine* (1985), which Adam had also enjoyed as a child. But the *Terminator* films were about the only ones I worked on extensively that Skylor really found interesting. Apparently Arnold is a can't-miss with little boys.

I subsequently wrote books on animated television programs and on films derived from comic books, partly because I thought those might be things Skylor could enjoy watching with me. I have tried to watch a few things with him just for fun, such as all 145 episodes of *Buffy the Vampire Slayer* in the fall of 2006, an experience that still ranks as our most enjoyable mutual viewing ever. I was pleased that Skylor seemed to recognize that *Buffy* was a cut above the typical television program in quality; unfortunately, the experience did not render him immune to the insipid (and possibly sinister—see chapter 2) sitcoms-for-kids that populate the Disney cable/satellite television channel and that have subsequently joined *Buffy, South Park,* and *Family Guy* as his television viewing of choice.

By the beginning of 2007, young Benjamin, approaching two, was ready to start viewing television and film. He, the child of my dotage, born when I was nearly fifty-two, was the first of my sons to be born into the home of a professional scholar of film and television, and I resolved early on (having been unsatisfied with the job I had done with Adam and so far with Skylor) to try to put my expertise to use in helping him to learn to deal with the barrage of popular culture with which he would inevitably be bombarded throughout his life. So I've changed my strategy significantly, encouraging him to watch children's film (though we avoid children's television), but at the same time learning as much about them as I could so that I could help him begin to negotiate, through his engagement with film, the potentially treacherous terrain of American popular culture. The result has been a journey for me through the world of children's film, sometimes accompanied by Benjamin and/or Skylor, sometimes not. It's been a long, strange trip through a foreign land, filled with surprises, both good and bad. I've discovered encouraging gems and disturbing atrocities. This book is my report back to the world of adults.

I am particularly concerned in this report with the political and ideological messages that are conveyed (intentionally or otherwise) to impressionable young viewers by children's film. Here, I adhere largely to the view of the French Marxist theorist Louis Althusser, who felt that the array of ideological messages to which we are exposed throughout our lives does not simply influence us to think about the world in certain ways but is quite literally responsible for calling us into being as thinking individuals and for making us who we are. Further, Althusser identifies ideology not simply as an illusion that hides the truth of social practices but as the material fabric within which those practices are necessarily carried out. Althusser's goal, then, is not to avoid or overcome ideology (which would be impossible), but to attempt to understand and delineate its workings so that individual subjects can interact with ideology in more critical and productive ways. In this same way, I hope in this book to help adults better understand the messages encoded in children's film so that they can help the children in their lives engage these messages in productive (and, possibly, resistant) ways.

This Althusserian line of reasoning also implies that, more than responding to children's tastes and desires, children's films largely shape those tastes and desires, molding young viewers into ideal consumers not only for children's films but for the other products produced by our consumerist society. One might, of course, make this same claim about popular culture in general (though the exact mechanisms involved are the subject of much debate in the field of cultural studies), but the question is particularly urgent when it involves young viewers who are presumably much more impressionable and susceptible to suggestion than older and more sophisticated audiences.

Given the inexperience of young viewers, it seems pretty clear that movies go a long way toward creating the tastes of young audiences. However, it is also the case that young children who watch movies are exposed to a variety of other stimuli that help to shape them as individuals and determine the kinds of things that they find entertaining. Television, of course, is foremost among these, and as such the specter of television haunts the margins of my account of children's film. I will, however, have relatively little to say about television in this account, other than to say that my limited experience in watching kids' TV leads me to believe that it is a fundamentally different phenomenon than children's film. For one thing, children's films tend to be doubly coded, containing some elements that are designed to appeal to (and send messages to) young viewers and others that are designed for the adults who accompany the youngsters to the movie theater. Indeed, because filmmakers now tend to perceive children's films as potential blockbusters, they tend to try to appeal to the largest possible audience, so that even the children's elements of these films are designed for a range of ages; thus, Skylor and Benjamin can often enjoy the same films, even if they enjoy them for different reasons. Television, on the other hand, seems aimed at a much more focused demographic, with some programming aimed at, say, three- and four-year-olds, some for nine- and ten-year olds, some for teenagers, and so on. One suspects, in addition, that kids' TV does not worry much about appealing to adults because there is much less expectation that adults will watch the programming along with the kids, however much they should. Indeed, it appears that much of the point of such programming is to serve as a surrogate parent, keeping kids occupied for a few moments while their parents do other things. Meanwhile, having removed young viewers from adult supervision, the programs can do their real work, which is get the kids positioned in front of the TV so that they can be hit with niche advertising, aimed at their particular demographic. For this reason, I discourage Benjamin, especially, from watching commercial television and try to limit his viewing as much as possible to commercial films. Even so, he does occasionally see some TV, and I can report that, even at his young age he responds very directly to advertising, proclaiming "I wish I had that!" in response to virtually every ad he sees.

Indeed, if one wishes to find sinister threats to our children in the media, I suspect that the main culprit is almost certainly television advertising, not films, or even television programming. Not a very controversial claim, I know, but it is also the case that, however sinister, television advertising aimed at children has received very little serious study, partly because it is a vast yet ephemeral text that is incredibly difficult to get a handle on. Children's film, on the other hand, is a different matter. Though there are a slew of made-for-TV and straight-to-video children's films, major theatrical films for children are relatively small in number. They also have unusually long lives, living (especially on DVD) well beyond their presence in theaters. This fact makes children's film as a phenomenon manageable for a critic like me, and also makes individual children's films particularly important because they are often viewed again and again, thus becoming integral parts of children's worlds. Parents and others who care about children, then, should be particularly interested in learning what these films are really saying—as should readers who are simply fascinated by the enduringly provocative subtexts of some of America's most popular movies.

——— 1 ———

Disney Does America: A Political History of Children's Film

While films that might appeal to children are essentially as old as film itself, it is also the case that the entire medium had such an unsavory reputation in its early years that, in the eyes of many, filmgoing was by definition an unacceptable activity for children. It was not, indeed, until the Hollywood film industry exploded in importance in the 1930s that feature-length films that might be characterized as "children's films" began to emerge as an identifiable cultural phenomenon. Even then, many of these films, which often featured child stars such as Shirley Temple, Mickey Rooney, and Judy Garland, were not oriented so much toward children as toward families, hoping to appeal to parents while at the same time assuring parents that it was okay to bring along the kids. One could, in fact, make a very good argument that the first genuine feature-length children's film was Walt Disney's inaugural feature, the 1937 classic *Snow White and the Seven Dwarfs*. Meanwhile, that this film was also the first animated feature is no coincidence, but indicates the close relationship that has existed ever since between children's film and animated film.

Snow White was a watershed film in a number of ways, building upon Disney's earlier animated shorts to establish many of the conventions that would dominate children's film for decades. These conventions, of course, involve among other things a number of basic suppositions about what is appropriate for children, but they also involve a number of fundamental assumptions about what children themselves are like—or should be like. A quick look at *Snow White* shows that Disney, early on, was working with these assumptions about the tastes (and needs) of young viewers (in addition to the basic assumption that children like animation and find animated characters and settings appealing). These might be called the structural assumptions of Disney animated films, and should be carefully distinguished from the ideology embodied in these films:

- Animated animals (presented so as to appear friendly and unthreatening to humans) have an innocence that makes them especially appealing to children. These animals can serve as stand-ins for children, and thus the films need not have children as characters.
- Children enjoy music, and strategically inserted musical numbers help to hold the attention of young viewers.
- Magic is an especially effective and appealing motif for young viewers.
- Children find slapstick violence quite entertaining, especially as animated characters can emerge unscathed from such violence.
- While a certain amount of violence and danger help to keep children interested in the plot, all threats must be successfully banished, leading to a joyful, happy ending.
- Children must be protected from any hint of sexuality, up to and including the virtual elimination of parents from the lives of the characters.
- If physical labor is depicted, it must be shown to be pleasant, enjoyable, and highly rewarding as an activity in its own right.

Snow White is an absolutely charming film, though it is, in fact, a bit dated now, despite its supposedly timeless fairy-tale subject matter. Thus, while the film contains enduring songs such as "Whistle While You Work" and "Heigh-ho," the singing style, especially the quivering coloratura of Snow White herself (as performed by Adriana Caselotti), seems decidedly old-fashioned to twenty-first-century ears. (Skylor's take: "They thought that sounded *good?*") Similarly, the famous opening, which shows the opening of a book of fairy tales to begin the story, was at the time reasonably clever (and appropriate, given that the film opened a new chapter in cinema history). But it has been replicated so many times that it is now a cliché, mocked as such even in the opening of Disney's own *Chicken Little* (2005). The same might be said for the film's ending, which shows Snow White and Prince Charming riding away together on a gallant steed (she riding demurely sidesaddle, of course), followed by on-screen text assuring us that "they lived happily ever after." Much about the actual content of the film seems dated as well. For example, the highly condescending treatment of the dwarfs through most of the film would probably never pass muster in today's politically correct environment, though it was absolutely uncontroversial in the 1930s. Meanwhile, the film depicts Snow White as an essentially helpless victim who must be saved by a man and whose main talents seem to involve singing and doing housework. It is certainly the case that Disney's treatment of gender—especially in the representation of the long line of Disney princesses—has been problematic over the years. And much of the considerable criticism of Disney on this score is quite justified. After all, if children's movies, far more than adult movies, present their audiences with role models that are crucial to the development of their own identities, then such issues are of crucial importance. Indeed, Amy M. Davis, in her recent book *Good Girls and Wicked Witches* (2007), has argued that Disney's films have been perhaps the single most powerful force in determining expectations about feminine behavior in American society as a whole since the 1930s. For my part, my kids are all boys, but if any were girls, I'd be especially worried about the Disney princess, passively waiting until "some day my prince will come," as a role model. I also worry about the images of girls that my boys might develop from such models. On the other hand, the depiction of Snow White is certainly no more stereotypically sexist than were the depictions of women in many other films of the day, even though it is also the case that specific stars (such as Katharine Hepburn and Bette Davis) were at that time projecting feminine strength and independence that went against this grain.

Maybe the old-fashioned feel of *Snow White* (and it seems designed to have that sort of feel, kicked off by the absolute anteriority of its "once upon a time" beginning), even in 1937, explains why Benjamin simply won't watch it. He's accustomed to the more high-energy feel of the Pixar and *Shrek* films, after all. Skylor doesn't much like it, either, though I must admit that he is highly entertained by what to me is the most troubling aspect of the film, that being the consistent pummeling taken by the poor dwarf Dopey, who is the object of most of the film's slapstick violence. Dopey is at least a generation younger than the other dwarfs (though there is no indication that any of them might be his father), but (as his name indicates) he is clearly mentally challenged, which is what makes his treatment in the films seem so troubling to me. On the other hand, when I expressed this concern to Skylor, he told me to lighten up, and maybe he was right, though I still haven't quite figured out what to make of his follow-up comment that "smart people just aren't funny."

Anyway, while Disney certainly does considerable violence to the original Brothers Grimm fairy tale from which its story is taken, it does produce a fairy-tale feel. For example, the requisite prince does come to save the day (with an assist from the seven dwarfs), defeating the designs of the evil queen and riding away with Snow White, presumably to make her his princess. Then again, one has to ask whether this is really a fairy-tale ending or just a Hollywood ending. After all, many Hollywood films of the day ended rather similarly, though of course this ending (like the dreamlike texture of the entire film) has a special resonance within the dark Depression years of the 1930s, when any number of Hollywood filmmakers subscribed to the theory that they could best serve (or at least attract) filmgoers by providing them with escapist fare that would get their minds off their very real day-to-day troubles.

My point here concerns the way in which children's films and Disney films in particular have conscripted the fairy tale and produced a Hollywoodized or Disneyfied version that has long been the principal way in which fairy tales are experienced by American children. Thus, *Snow White and the Seven Dwarfs* is not just the Disney version of that particular tale: it is the only version that many children in the past seven decades have ever experienced. Further, *Snow White* serves as the prototype for all subsequent fairy-tale films, which makes it particularly important to be cognizant of the fact that Disney made such dramatic changes to the meaning of the tale in the film adaptation. As fairy-tale scholar Jack Zipes notes, the original story is based on a rather medieval form of "might makes right" ideology in which the evil queen and Snow White battle for supremacy, with the latter coming out on top. The film, on the other hand, is a much more subtle argument in favor of obedience, conformism, and orderliness. As Zipes puts it, the images of the home of the seven dwarfs "are all clean-cut, suggesting trimmed lawns of suburban America and symmetrical living as models. To know your place and do your job dutifully are the categorical imperatives of the film" (128). Zipes further notes the crucial role played by the dwarfs in Disney's cleansed and saccharine version of the tale, serving as they do as happily obedient model workers who contrast sharply with the sometimes unruly work-force of 1930s America (and, oddly enough, the soon-to-be unruly workforce in Disney's own studios).

One might add that the tidy home of the dwarfs is actually a mess until Snow White arrives to clean it up, with an assist from her little animal pals. In other words, a tidy suburban home is a female prov-ince; men are supposed to go out into the world and work for pay, happy in the confident knowledge that no matter how lowly their posi-tion in the workplace, they can go home at night to become kings of their own castle, kept for them by the little woman. In addition, one might add that, in its own way, Disney's version of the tale is just as much about power as is the Brothers Grimm version, except that the original tale is based on a medieval conception of power as a matter of physical force, while the Disney version is based on a much more modern (and sophisticated) vision of power as a matter of much more subtle psychological manipulation. More importantly, the workings of power are, in the Disney film, displaced from the characters inside the tale to the audience outside it, as the film pursues its openly didactic course of providing models for proper behavior.

Of course, Disney was hardly a dominant force in American culture when *Snow White* was released in 1937, though Disney's short car-toons had already become an important part of the mediascape. Mickey Mouse had become a cultural icon, well known not only through the short films in which he was featured but also through the extensive (and pioneering) co-marketing campaign through which Mickey Mouse merchandise had become a prominent presence in mil-lions of American homes. *Snow White* (referred to throughout the film industry as "Walt's folly" during its making) was a surprising success and certainly helped to propel the Disney company into the future, but it is only in retrospect that it can be seen as such a prototype for later films. Seen through the optic of the later films that followed, *Snow White*, in addition to its obvious assumptions about the elements that go into the making of a successful animated film for children, al-ready begins to show the beginnings of what would come to be a well-developed discourse of Disney animated films, embodying a number of fundamental assumptions about the world and children's relationship to it.

As numerous commentators have noted, Disney's animated films seem predicated upon an assumption of childhood as a time of innocence, with maturation into adulthood involving a loss of this innocence. I would go further, to suggest that Disney's animated films also seem to assume a model of history in which the passage through time of American civilization mirrors the growth of an individual child, making the past a locus of innocence (and the further back in the past, the more innocent the time), with the progression into modernity involving a loss of that innocence. This dual narrative of individual and social maturation as loss of innocence tends to give Disney's animated films a strongly nostalgic air, because the past is always a better time than the present, assuming (as Disney's films generally do) that innocence is preferable. In addition, it is important to examine just what constitutes Disney's particular definition of what innocence entails.

Most obviously, Disney's definition of innocence involves a sense of wonder and magic: for Disney children believe in magic and live lives that are filled with wonder, just as earlier generations of human beings had a greater experience of the magical. Magic, indeed, is one of the key ingredients of everything Disney: the Magic Kingdom is not only the designation of the central attraction at both Disneyland and Disney World, but might also be used to designate the overall world of Disney's animated films. In this sense, Disney pretty much adheres to the vision of history put forth by the pioneering German sociologist Max Weber, who felt that capitalist modernization had impoverished human experience by stripping the world of magic. Weber argues that the worldviews of Protestantism and of capitalist modernity share numerous important characteristics and that Protestantism is a rationalized form of religion that lacks the reliance on magic of many other religions, including Catholicism. Working in the early years of the twentieth century, Weber believed that the growth of Western capitalism (aided by the spread of Protestantism) had led to a thoroughly rationalized view of the world. In it, every aspect of life (including religion) is understood through and regulated by scientific principles, leading to a sense of reality that is completely stripped of any sense of wonder and magic.[1]

Less obvious (but potentially more important) is the way in which Disney's animated films have consistently associated innocence with a constellation of images involving the natural, the real, and the authentic. This cult of authenticity is perhaps the most crucial element that underlies the discourse of the Disney animated film from the very beginning. Snow White, like so many Disney protagonists after her, is faced with a threat that makes it impossible for her to be her true self and to occupy her rightful role in life. The resolution of the plot then entails her success in surmounting this difficulty to assume her natural place in life and to return to her authentic self as a princess. The key-words associated with this discourse—"authentic," "true," "real," "natural," "rightful," and so on—all sound good, but this emphasis has troubling implications that run directly counter to the mainstream ideology of American capitalism, an ideology Disney films have often been assumed to exemplify. After all, one of the key elements of American ideology is the notion of virtually unlimited upward mobility, which assumes that anyone can be anything if they want it passionately enough and work for it long enough and hard enough. This notion involves an extremely fluid notion of identity which assumes that our identities are not determined by our origins but our actions. The Disney vision that we have a true, real, authentic, natural, original identity runs directly counter to this ethos of mobility and is in fact quite central to the worldview of medieval Europe, which saw identity as fixed and determined by birth, while at the same time viewing society itself as ideally stable, any change necessarily involving decay.

That Disney's animated films seem informed by a medieval view of individual identity and social history might explain the fact that these films have had their greatest successes in settings that are essentially medieval, involving protagonists who are born aristocrats, fated for greatness. But this medieval worldview directly contradicts not only the liberal bourgeois vision that is central to American democracy, but also the ostensible ideology of the films themselves, which have so often been taken (with the encouragement of the Disney company) as paradigms of the representation of American ideology in popular culture. Disney films are in fact shot through with such contradictions, sending decidedly mixed messages that must surely be confusing to young audiences.

To see that this emphasis on the rightness of the natural order of things is a distinct property of Disney films and not necessarily one of children's films in general (though Disney would soon come to define the terms of those films), one need only look at the next great children's film to appear after *Snow White*, but one that appeared early enough that the entire discourse of children's film had not yet come to be dominated by Disney. This film, *The Wizard of Oz* (1939), was produced by MGM, one of the biggest of the major studios, thus announcing that children's film was potentially becoming big business, though the then-tiny Disney would continue to dominate the field for decades to come. *The Wizard of Oz* is still considered by many to be the greatest children's film of all time. I can remember that, with no access to recorded video, the annual television broadcast of the film was one of the most important and eagerly anticipated cultural phenomena of my own childhood, even though we only had a small black-and-white TV and I didn't realize until much later that most of the film was actually in color. My kids are lucky enough to see the film in color on a big-screen TV, and Benjamin loves it, though Skylor finds it too slow and plodding for his tastes. (He is also disappointed by the wicked witch's flying monkeys, which I assured him would be really scary, but which he merely finds silly looking.) In any case, *The Wizard of Oz* ranks tenth on the American Film Institute's latest list of the top 100 American films of all time, making it the highest-rated children's film on the list.[2] Steven Spielberg's *E.T. the Extra-Terrestrial*, which might be considered a children's film, is second at twenty-fourth on the list, while *Snow White* (still the top-ranking animated film on that list) comes in at thirty-fourth. The only other children's film (or animated film) on the list is *Toy Story*, which barely makes it in at ninety-ninth.[3]

The Wizard of Oz is a live-action musical based on what was then a relatively recent novel, L. Frank Baum's *The Wonderful Wizard of Oz* (1900), and it was adapted to reflect the late-1930s Depression-era setting in which it was produced.[4] It would thus seem at first glance to have little in common with an animated, fairy-tale film like *Snow White*. On the other hand, slightly closer inspection shows that the two films have a surprising number of things in common, both featuring female protagonists who get help from charming, quirky sidekicks in defeating the machinations of an evil female witch/crone so that they can return from exile to their proper homes.

In fact, except for the lack of animation, *The Wizard of Oz* adheres quite closely to the seven basic structural characteristics I associated with *Snow White* earlier in this chapter. However, it lacks the celebration of the natural and the authentic that is embedded in *Snow White*, instead celebrating, through its figure of the lovable huckster wizard, image-making and sleight of hand. The very fact that it is a live-action film sets *The Wizard of Oz* apart from *Snow White* in important ways, immediately suggesting a greater engagement with contemporary reality, as opposed to the absolutely anterior setting of the Disney film, which disengages it from the world of contemporary reality. Similarly, the Russian theorist Mikhail Bakhtin argues that the novel differs from the epic most importantly in the way the former engages contemporary historical reality, while the epic is set in an absolute past that is entirely disconnected from the flow of history. Indeed, that the filmmakers clearly sought to engage their contemporary world is signaled by the fact that they added an extensive frame story set in Depression-era Kansas that goes well beyond the brief Kansas scenes in the novel. As part of this frame story, the film stipulates that Dorothy Gale's adventure in Oz is a mere dream she experiences while unconscious from a head injury, so that the film contains no real magic at all, as opposed to the genuine magic that inhabits the very center of the Disney universe. This is again a calculated deviation from Baum's book, in which Oz is real: Dorothy, in the sequels, ultimately returns there to enjoy its consumerist splendor with Uncle Henry and Auntie Em.

The Wizard of Oz also seems more realistic than *Snow White* in that its protagonist (memorably played by Judy Garland) is not a fairy-tale princess, but an ordinary Kansas farm girl. Further, she assumes the role of protagonist not because of her royal birth, but seemingly by chance, as she just happens to be in the right place at the right time to be blown (at least in her own mind) to Oz by a tornado that hits her farmhouse. Additionally, Dorothy ultimately succeeds by struggling against adversity and not because it is in her nature to succeed. She does get a little help from the (all-male) group of companions that she gradually accumulates while in Oz, but she lacks the help of a masculine rescuer in the mode of Prince Charming. Her would-be rescuer, instead, is the eponymous Wizard, a humbug who is anything but authentic and who ultimately does nothing to help Dorothy return home. Further, he helps her friends only through a quintessentially American strategy that is based largely on the notion that image is everything: the Tin Man gains a heart because he is given a testimonial to his goodness; the Scarecrow acquires a brain simply by getting a diploma, and the Cowardly Lion gets courage because he gets a medal attesting to his valor. This motif, of course, reflects a basic ideology of identity as performance that is virtually the polar opposite of the essentialist Disney emphasis on the true and the natural.

For her part, Dorothy learns that all she needs is to believe that she has the power to return home just by clicking the heels of her ruby slippers together, and magically she can do it. The film thus potentially delivers a message about feminine confidence and capability, even if the more fundamental point would seem merely to be an endorsement of good old American individualism and the power of positive thinking—a mode of thought that, in 1939, was becoming more and more difficult as the Depression lingered on year after year while the world drifted toward war.

That *The Wizard of Oz* is a thorough endorsement of Americanism can also be seen in its second, less obvious deviation from *Snow White*, the way in which it serves as an all-out celebration of capitalist consumerism. *Snow White* resides in a world outside of history, but it is roughly placed in a medieval, precapitalist setting; its nostalgic tone suggests, however vaguely, that there was something preferable about the good old days before the capitalist rat race. *The Wizard of Oz*, on the other hand, begins in contemporary Depression-era Kansas (the poverty of which is signaled by the film's sepia-toned opening scenes), then moves to the brilliant, Technicolor world of Oz. Importantly, however, this movement does not represent a step back in time, but forward in capitalist efficiency. Oz (especially the Emerald City) is a land of wealth, and the wizard—a sort of cross between Thomas Edison and P. T. Barnum—gets by on ingenuity and sleight of hand rather than magic as he leads the land to prosperity.

Baum's original novel, written and published just as consumerism was beginning its inexorable rise to the center of the American experience, is even more overt than the film in its endorsement of consumerist ideas. Indeed, William Leach, in *Land of Desire*, his impressive study of the rise of American consumerism at the beginning of the twentieth century, singles out Baum's novel and its sequels as a key marker in the historical development of the ethos of consumerism.

The film treats Dorothy's return to the reality of Kansas as a good thing, ultimately delivering its "there's no place like home" message in a manner clearly meant to be reassuring to Depression-era audiences. *The Wizard of Oz* provides both a thrilling Technicolor escape from the gray doldrums of the Depression and a simultaneous message that no such escape is really necessary. But Dorothy's return to Kansas is not a happily ever after triumph in the manner of *Snow White*, in which the natural order has been restored and therefore all

problems overcome. Indeed, the ending of *The Wizard of Oz* represents a disavowal of permanent, magical (and rather un-American)
solutions of the kind embodied in *Snow White*. Dorothy awakes in a
Kansas that is still poor and where her day-to-day problems will continue to be very real.

The Wizard of Oz was only a moderate commercial success upon its
initial release and did not really become the iconic film that it now
appears to be until the annual television showings that began in 1959
and that constituted such an important part of the cultural framework
of my own childhood. It did exert an obvious influence on subsequent
films, such as the 1940 Shirley Temple vehicle *The Blue Bird*, but the
onset of World War II largely put children's fantasy films on hold.[5]
Disney, however, having constructed a new studio with the profits
made from *Snow White*, stepped up production in the years leading up
to the war. This move nearly drove the company into bankruptcy, but
also put them in a position to emerge from the war as the unchallenged leader in the children's film market.

Disney's second feature-length film, *Pinocchio* (1940), is the most
down-to-earth of the classic Disney animated films, despite its "wish
upon a star" theme song and its continued use of magic as a crucial
motif. In particular, the film requires its protagonist to work to prove
his worth, which seems more in line with the ethos of capitalism than
do most of these films. *Pinocchio* even involves a sort of upward mobility plot in which the eponymous protagonist improves on his initial
status, as opposed to most Disney films, in which the protagonist simply regains the position he or she should have had in the first place.
The plot arc of *Pinocchio* is thus unusual for Disney films, in which
the plot typically begins with a disruption (typically magical) that displaces the protagonist from an initial position of authenticity and is
then resolved when the initial position is regained. *Pinocchio*, however, begins with a protagonist who is a mere manmade artifact, and
thus not natural. A magical intervention (on the part of the benevolent
Blue Fairy) then brings the eponymous puppet to life and sends him
on the road to authenticity as a "real boy," though he must work to
prove himself worthy of this new status.

The emphasis on the real and the authentic is thus preserved, how-
ever different the plot of *Pinocchio* might otherwise be from other
Disney animated films. Meanwhile, the particular plot structure of
Pinocchio helps to make it Disney's most overtly didactic film, the

one that offers the most in terms of practical lessons and advice for dealing with the world. Given life and the potential to be a real boy by the magical Blue Fairy, the wooden puppet Pinocchio can realize that potential only if he proves himself to be "brave, truthful, and unselfish." He ultimately does so, of course, thus fulfilling the dream of his loving creator Gepetto to have a son (without, apparently, the inconvenience of having to deal with the child's mother). There are, though, troubles along the way, and Pinocchio gets into considerable difficulty when he falls prey to the seductions of easy fun, rather than hard work, thus providing cautionary lessons to young viewers. The obvious message of the film is simply that kids should go to school rather than play hooky. However, as Nicholas Sammond points out, the real message of the movie is that "indulgence in the pleasures of the working class, of vaudeville, or of pool halls and amusement parks, led to a life as a beast of burden. Ultimately, one was either a manager or managed, and the choices one made determined the outcome" (78).[6]

Sammond very effectively demonstrates the crucial role played by Disney in the period 1930–1960 in evolving conceptions of what constituted a child (especially an American child), of what childhood should be like, and of how parents could best prepare their children for a successful future life. Not surprisingly, *Pinocchio* is for Sammond the central film in Disney's stable, because it is the one that most clearly seeks to help convey to children the "middle-class virtues of deferred gratification, self-denial, thrift, and perseverance, naturalized as the experience of the most average American" (78). For Sammond, however, Disney's films were only a small part of the company's efforts in this regard, which also included a whole panoply of public relations maneuvers, including the creation of an extensive personal mythology around the figure of Walt Disney himself, who became the embodiment of that "most average American."

Sammond's emphasis on middle-class virtues suggests that the overall political implications of the classic Disney films are not really right wing, as has sometimes been charged, but are, in fact, solidly middle-of-the-road, and calculatedly so. Disney films and other products have, in fact, tended to dismiss and denigrate working-class culture, but in the very all-American mode that has seen working-class American parents, certainly since the difficult days of the 1930s, themselves almost universally hoping that their children could rise to become middle class. However, within this middle-class ethos, Disney is consistently conservative in its easy naturalization of the class structure of contemporary capitalism and its assumption that there will always be winners and losers (managers and managed, as Sammònd puts it), so that the best parents can hope for is to teach their children to be one of the winners.

Indeed, there are more contradictions in the ideology of the classic Disney films than Sammond indicates, partly because he puts so much emphasis on *Pinocchio*, the most solidly middle class of all of these films. Among other things, Disney's emphasis on the real, the natural, and the authentic implies that children are naturally either winners or losers by birth, which seems contrary to the official American vision. Granted, Disney's vision of a preordained, proper status for each individual does sometimes seem to echo belief in predestination that is central to Calvinism, which Weber and others have seen as a crucial component of the historical rise of capitalism. Indeed, the New England Puritans, so crucial to the development of the modern American mindset, were Calvinists. However, Disney's vision of the natural and the authentic, based more on heredity than election, seems more medieval than Calvinist, especially given the proclivity toward medieval settings in the classic Disney films. (Tellingly, *Pinocchio* has a vaguely nineteenth-century setting.)

That Disney films are so often taken (for better or for ill) to embody typical all-American virtues is a testament to the overall power of American ideology, which has so effectively instilled the vast majority of Americans with a confident belief that all things good and wholesome are associated with Americanness, while anything opposed to the American way must be vile and depraved. Disney films are overtly designed to appear good and wholesome; ergo, they must well represent traditional American values. Thus, parents who, like myself, would want their children to question whether society must or even should be structured according to an opposition between winners and losers, will find little support in Disney films—or in most other American films, for that matter. However, the Disney version of a world made up of winners and losers differs from the official American version in that, in the world of the classic Disney animated films, the winners win because they are fated to do so, not because they do the right things (presumably through rectitude and hard work, though surely talent, opportunity, and luck are involved as well) to succeed.

The dog-eat-dog worldview of capitalism is a fairly brutal one, but the Disney notion of success via entitlement is a real killer, leaving no room for those who are not winners by birth to ever have a chance at success. This is not to say that the Disney company is engaged in a nefarious plot to foist this vision on America's children—or even that they themselves are aware that this vision is embedded in their classic films. To some extent, this vision simply comes about as a natural result of the proclivity for medieval settings in Disney's early films. The medieval horror of change and insistence on everyone staying in their natural places in many ways runs directly contrary to the Disney company's characteristic pride in its own innovations, both techno- logical and aesthetic, though the latter occurred mostly in the com- pany's early years. *Snow White* was certainly a major breakthrough in the art of animation, putting Disney at the very forefront of the form. *Pinocchio*, however, shows only minor technical advancements over *Snow White*. *Pinocchio* was also a very expensive film to make and one that did not do well at the box office, leaving the Disney company in financial disarray—which makes it all the more impressive that Disney would then immediately embark not on a quest for cash but on its most ambitious and innovative period of aesthetic innovation, in the form of two remarkablly experimental, even avant-garde, films: *Fantasia* (1940) and *Dumbo* (1941).

Fantasia is essentially a series of music videos (thus making Disney one of the inventors of that form) in which various well-known refrains from classical music are accompanied by animated on-screen sequences featuring everything from dancing hippos to abstract explo- sions of psychedelic color. Due to the latter, incidentally, the film gained a certain reputation in the 1960s as an excellent "drug movie," but it has primarily been discussed as an effort on the part of the Dis- ney company either to gain some artistic prestige for itself or to bring high culture to the masses. I have no desire to enter into those discus- sions here, because *Fantasia* is not really a children's film, though it is a fascinating one. My interest here is primarily in *Dumbo*, which immediately followed *Fantasia* and which showed many of the same aesthetic sensibilities, but in a film that was clearly designed to appeal to children.

Dumbo is, in my opinion, a stunning masterpiece, the pinnacle of the artistic achievement of the Disney company and one of the aes- thetic high points in the history of American film. It's another of those famous Disney animated films that I never saw as a child and in fact only saw for the first time with Benjamin and Skylor. Skylor, incidentally, doesn't share my enthusiasm for the film, but Benjamin does, and it now ranks as one of his absolute favorites. Compared to *Pinocchio*, *Dumbo* was a low-budget effort, employing watercolor backgrounds and relatively simple animation. But it is also a daring film that takes numerous chances with both the music and the visuals, possibly precisely because of the low budget. It also takes a number of narrative chances, such as employing a protagonist who does not speak throughout the film, but relies entirely on nonverbal expressions to gain audience sympathy and identification. *Dumbo* was a great commercial success that, after the back-to-back financial fiascos of *Pinocchio* and *Fantasia*, saved the Disney company from economic ruin. Unfortunately, the film (the making of which was punctuated by the bitter Disney animators' strike of the spring of 1941)[7] also marked the end of Disney as a pioneer in the exploration of genuinely new artistic territory. After *Dumbo*, the Disney company became a corporate film factory, even though a very important one. Partly because of World War II, the company moved away from its emphasis on animated films in the next few years. After the war they continued to move more and more into live-action film, never again focusing on animation to the extent they had in the early years. Indeed, their most important innovations in animation in the years after *Dumbo* involved the mixing of live action with animation rather than anything truly original in the animation itself.

Dumbo begins with a relatively unpromising sequence in which a flock of storks bring newborn babies to various animal mothers (including a bear, a kangaroo, a hippo, and a tiger, though the mother elephant is left waiting) who are wintering with a circus in Florida. But this presentation of the most clichéd of all efforts to efface the sexual realities of reproduction does little to prepare us for what follows, beginning with the truly charming sequence in which the highly stylized circus train (the train is one of Benjamin's favorite characters in the film) is loaded up with animals and equipment. The train then heads north to begin the new circus season, at one point (despite the flat Florida terrain) having to struggle up a steep hill in the manner of the "little engine that could." On the way, Mrs. Jumbo, the mother elephant, finally has her offspring delivered (elephants do, after all, have an unusually long gestation period). Unfortunately, the adorable

Jumbo, Jr., comes equipped with gigantic ears that make him the object of mockery among the pretentious biddies who constitute the remainder of the circus's elephant brigade. The biddies rename the baby Dumbo, and the name sticks, though the baby seems unconcerned thanks to his mother's solicitous care.

Eventually, the train arrives at its initial destination, leading to the film's first truly standout sequence, in which the elephants aid the circus's contingent of roustabouts in putting up the big top and preparing for the circus to begin. The human workers in this scene are all black and completely faceless, which can be taken either as a racist and classist dismissal of their value as individual human beings or as a critique of their treatment as commodities by their bosses. Indeed, this whole sequence seems poised precariously between genuine proletarian art and racist antiworker propaganda. Some of the lyrics in this song are problematic and seem to denigrate the workers as irresponsible (they sing, for example of throwing their pay away as soon as they get it), while their declaration of themselves as "happy-hearted" despite their exploitative treatment by the circus seems to make light of the genuine difficulty of their lives. And yet there is an earthy vitality to their chant-like song, which suggests something admirable about their ability to maintain their spirits despite the conditions under which they live. Meanwhile, their interchangeability and facelessness also contribute to their ability to work rhythmically together in the collective enterprise of raising the tent.

Any reading of the treatment of labor in *Dumbo* (and it is the Disney film that treats the issue most extensively) must, of course, be read through the bitterness of the animators' strike that shattered the tranquility of the Disney studios just as the production of *Dumbo* was drawing to its conclusion. The strike was organized by the Screen Cartoonists' Guild in response to Disney's arbitrary and inconsistent labor policies and the apparent efforts of the company to prevent unionization of its employees, including the firing of key animator Art Babbitt, perceived by the company as a pro-union troublemaker. The strike lasted five weeks but had repercussions that lasted much longer. Indeed, though a federal mediator helped end the strike reasonably quickly (ruling in favor of the strikers on every point), the studio was never again the same. Most of the strike leaders left (or were driven out of) the company soon after the end of the strike, and many felt that the exodus left the company seriously short of creative talent. Some of the most important animators to leave Disney in the wake of the strike, figures such as Zack Schwartz, Dave Hilberman, and John Hubley, went on to found their own animation studio, United Productions of America (UPA). These founders were eventually joined at UPA by several other former Disney animators; by the early 1950s, UPA had earned a reputation as the leading force for innovation in animation, even if they never achieved the commercial success of Disney or its chief rival in the world of animated shorts, Warner Brothers. UPA productions of this era, such as the series of *Gerald McBoing-Boing* shorts (the first of which was written by Dr. Seuss) are some of the most visually innovative works of postwar American culture as a whole, drawing some of their energy from leftist cultural traditions that had otherwise been largely squashed by the early years of the Cold War.

One is tempted to read the conflicted implications of the roustabouts scene in *Dumbo* as a sign of ambivalence about the strike on the part of those who stayed to see the film through to its end. It certainly seems appropriate to see the roustabouts as stand-ins for Disney's animators, especially when they sing of getting the true rewards for their work by seeing the joy that children receive from the show they help put on. Read ironically, these lines could imply a critique of the Disney company, suggesting that the company expected their animators to take their gratification from the joy of producing a good product—even if they didn't receive fair monetary consideration or work under equitable conditions. Then again, one could also read these lines literally—as an implicit criticism of the strikers, who might thereby seem to be portrayed as abandoning their young constituents in favor of their own selfish interests. Meanwhile, one might find a similar criticism of the workers in a later scene in which a group of drunken clowns (buoyed by the success of a recent scene in which Dumbo really did all the work) babble about hitting the boss up for a raise. I myself have never quite figured out what to try to tell a three-year-old like Benjamin about all of this. So far, I've just told him that the scene shows how hard the workers work and how important they are to the success of the circus. Maybe we'll discuss more complex readings later. For his part, he just likes their song, which is his favorite in the entire film.

As the circus gets underway, Dumbo's mother attempts to protect her son from a thuggish, red-haired, freckled youth who looks like a refugee from *Pinocchio*'s Pleasure Island. He is, in short, a standard Disney representation of working-class youth. In a heartbreaking scene, Mrs. Jumbo's reaction to the kid's taunts causes her to be brutally attacked by the ringmaster and his minions, who declare her a rogue elephant and lock her away in solitary confinement, leaving the bewildered baby Dumbo virtually alone in the cruel world of the circus.

Luckily, Dumbo is befriended by the streetwise but benevolent Timothy Q. Mouse (mice are almost always benevolent in the Disney universe), so the poor infant (apparently still too young to talk, though the other animals in the circus are quite articulate) does have a guide to the world. Oddly enough, however, this guide does him very little good, and it is partly due to Timothy's help that Dumbo lands a key role in the elephant show, only to make a mistake during a performance that leads to a disaster in which the entire circus tent collapses, sending the patrons scurrying for safety. Dumbo is expelled from membership in the elephant clan, leaving the confused infant more alone than ever, consigned to duty as a buffoon in the clown show.

Dumbo and Timothy soon get into trouble again when they accidentally imbibe some sort of bubbly alcohol (it seems stronger than champagne) left behind by the drunken clowns. The subsequent drunkenness of the elephant—mouse duo then leads to perhaps the strangest scene of the entire film, a sort of pocket version of *Fantasia* in which a montage of musical styles provides accompaniment to a series of alcohol-induced hallucinations, centrally involving pink elephants, presented in a variety of surreal manifestations. One can only describe the art of this sequence as avant-garde, leaving little doubt that at least some of Disney's animators of the time saw themselves as participating in a cutting-edge aesthetic endeavor.

In the course of his drunken stupor, Dumbo unknowingly flaps his huge ears and flies up into a tall tree, taking Timothy with him. They both fall asleep in the tree, later to be awakened by a herd of crows, presented as outrageously stereotypical African Americans. While the overt racialization of these crows is just a bit offensive, it is not quite fair to see them as evidence of overt racism on the part of the Disney company, as some critics have done. After all, the crows, buffoonish as they are in some ways, turn out to be benevolent figures who help Dumbo get in touch with and accept his true self and to realize that he can, in fact, fly. Their extreme representation is certainly a sign of racial insensitivity on the part of the Disney company, though, and I can imagine that African American parents, viewing the film with their children, would find the scene uncomfortable indeed.

Disney followed *Dumbo* with another classic featuring animal characters, *Bambi* (1942). Indeed, *Bambi* shows no human characters on-screen at all, featuring "Man" only as a dangerous and destruction off-screen presence that sometimes appears to disrupt the tranquil environment of Bambi's forest, most notably in a famous scene mid-way through the film in which Bambi's mother is shot down (off screen) by hunters, leaving the baby deer essentially alone in the world—and leaving generations of filmgoers in tears. *Bambi* is a charming film whose principal political message seems to involve showing the dark side of hunting by presenting it from the perspective of the animals. One could take this as an anti-gun message as well, as numerous critics have. To this extent, the film would seem to be aligned with political positions that are usually associated with liberalism. However, it is also the case that Bambi is a young prince, the son of the Great Prince, a mighty old stag who rules the forest (making him, like so many fathers of the 1940s, too busy with his work to provide very much child care).[8] And the film makes it abundantly clear that this accident of birth makes Bambi someone worthy of special consideration (he deserves to be a prince because he was born a prince), thus making the film the forerunner of the decidedly retrograde royalist ideology that runs through so much of the Disney oeuvre, perhaps most outrageously in their most commercially successful animated film, *The Lion King* (1994).

Among other things, *Bambi* turned almost completely away from the avant-garde tendencies of *Fantasia* and *Dumbo* and toward a much more realistic (and less interesting) style of animation. Meanwhile, its focus on the depiction of animals living in nature makes it an important forerunner of the numerous nature documentaries (marketed as "True-Life Adventures") that would become one of Disney's most important products in the coming years, winning a total of eight Academy Awards and gaining considerable prestige for the company. I can attest that Benjamin and Skylor both find many of the nature scenes in these films highly entertaining, though the voiceover narrations of the films, which present highly anthropomorphized descriptions of animal behavior, seem a bit dated. Most of those "True-Life Adventures" are available on DVD today, though they've never been big sellers, perhaps because of the dated narration, though the action is a bit slow by today's standards as well. The same is true of the fictional live-action films that Disney produced over the coming decades, which cannot really compete with the high-action special-effects extravanganzas to which today's children have become accustomed. Still, films such as *Treasure Island* (1950) and *Swiss Family Robinson* (1960) have their moments. I've managed to get Skylor to sit through both films, at least, and I can report that he, very much a devotee of state-of-the-art special effects, still finds the whole sequence in the latter film involving the battle with the pirates who invade the Robinsons' island sanctuary pretty entertaining. But it isn't something that he can watch again and again as he does with certain sequences in contemporary high-action films such as *Hellboy* (2004), his personal favorite.

The "True-Life Adventures" are particularly interesting for the way they resonate with Disney's consistent celebration of the natural, even as they are actually highly scripted presentations of animal behavior that seem, consciously or not, designed to overcome the rift between Disney's medieval naturalism and its purported Americanism by simply collapsing the two together. Thus Americanism *is* natural (not ideological), and the Disney celebration of the natural and the authentic becomes American after all. Sammond presents an excellent reading of this aspect of the "True-Life Adventures," noting that they presented a world of nature "that reproduced the social world of the American suburb." They thus "reconfigured as natural and universal a place and a set of practices that were taxonomically and historically specific" (202).

Among other things, the fascination with animals that underlies the "True-Life Adventures" resonates with the prominent role played by animals in Disney's animated films—and with the consistent Disney emphasis on seeking and maintaining one's natural place in the world. Animals, after all, would seem by definition to be closer to nature than humans, more likely to be bound by their inherited roles than to seek to go beyond them. The same, of course, might also be said for children, who are, in the Disney version (and contrary to the Calvinist notion of human inborn total depravity), something like animals, innocent and natural and free of the corruption that comes with age and experience. This latter fact helps to explain why children in Disney films can so often see things that their older and presumably wiser counterparts cannot—and why children often have to come to the rescue of adults. The same might be said for women, who, despite representing a civilizing force in Disney films, can do so partly because they have a greater clarity of vision that comes from a more simple and natural view of the world. One might, of course, see this vision of innocence as a positive portrayal of children or women, but it is also possible to see it is a condescending vision of both as being like little animals and as less fully human than adult males. Disney means, I think, to valorize childhood (if only to make their films more appealing to young audiences), but this valorization is tempered by another of the many contradictions with which Disney's films are shot through: the fact that maturity and responsibility are almost portrayed as positive goals to which children should aspire.

The impressive staying power of Disney's animated films (they are specifically—and successfully—marketed as "timeless classics" relative to their live-action films probably accounts for the fact that Disney is so often thought of largely as an animation studio, even if animated films have not been their main product since *Bambi*. The fact is that when *Bambi* was released, Disney was already moving away from animation toward the much less expensive live-action format. Through the rest of the 1940s, for example, their most prominent effort in animation was the notorious *Song of the South* (1946), which mixed live action and animation in a concoction deemed by many so racist that even Disney (whose corporate strategy, at least in the days before DVD, depended so heavily on the periodic rerelease of their animated films) now seems ashamed of it and determined to keep it out of theaters and off DVD.[9] *Song of the South* has its charming moments, and its key song, the Oscar-winning "Zip-a-Dee-Doo-Dah," is a Disney staple, with a life of its own apart from the film. And there is nothing mean-spirited about *Song of the South*; the film comes off as simply insensitive, oblivious to the potential offensiveness of its stunningly stereotypical images of happy dancing former slaves (clearly depicted as being closer to nature than their white counterparts) who seem to have loyally stayed to work on the Southern plantations on which they were once mere property, still obediently obeying their former masters.

Disney seemingly returned to form in 1950 with the release of *Cinderella*, at that time perhaps the most paradigmatically Disneyesque film to have been released by the company since *Snow White*. The film, which had actually been in the planning stages even before World War II, again employs the standard formula of the fairy-tale princess cheated of her birthright by evil foes only to win it back with the help of a handsome prince. This time all the humans are white, so race is no issue, though there are of course also lots of charming non-human characters, especially the playful singing mice who are Cinderella's primary supporters during her time of troubles with her evil stepmother and stepsisters. These mice are a Disney trademark, of course, and a key marker of the way in which the film Disneyfies the original Perrault fairy tale. Cinderella survives her travails by the very Disneyesque strategy of turning away from reality and living very much in her dreams. Indeed, the film places great emphasis on her ability to go on dreaming, despite everything, which seems to recommend escapist fantasy (rather than political action) as the appropriate means for dealing with injustice in the world. If you're treated unfairly, just wait and try to endure. Hopefully something will come along, like a fairy godmother and/or a handsome prince.

Cinderella ultimately triumphs not by overthrowing or even revising the social order. Instead, she merely restores it to its appropriate and natural form (with everyone resuming their proper places as determined by birth), which had been distorted by the machinations of her stepfamily. Cinderella becomes a princess because she was a natural aristocrat all along, as signaled by her delicate feet. This basic endorsement of a static social order might itself be a bit boring, of course, were it not that the film is so punctuated by magic and music, two tried-and-true Disney devices. Meanwhile, there is also the trademark Disney violence: a surprising percentage of the film's seventy-four minutes is spent on scenes in which the evil cat Lucifer attempts (unsuccessfully, of course) to murder and devour various cute and cuddly mice, while one of the film's most extended scenes shows the local king attempting to dismember the duke, his most trusted advisor, with the royal sword.

The cartoon format and the idyllic ending of *Cinderella* presumably ensure that children will not be traumatized by these scenes of violence. In fact, this ending aims to leave no room for lingering doubt that all is well in the kingdom or in the life of Cinderella, even though she moves directly from the domination of her stepmother and stepsisters into the control of a powerful man whom she hardly knows. Meanwhile, *Cinderella* is not just a fantasy of marrying well, but also a consumerist fantasy, which might not be surprising in the first major Disney animated film to be introduced during the postwar economic boom. Thus, the fairy godmother seems almost like a stand-in for the emergent consumer capitalist system of the era as she produces a variety of expensive goods seemingly from thin air. Then again, the disappearance of all these goods at midnight might be taken as an inadvertent reminder of the tenuousness of capitalist wealth, as all that had been solid suddenly melts back into the air from which it came. But, deserving as she is, Cinderella need not fear. She not only finds love, but love with someone who is very rich and can resume the flow of fancy commodities begun by the magic of the fairy godmother.

Disney turned away from fairy tales and princesses proper with the release of *Alice in Wonderland* in 1951, an adaptation that required considerable bowdlerization of the Lewis Carroll original, though Carroll's work lends itself well to animation in the sense that it includes a number of strange situations and absurd characters that are perfect for visual representation through animation.[10] These visuals (which show vestiges of the experimentalism of the *Dumbo* era) are the heart of the film; it includes very little in the way of an actual story, but instead simply takes Alice almost randomly from one bizarre, dreamlike situation to another as she gradually makes her way back home after following a white rabbit down its hole into Wonderland. Alice is another in the long line of Disney dreamers, daydreaming, as the film begins, of living another life in an alternative world constructed according to the dictates of her own imagination. Wonderland then becomes that dream, but is in fact more like a nightmare, as she careens from one dangerous situation to another before returning, like Dorothy Gale, to the safety of home.

Thus, *Alice in Wonderland* is another in the long line of Disney films that seem to celebrate the individual imagination only ultimately to advise individuals to accept the status quo. The Queen of Hearts (another of Disney's evil, threatening women) is a particularly important character. Portrayed in the film as large, uncouth, and extremely masculine (as opposed to the small, effeminate King of Hearts, whom she clearly dominates), the Queen of Hearts here functions rather clearly as an image of the woman who refuses to accept her naturally feminine, subservient domestic role. Indeed, her penchant for decapitation could not be more obvious as an emblem of her status as the castrating female. Asserting her authority despite her gender, she becomes a sinister and threatening figure, the polar opposite of Alice, who remains throughout the film passive, demure, and unequivocally feminine, returning in the end to her proper place, having learned a valuable lesson about the dangers of venturing out of the domestic sphere.

If films such as *Cinderella* and *Alice in Wonderland* seem to celebrate the imagination, only to counsel conformism, *Peter Pan* (1953), widely seen as a celebration of childhood, actually advised the putting away of childish things. In the film, young Wendy Darling forays into Neverland (something like a forerunner of the Disneyland theme park, plans for which were then well advanced), home of the impish Peter Pan and the swarthy, beak-nosed Captain Hook, whose basic vileness is coded in his ethnicized appearance. This theme-park world has its attractions, but in the end Wendy returns to her proper British bourgeois home to face her domestic responsibilities. In particular, a maturing girl in early puberty, Wendy prepares to enter the sexual economy and do her natural duty of producing children of her own, so that the cycle can continue.

Indeed, the implied sexualization of Wendy's maturation is one of the most striking things about *Peter Pan*. She seems to be the first girl to have ever entered Neverland, previously the province only of boys, several of whom (the "lost boys") have come there to live permanently. Normal females (this would exclude Tinker Bell and the cartoonish Indian squaws who feature in the film) do not really belong in the adventure world of Neverland, because women belong, in the ideology of the 1950s in general and of 1950s Disney films in particular, in the routinized domestic space of the home. According to this vision, boys will be boys, and it is the job of females to tame them and turn them into responsible men who will settle down, get jobs, and produce and support families. To a large extent, the key message of all of Disney's films of the 1950s is the necessity of maturation and acceptance of responsibility, which helps to explain why Disney protagonists from the period are so often female. According to this view, females may be limited in many ways, but they are expected to mature first (probably because they have a less complicated procedure to go through, being mere females), providing an anchor for wayward men. In films such as *Cinderella* and *Sleeping Beauty*, the princes play active roles, while the princesses wait to be saved, but it is the princesses who galvanize the princes into action and convince them to act like heroes—then settle down and marry.

The vague subtext of feminine threat that underlies the main plot of *Peter Pan* is also informed by a self-contradictory message: the film suggests that sexual maturity for men is, however necessary, a form of entrapment (note how thoroughly tamed the Darling father appears to be), with feminine sexual allure serving as a snare that ends up spoiling boyhood fun. After all, Wendy with her budding breasts and hips just beginning to flare, nearly leads Peter Pan to his death.

In the same vein, *Lady and the Tramp* (1955) features a free-spirited male dog (the eponymous Tramp) who is domesticated by the sexual allures of the prissy Lady, a suburban cocker spaniel. Indeed, as Nadel notes, this film was a classic case of the attempt during the long 1950s to promote "the cult of domesticity as a form of political and social containment of the sexual energies of post—World War II teenagers and young adults, congruent to and commensurate with the American foreign and domestic policy of containing communism" (117).

Lady and the Tramp is especially rich in allegorical energies. Driven from her posh suburban home by two evil Siamese cats, Lady runs away to the city, where Tramp, a streetwise stray, proudly shows her the ropes. Tramp clearly regards his unfettered life in the city's slums as preferable to the routinized confines of Lady's suburbia, a land of fences, collars, and leashes. Standing in for the urban underclasses, Tramp lives high on the hog from handouts he gets from various families and restaurants, thus suggesting that the underclasses in general are largely composed of carefree beggars, happy to live off handouts, thus avoiding work and responsibility. The film, however, clearly recommends Lady's bourgeois attitude over the Bohemian lifestyle of Tramp. After a series of adventures, she and Tramp settle down and start their own family, living in domestic wedded bliss with Lady's original suburban family. Meanwhile, the film also reminds us that the irresponsible urban poor tend to be immigrants of suspect ethnicity. Thus, when Lady is briefly imprisoned in the dog pound, the denizens of the pound include a Mexican Chihuahua, a German (read Nazi) dachshund, and a Cockney (read working-class) bulldog. There is also a Gorky-quoting Russian wolfhound, whose portrayal associates the underclasses with Russians and communists.[11]

In its focus on dogs, *Lady and the Tramp* relies on animated animals even more than most Disney films. In fact, the humans are entirely marginal and generally appear on-screen in fleeting shots that show only parts of their bodies. Their faces are seldom seen at all. Presumably, this device is intended to suggest that we are seeing the humans as they might appear to Lady and the other dogs, but it is also the case that this technique further marginalizes the humans and increases the film's focus on the dogs, which are easier than humans to animate convincingly but which are also easier to portray sympathetically. The Disney company was quite well aware that one of the principal features of bourgeois ideology is an intense sentimentality that tends to focus on animals, kindness to animals thus serving as a utopian compensation for the cruelty and alienation to which humans are subjected in a capitalist environment. After all, even the Nazis were notoriously fond of dogs.[12]

Of course, in the Disney universe, this same sentimentality is not extended to cats. The sworn enemies of the mice so beloved by the Disney company, cats predictably appear as sinister, sneaky, and conniving creatures. The film would also have us believe that dogs, unlike cats, are naturally suited to be pets, even though that status would seem to remove them from nature. What is particularly significant here is the film's emphasis on the fact that the cats in the film are Siamese, that is, Oriental, driven home at great length in their performance of an ostentatiously Oriental song ("we are Siamee-uz, if you plee-uz") and accompanying slinky Oriental dance. In fact, the sneakiness and treachery of the slanty-eyed cats are closely associated with their Oriental ethnicity, suggesting that such behavior is only to be expected of Orientals and producing some of the most strikingly Orientalist images in the entire Disney oeuvre. As Eleanor Byrne and Martin McQuillan put it, the cats are depicted as "wily, duplicitous, troublemaking, freeloading, Asian illegal immigrants" (97).

Of course, the United States had a long history of suspicion toward Asian immigrants, as can be seen in the Chinese Exclusion Act of 1882. The virulent racism of anti-Japanese propaganda (and the oppression of Japanese Americans) during World War II indicated that Orientalist racism was still alive and well. Indeed, Nadel notes that the depiction of the cats "draws heavily on the images of the Asian associated with World War II and Korean War propaganda" (122). Guilt feelings over the atomic bombings of Hiroshima and Nagasaki gave this racism a new nervous edge in the long 1950s, and this nervousness was quickly exacerbated by the successful

another of Disney's sinister female villains. Indeed, Cruella master-
minds the kidnapping of 99 Dalmatian puppies with the macabre
intention (somewhat shocking in a Disney film) of killing them and
skinning them for fur coats. She may thus be the most despicable of
Disney's female villains, though she is presented as comically inept,
presumably to avoid frightening small children. In this film, meanwhile, all animals are kind and good, even including a cat, so that the
film is essentially structured around a polar opposition between good
animals and bad humans, a motif that looks back to *Bambi* and power-
fully reinforces the sentimental bourgeois tendency to feel more sympathy for animals than for humans. However, as with so many polar
oppositions in the long 1950s, this human-animal dichotomy is not a
simple one. As Patrick Murphy points out, "the animals are most
noble when most nearly 'human,' while the human is most ignoble
when most nearly 'inhuman'" (128).

Otherwise, *One Hundred and One Dalmatians* is a relatively slight
work, lacking the mythic resonances of many of the Disney animated
classics of the long 1950s. In fact, the film can be taken as the marker
of the beginning of a period of decline in Disney animation. The Disney company attempted another (rather unsuccessful) animated story
with mythic proportions in *The Sword in the Stone* (1963), based on
the Arthurian legends, and it scored a major hit with the release of
The Jungle Book (1967), perhaps the height (or depth) of Disneyfied
racist Orientalism. By and large, though, the ideology of this film is
unusually garbled and confused. It features a young boy (Mowgli),
who grows up in a natural state in the jungle, raised initially by
wolves in the mode of Romulus and Remus, but ultimately concludes
that it is unnatural for humans to live so naturally and that Mowgli's
proper place is with other humans in civilization. Despite the fact that
the boy-protagonist Mowgli loves the jungle and the animals who
have befriended him there, he ultimately returns to human society,
because that is where (the film assumes) he belongs. Some, of course,
might feel that Mowgli's brown skin subtly suggests that he was
able to survive among the animals at all because he is closer to their
state by virtue of being nonwhite and non-Western. But the story is
set in India, so it makes perfect sense for Mowgli to be Indian (as he
was in the source material, the stories of Rudyard Kipling). Therefore,
I do not think it is fair to complain about his brown skin as an inherently racist image. One might even find progressive implications in

the fact that the film has a nonwhite protagonist, though Douglas Brode (as he generally does when defending Disney) surely overstates the case when he gushes that Mowgli "provided American children, including those in the deep South, with their first animated youth hero of color" (*Multiculturalism* 263). In point of fact, Mowgli is Americanized enough not to seem very Indian, and he is certainly not presented as a role model for African American or other American children of color.

Indeed, the film's Americanization of all of Kipling's original materials—including giving the otherwise exotic jungle animals familiar American personalities and ethnicities—could be seen as a form of cultural imperialism. Moreover, this film's grotesquely African American monkeys (and their king, Louis, who is, inexplicably, an orangutan)[14] are perhaps the most racist images in any Disney film outside of *Song of the South*. These monkeys and their ape king are the clear descendents of the crows of *Dumbo*, except that they are a conniving and sinister group who work against Mowgli, rather than helping him as the crows do Dumbo. Meanwhile, associating Africans and African Americans with monkeys and apes has a long and baleful legacy in the discourse of American racism, a fact that is further exacerbated in *The Jungle Book* by the fact that the ape king sings suggestively of his desire to be human, claiming that "an ape like me" can be human, too, with just a hint of training—reinforcing the standard racist notion that African Americans are subhuman simian creatures simply seeking to pass themselves off as human.

Such images, shockingly racist by the standards of the twenty-first century, were not quite as obvious in 1967, but they should have been obvious enough to anyone who was paying attention. One suspects, however, that the Disney company, still coming to grips with the death of Walt Disney in late 1966, probably wasn't paying attention. I do not believe that one can conclude from the evidence of *The Jungle Book* that Disney was consciously attempting to convey racist notions to American children. Instead, it seems likely to me that they were simply careless, not bothering to worry that they might be conveying such ideas, and simply calling upon tried-and-true images from the collective Disney memory to produce effective entertainment for children (and substantial profits for the corporation).

Such carelessness is, of course, rife not only in the Disney oeuvre but in the legacy of American children's film as a whole. The makers of children's film have all too often assumed that the innocence of their audiences will somehow protect those audiences from any potentially harmful readings of the films. On this view, children viewing *The Jungle Book*, having no racist inclinations, will not read the portrayal of the monkeys as racist or derive from it any suggestion that African Americans resemble apes or monkeys. This assumption does not strike me as a good one. For one thing, specifically American visions of childhood innocence are part of a discourse about American childhood and not necessarily accurate descriptions of actual children. And, even if all children are born innocent (religious notions of original sin can be safely discounted), they are quickly acculturated and rapidly move away from that initial innocence under the impetus of the various social stimuli to which they are exposed, such as movies.

In addition, the discourse of childhood innocence developed over the years from roughly the 1920s to the 1950s (when it reached its fully articulated form) under careful cultivation by a variety of forces in American culture, forces that have profited immensely by the extent to which this discourse has been accepted by the American public. In this view, the innate innocence of children made potentially negative influences (such as immoral movies or other forms of popular culture) especially dangerous. As Sammond has effectively outlined, the Disney company played a leading role in this effort, which not only involved the portrayal of the company as a bastion against the corrupting influence of other forms of popular culture (especially film), but also included a careful coding of the "normal" and "natural" American child as "white (largely male), Protestant" and as having "middle-class origins" (10). In particular, the Disney company was able shrewdly to build upon concerns that movies were bad for children (and might introduce unsavory influences into their lives— often emanating from the lower classes or from immigrants) by portraying itself as the antithesis of such bad movies. According to this carefully administered marketing plan, the antidote to bad influences in the movies was not to try to keep children away from movies altogether, but to satisfy their desire to see movies by supplying them with the kind of wholesome alternatives that Disney was in the business of producing. Sammond shows that this strategy was centered on images of consumption, in which children were viewed as imbibing good American values (embodied by Walt Disney himself) at the same time they were taking in Disney films. Focusing on the marketing of and response to *Pinocchio*, Sammond argues that the film became part of an extensive discourse that conveyed the notion that "to watch *Pinocchio* was to consume Pinocchio; to consume Pinocchio was to consume Walt Disney. To consume Walt Disney was to ingest the qualities essential to Americanness that were required for its reproduction in subsequent generations" (113).

It seems clear to me that the Disney company not only conveyed such ideas but also literally believed them, buying into its own messages. Thus, the racist images in films such as *The Jungle Book* did not strike the company as problematic precisely because the company was so focused on its own white, male, middle-class perspective that other perspectives literally became unthinkable. The same might be said for the sexist imagery for which Disney films have been so roundly criticized. Less has been said about the portrayal of class than of race and gender in Disney films, which on the surface participate in a broad discourse that is common to American films in general, a discourse in which the importance of class is largely effaced. In American film as a whole, the rich are typically portrayed as bumbling, effete, and corrupt, and Disney films are no exception. Meanwhile, the earnest, hardworking members of the middle class are portrayed as more honest, dependable, and capable. However, I think the Disney company, in its classic films, does more than most studios to suggest that the poor (especially the immigrant or nonwhite poor) tend to be either shiftless, conniving, and dishonest or simply to be happy with their lot, living in a state of nature and delighted not to have to deal with the complex financial matters that plague their economic betters.

Again, however, I do not think Disney films are specifically designed to denigrate poor immigrants so much as that they are so caught up in their own white, middle-class perspective that they are oblivious to the implications of their films. One can see this tendency in, for example, the clearly ethnic villains of *Dumbo* (the ringmaster) or *Pinocchio* (Stromboli), both of whom are possibly meant to be gypsies. Even more telling, however, are certain moments in films such as *Mary Poppins* (1964), the mostly live-action film (though it includes an animated sequence) that was the biggest hit produced by the company during Walt Disney's lifetime. It is still one of the most fondly remembered films of its era, and most people of my age seem to think of it as one of the most charming films of their childhoods. I didn't see it when I was a kid, I must admit. In fact, I didn't see it until I was working on this book and decided to watch it with Skylor. He thought it was boring; I thought it was fascinating, though maybe not quite for the same reasons as most people. For one thing, it seems to function largely as a scathing condemnation of the way in which capitalist modernization is turning life into a soulless, regimented routine, stripping life of all magic. That, of course, is where the magical nanny Mary Poppins (Julie Andrews) comes in, restoring said magic to the lives of the Banks family, including the emancipation of Mr. Banks from a soul-destroying job as a ruthless banker. In this sense, of course, the film would seem to be one of Disney's most overtly anticapitalist statements, but it is one that should be viewed with a certain amount of skepticism. For one thing, the film is based primarily on a 1934 children's book of the same title by P. L. Travers, but the filmmakers decided to move the setting back in time to the Edwardian era, thus both making it seem more quaint and avoiding any engagement with the nasty issue of the Depression of the 1930s, which might have given the film's implicit critique of capitalism a bit too much bite. After all, that the film is ultimately quite insensitive to the injustices perpetuated by capitalism can be seen in a number of ways, perhaps the most striking of which is the film's best-known musical production number, in which the Oscar-winning song "Chim Chim Che-ree" is performed by a group of happy, carefree chimney sweeps, cavorting about on London's rooftops. We know from British history (and British literature by the likes of William Blake and Charles Dickens) that chimney sweeps were among the most oppressed workers in a rapidly modernizing London of the eighteenth and nineteenth centuries, doing grim, dirty, hazardous work under horrific conditions for extremely low pay—and usually dying young from job-related diseases. To depict them as lighthearted, free spirits whose work allowed them to escape the mind-numbing routine encountered by Banks at his clean, well-paying office job would thus seem to embody the worst kind of insensitivity to the real suffering of such workers. It was just as insensitive that this number won the Oscar for best song and that virtually no one who saw the film at the time seemed to be outraged by the happy, dancing claim that although he lives in smoke and grime, "In this 'ole wide world / There's no 'appier bloke."[15]

When I first saw this number I was so stunned that I had to rewind and watch it several times, much to Skylor's displeasure. I simply

couldn't believe what I was seeing. For me, this number alone qualifies *Mary Poppins* for the children's film hall of shame, because it
presents viewers too young to know any better with a patently falsified version of historical reality, declaring that the main victims of
capitalism are the rich bankers who end up having no fun because
they have to spend so much time counting their money. Poor people,
on the other hand, are free of such concerns and thus do not suffer
from the routinization of life under capitalism, remaining in a more
natural and authentic state. Such suggestions are not just silly, and
they are not just lies. They are potentially harmful lies that give children a vision of the world in which they live that is not only false but
false in ways that will make it easier for the powers that be in this
world to manipulate and exploit them as they grow up under the illusion that the poor are happy workers.

Mary Poppins is distasteful in other ways as well, as when it
presents the suffragette activism of Mrs. Banks as comically silly,
thus dismissing the historical oppression of women as a fantasy of
bored housewives and, by extension, making present-day feminists
seem silly as well. Ultimately, having gotten over my initial shock at
the chimney sweep dance, I think the thing that bothers we most about
Mary Poppins is the sheer hypocrisy of the Disney company's attempt
to cash in on an overt critique of capitalist routinization of which their
own highly organized production practices are a prime example. The
attempt here seems particularly cynical, even though the same sort of
critique had been implicit in the company's marketing of "magic" all
along.

There is, of course, great positive value in Disney's continual production of magical narratives (if only to remind us of some of the
things we have lost as a result of capitalist routinization). Still, it is
also the case that the true genius of the Disney company has always
been in its ability to employ capitalist routine in a particularly efficient way.[16] Both parts of the widely used term describing Hollywood
as a "dream factory" apply to Disney more than perhaps to any other
studio: not only is Disney quite openly in the business of manufactur-
ing and marketing dreams, but they do so in a very business- and fac-
tory-like way. Walt Disney's greatest contribution to American
culture might not be his co-invention of an anthropomorphic mouse
or his realized dream of vast, high-tech theme parks so much as his
understanding of how to employ Fordist techniques of assembly line

production in the making of his films. It is thus telling that the name Disney signifies the products of a particularly corporate entity rather than the works of an individual film *auteur*, in the way the name Hitchcock might. Walt Disney, after all, never directed a feature-length film in his life. What he did was develop and employ management skills that produced one film after another in very much the same mode once that mode was set in place. It is not for nothing (even if it is also not entirely fair) that the term "Disneyfication" evokes visions of a giant stamping machine crunching out cookie-cutter copies of the same basic film, whatever the source material—which usually came, as Schickel has pointed out, from "literature's bargain basement" (345). This crank-them-out tendency has, in recent years, been extended by the Disney company in a flurry of straight-to-DVD sequels to its successful theatrical releases. Indeed, as I write this in early 2009, the Disney company seems more and more to be going for quantity over quality in a variety of venues, depending on its one yearly Pixar release to maintain the company's prestige as a maker of children's films. The recent productions of Disney and its now-subsidiary Pixar are discussed in the next two chapters.

——2——

Disney after Disney: The Fall and Rise and Fall of Disney's Dominance in Children's Film

The period between 1967 and 1989 was a virtual wasteland in the production of children's animated film, but that long dry spell came to an abrupt halt in 1989 with the release of *The Little Mermaid*, which announced the beginning of a new string of successful animated films that ran through the 1990s, resurrecting numerous motifs (including sexist and racist ones) from the 1950s in a clear nostalgia play. Indeed, the Disney renaissance initiated by *The Little Mermaid* is most remarkable not because it introduced new themes or techniques, but because it largely didn't, representing an attempt instead to reproduce the magic of the earlier classic Disney animated films from *Snow White* to *The Jungle Book*. However, it means one thing to make *Snow White* in 1937 and something entirely different to remake it half a century later. Thus, the element of nostalgia for an earlier and presumably more authentic time that was already present in the earlier films becomes significantly stronger in films such as *The Little Mermaid, Beauty and the Beast* (1991), and *The Lion King* (1994), because these films now have the added element of being nostalgic for the earlier films. Further, given the tendency in the Disney universe to make nostalgia a quest for authenticity, this phenomenon implies that the earlier films are symbolically regarded as authentic classics, while the later films are postmodern pastiches of the earlier classic films. In this way, the new wave of Disney films that began with *The Little Mermaid* can be regarded as a key instance of postmodern culture as described by the important theorist Fredric Jameson, who sees nostalgia as a key mode of such culture and regards pastiche as its principal technique.

It is the tendency to reproduce both the style and the content of earlier works from various periods that Jameson describes as "pastiche," which is, "like parody, the imitation of a peculiar or unique, idiosyncratic style, the wearing of a stylistic mask, speech in a dead language. But it is a neutral practice of such mimicry, without any of parody's ulterior motives, amputated of the satiric impulse, devoid of any laughter and of any conviction that alongside the abnormal tongue you have momentarily borrowed, some healthy linguistic normality still exists" (*Postmodernism* 17). Among other things, Jameson sees this reliance on the styles of the past as an indication of the particular kind of nostalgia that is one of the defining characteristics of postmodern art. In addition, this "random cannibalization of all the styles of the past" reduces the past to a series of spectacles, a collection of images disconnected from any genuine sense of historical process.

It should be noted that, at the time of the release of *The Little Mermaid*, the Disney company had been struggling for decades to find a new identity for itself—only ultimately to fall back upon a reproduction of its earlier identity. After all, for the three decades between the release of *Snow White and the Seven Dwarfs* in 1937 and his death in 1966, Walt Disney was virtually synonymous in the public mind with the company that bore his name. Perhaps it should come as no surprise, then, that the Disney film business experienced an extended identity crisis in the two decades after Disney's death. The fact is, however, that in some ways Disney's film business had been in decline for quite a while before Disney's death—and that the animated children's films for which the company is best known had become an increasingly small portion of its revenue stream. Only three animated films had been released in the last decade of Disney's life: *Sleeping Beauty* (1959), *One Hundred and One Dalmatians* (1961), and *The Sword in the Stone* (1963). The last of these, based on the legend of King Arthur, is one of the most obscure in the Disney animated canon, and did not do well at the box office on its initial release or on its rerelease in 1983. *Sleeping Beauty* fared a bit better at the box office and is, in fact, one of Disney's best-known films, returning to the fairy-tale mode that made the company successful in the first place. Yet it is a flawed and muddled film that for many lacks the charm of *Snow White*, whatever the technical virtuosity of its animation. Richard Schickel, for example, calls *Sleeping Beauty* "Disney's greatest animated failure" (234). Meanwhile, *One Hundred and One Dalmatians* initially did poorly at the box office, though it turned out to have a certain staying power and has fared better and better in each of its four rereleases, grossing more than $60 million at the domestic box office in 1991, when it was able to take advantage of what was then a resurgence of interest in Disneyfied animation.

The huge success of *Mary Poppins* provided a certain justification for the company's increasing emphasis on live-action pictures, which were simpler and less expensive to produce than animated films and seemingly offered broader possibilities for pulling in diverse audiences. But live-action films are hardly guaranteed to succeed, and the Disney company floundered through the late 1960s and the whole decade of the 1970s, though they did produce an occasional interesting effort that is still watchable today. Benjamin is particularly fond of *The Cat from Outer Space* (1978), a lighthearted, low-budget children's science fiction film that features a benevolent visitor from outer space who happens to look exactly like an ordinary house cat. However, the crystals on its collar amplify the power of its mind, giving it extensive capabilities to manipulate the world around it. It's still a lovable cat, though, and thus something of a forerunner of Spielberg's pet-like E.T., who appeared only a few years later, in 1982—not to mention Disney's own extraterrestrial-monster-turned-pet, Stitch, from *Lilo & Stitch* (2002). Actually, *The Cat from Outer Space* is in some ways ahead of its time, especially in the way it satirizes the paranoid response of the American military authorities to the arrival of the cat (among other things initially scanning the cat's ship for signs of a hammer-and-sickle insignia). Of course, this satire is rather mild, and the authorities eventually make peace with the cat, while the real villain of the peace turns out to be Mr. Olympus (William Prince), an international criminal kingpin who seems to have been borrowed from a James Bond film. This film is part of a long legacy of Disney films that foray into the realm of science fiction, such as 1969's *The Computer Wore Tennis Shoes*, starring a young Kurt Russell and featuring a plot that involves the downloading of the capabilities of a computer into the mind of a college student, thus to some extent anticipating the later evolution of cyberpunk science fiction in the 1980s.[1]

Disney tried to move into more mainstream science fiction with *The Black Hole* (1979), an expensive live-action film that attempted to cash in on the science fiction film craze initiated by the success of *Star Wars* (1977) and *Close Encounters of the Third Kind* (1977), films that were quickly followed by such science fiction classics as *Star Trek: The Motion Picture* (1979), *Alien* (1979), *E.T. the Extra-Terrestrial* (1982), *Blade Runner* (1982), and *The Terminator* (1984), making the period 1977–1984 perhaps the richest in science fiction film history. *The Black Hole*, however, was a dud in pretty much every way possible. A confused mess as a movie (though with occasionally interesting special effects), it also failed to meet the high expectations that the Disney corporation had for it at the box office, leaving the Disney film business in more disarray than ever—though other ventures of the company (Walt Disney World Resort had opened in Orlando in 1971 and was a big moneymaker through the decade) were still doing well.

The 1980s didn't start out much better for the Disney film unit (reconstituted as Walt Disney Pictures in 1983), though 1981 did see the release of a moderately successful (in financial terms) animated film, *The Fox and the Hound*. This film was touted as the beginning of a new age for Disney animation, mainly because it was made largely by a group of new, younger animators, replacing the old guard of Disney animators, some of whom had been around for decades. And this new team included some impressive talents, including future superstar director Tim Burton and future Pixar principal (and eventual Disney executive) John Lasseter. Other new animators included Brad Bird, who would go on to become one of the movers and shakers behind the television series *The Simpsons* and enjoy future success as the director of such important animated films as *The Iron Giant* (1999) and Pixar's *The Incredibles* (2004) and *Ratatouille* (2007). *The Fox and the Hound* was indeed something of a departure for Disney in that it was based on relatively contemporary material (a 1967 novel by Daniel Mannix) and contained a certain amount of social commentary, including a critique of prejudice, which went against the grain of the long legacy of racial insensitivity in Disney films. Still, the film was an aesthetic and technical disappointment to many because it pretty much adhered to the conventional Disney style and added very little in the way of animation innovation, despite the supposed changing of the guard among Disney's animators. The film can be read as an allegory about racism, based on the relationship between a fox and a hound who grow up together as friends but are then forced apart because society expects them to be racial enemies. They ultimately decide that their personal bond supercedes their species difference, which presumably teaches viewers that each of us should be viewed as individuals and judged on our own merits rather than slotted into racial categories. The problem, however, is that, as the film ends, the fox and hound are once again friends but must enjoy that friendship from afar, each having to live in his own separate world: the fox assumes his natural place in the woods, while the hound assumes his so-called natural place as a pet. One could easily, then, see this film as suggesting that people of different races can get along fine as long as they stay in their places and don't attempt to intrude into each other's spheres.

Disney's most interesting early 1980s film was probably *Tron* (1982)—and that mostly because of the way it presaged future directions in computer-generated filmmaking, though it did become something of a cult favorite in its own right. *Tron* was another science fiction film and not aimed at children. All in all, Disney in the early 1980s was going nowhere fast as a maker of children's film, and especially of animated films. There were even rumors that the Disney company might sell off the film unit and get out of the movie business altogether. Then came the Orwellian year of 1984, when Michael Eisner, the highly successful former president and CEO of Paramount Pictures, was brought in as the chairman and CEO of the Walt Disney Company with a special mandate to try to revitalize Walt Disney Pictures. Ultimately, Eisner succeeded big time, though his abrasive and ruthless management style did little to untarnish Disney's already problematic image as a company perfectly willing to manipulate childhood innocence in its efforts to make a buck at any cost. Indeed, Eisner features as the principal villain in Carl Hiaasen's *Team Rodent: How Disney Devours the World* (1998), perhaps the most bitter critique of Disney's corporate culture produced to date. Even Roy E. Disney, Walt's nephew, saw Eisner as a heartless purveyor of capitalist routinization and accused him of making the Disney company a "rapacious, soul-less company," ultimately leading a successful fight to oust Eisner from his position as CEO in 2005. In the meantime, friction between Eisner and Jeffrey Katzenberg, the head of Disney's film unit (whom Eisner had brought with him from Paramount), led to

Katzenberg's departure from Disney in 1994, a move that was particularly important because it led to Katzenberg's founding, along with Steven Spielberg and David Geffen, DreamWorks SKG, the studio that would go on to become the most important rival to the revitalized Disney film company in the realm of animated movies.

Actually, the Eisner/Katzenberg era at Disney studios got off to something less than a spectacular start, especially in the realm of animated film. *The Black Cauldron* (1985), the first film released under the new regime (though work on it had begun earlier), was Disney's first PG animated film. It was also, at around $25 million in production costs, the most expensive animated film ever made to that date. *The Black Cauldron* employed a number of technical innovations, including a new photographic transfer process. It was also the first Disney animated film to make use of computer-generated imagery, though it used mostly traditional animation. But it took in only about $10 million in U.S. box-office receipts and produced very little in the way of auxiliary revenues from merchandising and other sources. Its failure, however, had less to do with its perceived darkness than with its uninspired animation and storytelling. Disney then followed with the equally uninspired *The Great Mouse Detective* (1986), which was somewhat more in the traditional Disney vein, though its rodent version of Sherlock Holmes wasn't much of a hit, either. Indeed, this moused-up adaptation of the Sir Arthur Conan Doyle stories comes off as basically silly, suggesting, if anything, that any cultural artifacts more than a few years old are not worthy of being taken seriously, probably about the last message that needs to be delivered to American children, who tend to feel that way already.

Probably the most interesting animated Disney film during the early Eisner/Katzenberg period was *The Brave Little Toaster*, which wasn't even made at Disney per se, but was abandoned by the studio during the production process. Indeed, the film's original director, the young animator John Lasseter, was fired by the studio, which saw little promise in the computer animation techniques he wanted to use to make the film. Lasseter would eventually end up with the new Pixar, while *The Brave Little Toaster* was completed at the loosely affiliated Hyperion Pictures after the former Disney employees who founded the latter (named for the street on which the original Disney studio was located) acquired the rights to make the film. Disney was still slated to distribute; however, after the film was finished (and premiered at the Sundance Film Festival in 1988, becoming the first animated film exhibited there), Disney opted out of theatrical distribution altogether, and the film saw only limited theatrical showings due to Hyperion's own lack of distribution abilities. It was finally released on Disney Home Video in 1991, however, and became something of a rental-market classic in its own right in the midst of the animated renaissance of the 1990s.

Disney's pass on distribution of *The Brave Little Toaster* might seem, in retrospect, to be an error in judgment (especially as Disney's own animated films were doing so poorly at the time), but the fact remains that the film is not really a Disney film, however interesting it might be. For one thing, its relatively simple animation lacks the polished (some would say *too* polished) virtuosity of most Disney animated films. On the other hand, except for the crude animation, *Toaster* might be seen as a sort of proto-Pixar film. This observation might help to illuminate the reasons why Disney films and Pixar films are not really the same thing, even in the post-2006 world in which Pixar is a wholly owned subsidiary of Disney; former Pixar head Steve Jobs is Disney's largest shareholder, and Pixar's Lasseter, a former Disney reject, is now a famed computer animation guru who is the chief creative officer of the animation studios of both Disney and Pixar. Indeed, Lasseter himself remained peripherally involved with the making of *Toaster* at Hyperion, while the film was cowritten by Joe Ranft. Ranft went on to do a considerable amount of voicing and writing for Pixar films, ultimately becoming the head of the studio's story department before his death in an auto crash in 2005.

Toaster is worth considering in detail for its very difference from traditional Disney films. Basically, it tells the story of a group of anthropomorphic household appliances, including the toaster of the title (voiced by Deanna Oliver), an old tube-driven radio that still broadcasts material mostly from the 1940s and 1950s (Jon Lovitz), a desk lamp (Tim Stack), an infantile electric blanket (Timothy E. Day), and a self-propelled upright vacuum cleaner called Kirby (Thurl Ravenscroft, best known as the voice of Tony the Tiger in TV commercials for Frosted Flakes cereal). Disney, of course, is well known for anthropomorphizing animals without explanation (there is no reason given why Mickey Mouse can talk, he just can), but inanimate objects in Disney's animated films (as with the clock and candlestick of *Beauty and the Beast*, or even earlier examples, such as the crockery that is animated by Merlin's magic in the 1963 animated feature *The Sword in the Stone*) generally come to life with human characteristics only through the agency of magic.[2] Here, however, it is simply posited that the appliances are anthropomorphic (with vague hints that they hide this fact from humans), somewhat in the manner of the automobiles in *Cars*. In fact, one of the most striking scenes in *The Brave Little Toaster* takes place in a junkyard where a group of anthropomorphic cars are being crunched in a giant garbage compactor, singing eerily about their former lives as they go to their grisly fates.

As with Lightning McQueen and his cohorts in *Cars*, the fact that the appliances of *Toaster* are machines (all driven by electricity) places them clearly within the realm of technology rather than magic, which is the typical realm of the Disney film. Given that *Toaster* is based on a novella written by the esteemed science fiction writer Thomas M. Disch, one might say that it resides more in the realm of science fiction, while Disney films tend to inhabit the world of fantasy. On the other hand, the plot of *Toaster* is fairly typical of fantasy. As the film begins, the appliances that are the film's protagonists have seemingly been abandoned (for "2000 days") in a family's country cottage, now fallen into disuse. Tired of living alone with no humans to serve, the appliances decide to set out on a cross-country trek in search of their former owners, and in particular of the family's young son, initiating a quest motif of the kind found everywhere in works of fantasy, such as Tolkien's *Lord of the Rings*. On the other hand, the film itself reminds us that such quests are sometimes undertaken by loyal pets, recalling a whole family of children's films in which faithful animals attempt, against tremendous odds, to return to their masters. Indeed, the appliances adoringly refer to the family's son as "the Master," which further seems to place them in the category of pets, possibly in an attempt to make them more sympathetic. On the subsequent journey, the appliances encounter a series of strange adventures that in some ways reads like a trip through the history of American popular culture. In one sequence, for example, they travel through a dark and menacing forest of a kind common in fairy tales but that is especially reminiscent of the one through which Dorothy and her sidekicks travel in *The Wizard of Oz*. In another sequence, the appliances break through a thicket of ugly brambles and emerge into a brilliantly hued pocket paradise in which various species of animals happily frolic and sing, living in perfect harmony together. In other words, they suddenly find themselves in a scene from a classic Disney animated film. As machines, though, they are out of place in this world (and in any case, they must continue their quest to find the Master), so they depart this wonderful world of color and march forward into a series of adventures so perilous that they seem to abandon the realm of children's culture altogether.

In one action sequence of a kind we've all seen before in other contexts, the appliances attempt to get across a chasm below which a raging river seems to threaten them with sure death if they fall in. Yet fall in they do, except for Kirby, who is the biggest and strongest of them all. The heroic vacuum then leaps into the waters below, inflating his bag for flotation and rescuing all of his friends. Soon afterward, however, they all sink into a pool of quicksand in another stock scene from countless American films, especially Westerns. This time, however, they are all rescued by a seemingly innocuous, portly fellow by the name of Elmo St. Peters (voiced by Ranft). Unexpectedly, St. Peters tosses the appliances into the back of a giant-tired monster truck, which signals the film's sudden turn to the genre of the horror movie. It turns out that St. Peters is the proprietor of a used appliance-parts shop and is given to collecting old appliances that he can then cannibalize for their parts. In the subsequent sequence he is specifically compared to Dr. Frankenstein and is shown rather gruesomely cutting the motor out of a blender so that he can sell the motor to a customer. Then follows a rousing musical sequence in which the various appliances (some of them weirdly cobbled together from the parts of miscellaneous other appliances) sing to the newcomers, explaining to them (in case viewers missed the connection) that life (and death) in this little shop of horrors is like something from a terrifying movie. This song, "B-Movie Show," is one of several in the film by singer-songwriter Van Dyke Parks; it features a contemporary sound that is a far cry from the romanticized musical nostalgia of the classic Disney film, as well as lyrics that seem aimed more at adults than children, partly because of the rather grim content and partly because the full effect of the song depends upon recognition of its allusions to classic low-budget horror movies. On the other hand, the lively animated production number that accompanies the song is certainly entertaining to children (just ask Benjamin), even if they don't quite understand the song; it sounds a lot like something from *The Rocky Horror Picture Show* (1975).

The appliances manage to escape from the parts shop and even to make their way to the city apartment where the Master now lives with his mother, though there is no sign of a father. For that matter (in what one is tempted to take as an allusion to all those missing mothers in the classic Disney films), the mother herself is not fully present, either. In a truly odd motif, the mother is never shown on-screen. Instead, we merely hear her voice as she meekly offers to give up any appliances the Master would like to take with him on his impending trip to college. He opts instead to travel out to the country cottage to pick up his old childhood appliances for use at college, only to find, of course, that they are no longer there. Meanwhile, when the appliances arrive at the city apartment, the Master is no longer there, because he is seeking them at the cottage. The family's newer, high-tech appliances (including a home computer, a food processor, and a fancy toaster oven, among others) jealously toss the new arrivals in a dumpster, whence they are taken to the junkyard where we witness the bizarre scene of another elaborate musical number in which the morosely singing cars (voicing the almost surreal lyrics of the song "Worthless," again written by Parks) are sent to their deaths in the compactor. The appliances nearly meet the same fate (along with the Master himself, who eventually finds them there), but all are saved at the last moment, when the little toaster (in the act that gives the film its title) sacrificially throws himself into the gears driving the compactor, jamming the works and stopping the machine. (Oddly, the toaster until this point in the film is probably the least prominent and important of the film's five central appliance-protagonists.) All's well that ends well, and in the end the Master takes the old appliances (even the toaster, which he repairs) away to college with him.

The scene in the junkyard is definitely the strangest in this film, which is filled with odd moments—as when the air conditioner in the cottage turns out to have the voice of Jack Nicholson (imitated by Phil Hartman) or when a hanging lamp in St. Peters's shop has the appropriately creepy voice of Peter Lorre (also Hartman). Among other things, it would be easy to declare the compactor scene too frightening (or at least too existentially heavy) for small children. It is certainly the case that the vision of anthropomorphic automobiles, given lives and personalities, then crushed to death by the mighty compactor, seems absolutely gruesome. I can say, though, that three-year-old Benjamin loves this sequence and wants to watch it over and over on

DVD—just like, come to think of it, Adam loved watching and rewatching the scene in *Star Wars* where most of the main characters are nearly squashed in a compactor!

Benjamin's a smart kid, if I do say so myself, but his response to this scene may not be all that unusual. Kids in general are tougher, smarter, and more able to cope with things than they are often given credit for. Indeed, perhaps the most striking (and praiseworthy) aspect of *The Brave Little Toaster*—and the characteristic that may most set it apart from the classic Disney films—is that it does not patronize children or assume that they are incapable of anything other than the most literal and naïve of interpretations of what they are seeing on the screen. Still, the compactor sequence is potentially a very disturbing one. When I asked Benjamin if he wasn't sad that the cars were being crushed, he simply (and slightly impatiently) informed me that they were "just cartoons," so that I needn't worry. I complimented him for understanding this fact, but also informed him that there really were junkyards where real cars were compacted like in the film. His first response was to suspect that I was just pulling his leg ("You're kid-din', right?"), and he did seem to become a bit alarmed when I assured him I was telling the truth. But he thought about it, shrugged and said, "Yeah, but they're not alive like in the movie."

The Brave Little Toaster addresses the role of *things* in our lives in some very profound ways, if not so directly as something like the *Toy Story* movies, which are ultimately the Pixar films that it resembles most. After all, the choice of toys for exploring how kids relate to possessions seems an obvious one, while it is hard to imagine that very many children get particularly attached to toasters or vacuum cleaners. Indeed, as tools designed to do practical work, appliances inherently lack the charm of beloved toys, while—as products of technology—appliances are particularly prone to becoming outmoded and thus being discarded for newer and fancier models. It thus might seem an odd move to endow such objects with human personalities, though kids are so accustomed to seeing anthropomorphized objects, especially in animated films, that it probably doesn't strike most of them as very re-markable. The first time Benjamin and I watched the film, we got sev-eral minutes in before he suddenly looked up (I believe the blanket was talking at the time) and said, "Hey, it can talk!" But he tends to make the same observation about talking animated animals, and he certainly seemed happy to grant the premise in this case and play along.

The real significance of the living appliances in *The Brave Little Toaster* seems to me to pivot around the compactor scene in the junkyard, with its musical demonstration of the way in our contemporary society we put so much stress on objects and want so desperately (under the influence of advertising) to acquire them, then are perfectly happy to toss them aside when something seemingly more desirable comes along. The castaways are then declared worthless and sent to the garbage heap. The central emphasis on cars (which since at least the 1950s have been the major emblems of American consumerist prosperity) in the compactor scene serves to reinforce the point. Even these key commodities, which become such crucial and defining parts of our lives (more so than toasters or desk lamps), often for years at a time, are then typically tossed aside for newer models. That the five appliances are ultimately rescued (and taken with him to college by the Master) can then be taken as a vague criticism of this throwaway mentality, urging us to begin to consider the things in our lives for what they are and what they can do for us, rather than simply as commodities, objects of consumerist fascination, valued primarily as interchangeable targets of acquisition, then immediately tossed aside so we can acquire something else.[3] It can also be taken as a commentary on the insubstantiality of life in our contemporary capitalist world, where nothing lasts for long and change is the only constant.

That it is not quite possible to pin down the message of *The Brave Little Toaster* beyond these suggestions is not necessarily a weakness of the film, especially as a kids' movie. After all, three-year-olds like Benjamin would be unlikely to decode the meaning of the film in any detailed form, anyway—just as he doesn't get the allusions to Nicholson and Lorre or understand the radio's references to figures such as Franklin Roosevelt or Pee Wee Reese. Even adult non-baseball fans won't remember Reese as the shortstop for the Dodgers from 1940 to 1958 (with a break for service in World War II), although baseball fans will recognize him as an icon of a bygone era in the sport and in American culture as a whole.[4] Indeed, the film is sprinkled with "in" references, as when the radio directs the others to travel "north by northwest," then warns them to "watch out for low-flying aircraft"— referring to the famous scene in Alfred Hitchcock's *North by Northwest* in which protagonist Roger Thornhill (Cary Grant) barely avoids being hit as a low-flying crop duster swoops down on him. Granted, this scene is one of the most familiar in movie history, but three-year-olds can hardly be expected to recognize it, and some adults might not, either. It does, however, give parents a chance to sound knowledgeable and authoritative by explaining the reference to their kids, though I must admit that Benjamin didn't seem all that impressed by my learned exegesis on this topic. Skylor, on the other hand, did have a sudden moment of recognition when I explained it to him and he realized that he had seen the same scene spoofed in an episode of the *Family Guy* animated TV series.

Benjamin also doesn't understand (or seem to care) that the inclusion of Little Richard's "Tutti-Frutti" early in the soundtrack helps to establish that the appliances are relics from a bygone (but fondly remembered) era and that any sympathy that viewers have for them might be similar to complex cultural phenomena such as the 1950s nostalgia craze. On the one hand the 1950s were an era of repressive conformism; on the other hand, "Tutti-Frutti" is a great song and the 1950s did give birth to rock 'n' roll. Indeed, the inclusion of this song in the soundtrack tends to connect the outdated appliances with the culture of the past, suggesting that simply throwing away such obsolete goods is tantamount to throwing away the past itself and all the cultural legacy that goes with it. On this reading, however sensible it might be to discard outdated appliances, the mentality that accompanies such activities is part of a rage for the new that potentially deprives us of a great deal that is valuable in the old.

Again, such interpretations are available only to adults, not to the kids who respond to the film on a much more basic level as being about lovable animated figures seeking the security of a home guarded by a parent figure. Thus, among other things, *The Brave Little Toaster* is an excellent illustration of the way in which, especially in recent years, children's movies have come to be complex cultural artifacts that are consciously designed to be consumed on at least two different levels. While these films might be constructed first and foremost to attract and entertain children, they are also (mercifully) designed to offer a certain amount of entertainment to the adults who spend so much time watching the movies with kids. The *Shrek* series from DreamWorks might be the best illustration of this phenomenon, though this double-coding is also crucial to the success of all the Pixar films. Even Disney proper (as distinguished from Pixar) has gotten with the program and has offered, in its recent films, a panoply of cultural allusions and sly jokes that young children are almost certain not to understand but that make the films more pleasurable for adults.

In the case of *The Brave Little Toaster*, I think the gap between possible receptions of the film is particularly large. Thus, nine-year-old Skylor doesn't really like the film, because he is at an awkward in-between age: too old to see it with Benjamin's innocent appreciation of the basics and too young to be impressed by the more adult-oriented features, which can be quite complex. For example, one segment of the song "Worthless" is sung by an old wood-paneled station wagon, which begins its story by noting that it "once drove a surfer to sunset." This evocation of surf culture by this particular vehicle, of course, immediately recalls (for those old enough to remember) the 1963 hit "Surf City," by Jan and Dean, the first surf music song ever to hit No. 1 on the Billboard Chart. The song famously tells of a California beach where there are "two girls for every boy," which the singers are visiting in their old Ford "woodie." This song, of course, is particularly relevant here because the station wagon involved is described as being dilapidated (lacking, among other things, a back seat or a rear window), yet still usable and able to "get me where I wanna go."[5] This connection thus immediately calls into question whether the cars being crunched in this sequence of the film are really worthless or whether they might still have value to someone. To further this connection, "Surf City" was written by Beach Boys leader Brian Wilson, with whom Parks, the writer of "Worthless," has extensively collaborated over the years.

Meanwhile, the lyrics of this section of Parks's song go on, in their narration of this station wagon's past experiences, to provide the following description of California beach culture: "There were bikinis and buns; there were weenies. Fellini just couldn't forget." Even Skylor gets it that a line combining references to bikinis, buns, and weenies is not just about clothing and food, but is filled with sexual innuendo, though he lacks access to the way this line evokes the carefree sexual atmosphere of 1960s surf culture as described in "Surf City." But Skylor has no idea what to make of the truly surprisingly reference to Fellini, even after I tried to explain to him that Federico Fellini was a famous Italian filmmaker. I don't really understand the Fellini reference myself, other than suspecting that it's a sort of impressionistic reference that is not meant to be entirely explicable in rational terms. Yes, I know that Fellini's films often deal centrally with his own memories, real or manufactured. And I know that the he-donistic lifestyle described by the woodie in "Worthless" is reminis-cent of that which features in Fellini's most famous film, *La Dolce Vita* (1960), while beach scenes are particularly prominent in what might be Fellini's greatest film, *8 1/2* (1963). Indeed, *8 1/2* (released in the same year as "Surf City," for what it's worth) is, as much as any-thing, about the alienating effects of rampant modernization, which of course is pretty much what *The Brave Little Toaster* is about as well.

If this sort of modernist insider referencing seems a bit obscure even for most adults, it is certainly beyond the reach of three-year-olds. The question that arises, of course, is just what (if anything) parents who do have access to such aspects of the film should do to use that knowledge to illuminate the film for their children. My strat-egy is to explain, even to three-year-old Benjamin, my understanding of the text, even though I know perfectly well he will not understand most of what I am saying. Same with Skylor, though of course a nine-year-old can follow more than a three-year-old. After all, if children are to grow and learn they must by definition move beyond where they already are. It seems to me that exposing them to things that are a little beyond their reach can help them to stretch just a bit, while planting seeds for later, when (hopefully) they will experience so-that's-what-Dad-was-talking-about moments of recognition. Indeed, *The Brave Little Toaster* is ideal for just such a strategy, and one of the things I really like about it is that it does not take the least-common-denominator approach of so many children's films and does not assume that children are stupid and can't learn.

Disney, of course, has often been accused of doing just that, and it is not for nothing that "Disneyfication" is, among other things, a vir-tual synonym for "dumbing down." This charge is not entirely unfair, but it is not entirely fair, either. Among other things, it ignores the element of sheer magic that has made Disney films, especially the best animated ones, special—and that has provided some of the most effective protests against capitalist routinization in the past seventy years.

There are, in fact, a number of predecessors to *The Brave Little Toaster* in the Disney oeuvre of animated films, the most direct of which would be the 1952 short *Susie, the Little Blue Coupe*. Here, the car of the title starts out as a shiny new vehicle in a showroom, where she is quickly bought and goes to have a happy life out in the world.

Unfortunately, she eventually begins to grow old and to develop mechanical trouble, after which her owner trades her in for a newer model. Relegated to a used car lot, she is bought by a new down-and-out owner who takes poor care of her, sending her into a downward spiral in which she loses all self-respect. Ultimately, she is stolen and then crashed in a police chase, after which she is towed away to a junkyard. To this point, the film could be taken as a rather dark allegory of the human condition. However, this being 1952, the film ends on an upbeat note: Susie is bought (for $12.50) by a college boy who fixes her up and transforms her into a gleaming custom jalopy, once again full of pep and vigor.

If cars and other machines do not feature prominently in Disney's animated classics, the same cannot be said of the live-action films that became Disney's bread and butter in the 1960s. These films quite frequently featured cars in central roles, as with the flubber-powered flying Model T of *The Absent-Minded Professor* (1961) and its sequel, *Son of Flubber* (1963). These cars fly by technology (however far-fetched), rather than magic, but cars sometimes even invade the realm of Disney fantasy, as in *The Gnome-Mobile* (1967), in which a Rolls Royce Phantom II plays the title role. Surely the most prominent Disney auto, however, has been Herbie the Love Bug, an anthropomorphized Volkswagen Beetle that was the title character in the 1968 film *The Love Bug*. Herbie proved so popular that he helped spur sales of Volkswagen's signature auto, as well as inspired four theatrical sequels, the latest of which, *Herbie: Fully Loaded*, appeared as recently as 2005.

Still, *The Brave Little Toaster* shares relatively little with these Disney precedents in terms of its overall message or style, and it certainly did not trigger a move toward an emphasis on the mechanical in subsequent Disney animated films. On the contrary, the roughly contemporaneous *Oliver and Company* (1988), a sometimes amusing adaptation of Charles Dickens's 1838 novel *Oliver Twist*, features, in good Disney fashion, a cast of animated dogs. The film was reasonably successful at the box office, even if contains little of note rather than the basic idea of mining classic nineteenth-century British literature to find material for animated children's films.

And then came *The Little Mermaid*, featuring old-time Disney animated magic. Ariel (voiced by Jodi Benson) is the mermaid princess of the title, presumably updated for contemporary audiences by

making her spunkier and more independent than predecessors like the recumbent Sleeping Beauty. Ariel deviates from earlier Disney princesses in that she is willing to go against her essential nature as a mermaid (and go against the wishes of her father, the king of the Merpeople) in order to be with the dashing human Prince Eric (Christopher Daniel Barnes). She finally succeeds in winning his love (thanks largely to the traditional feminine virtues of physical beauty and a lovely singing voice), but only at the expense of becoming human herself, thus not only turning her back on her own cultural heritage, but even having to undergo a radical body modification in which her mermaid's fishlike tail is replaced by human legs.

The Little Mermaid also returned Disney animated film to its roots in the fairy tale, being based on one of the stories of Hans Christian Andersen. In his telling, however, the Little Mermaid does not win her man, but that sort of failure would not do in a Disney film, which was modified to produce a stereotypically happy ending—with happiness defined (for a woman) as the successful acquisition of a husband. One could thus see this film as going against the traditional Disney emphasis on the natural and the authentic, or one could simply take it as a declaration that the most authentic thing for a woman to do is fall in love and win a husband, regardless of what she might have to give up to do so. In short, *The Little Mermaid*, while including some stylistic updates (such as hipper music), is a definite throwback that seems almost entirely to ignore the gains made by the women's movement in the decades preceding its release. Meanwhile, the film continues the Disney tendency to regard parents as irrelevant or even as obstacles to be overcome, while including some of the most overt endorsements of consumerism to be found in any Disney film. In particular, it is clear that Ariel is fascinated not just by Eric, but by human beings in general, and particularly by the amazing (to her) objects that have been produced by that culture, which to her (in a direct, if inadvertent, dramatization of Marx's famous discussion in *Capital* of the commodity fetish) have an absolutely magical quality considering that she comes from a low-tech culture that seems mired in a preindustrial state.

Having learned that the Disney fairy-tale princess formula, left in disuse for decades, still had legs (as it were), the Disney company quickly followed, in 1991, with *Beauty and the Beast*, a $25 million film that pulled in $145 million at the domestic box office in its first run and would eventually take in nearly $400 in worldwide box-office receipts, almost twice the take of *The Little Mermaid*. *Beauty and the Beast*, which became the first animated film to be nominated for a Best Picture Oscar, was once again based on a traditional fairy tale, though one that had recently been reinforced in the popular consciousness by a television series that completed a three-year run on CBS in 1990. The film was touted by Disney as a statement against the shallowness of a society in which status is often based on looks, and would thus seem to be something of a departure from Disney tradition, in which beauty (at least for women) is consistently touted as the ultimate virtue. Indeed, the male lead (the beast of the title) is presented as grotesquely ugly (though he really isn't), but Belle, the female protagonist, is still young and beautiful, even if Disney once again tried to make her a bit stronger and more independent than earlier Disney princesses. Moreover, even the beast turns out in reality to be a handsome prince, cursed because of his own tendency to judge people by appearances to remain in the guise of a horrid monster until he can learn to love and win someone's love in return. Belle, meanwhile, falls into the clutches of the beast in an attempt to rescue her father from him, repeating a favorite Disney motif of children saving parents. Imprisoned in the beast's ramshackle castle, the young woman gradually comes to love the beast despite appearances. She ends up saving him as well (from angry villagers reminiscent of the mob in *Frankenstein*), returning him to his true (genuine, natural, authentic, original) form in the nick of time. The film then ends with another happy royal couple united in perpetual bliss.

As in most animated Disney films, then, *Beauty and the Beast* defines success as the reclamation of one's appropriate place in the world, just as Disney films as a whole tend to tout a surprisingly (given their seemingly thoroughgoing endorsement of the American way of life) static, almost medieval worldview in which almost all change is bad and in which the worst transgressions involve individuals who either seek to rise above their preordained station in life or to deny others the benefits of their own preordained station. Much of this worldview, of course, derives from the source material. Yet Disney is not hesitant to modify (sometimes dramatically) other aspects of the source materials, so this repeated counsel to stay in one's place represents a striking contradiction to the consistent endorsement of individualism that runs throughout Disney's oeuvre. However, this contradiction is not quite as strong as it at first appears. In Disney films, individualism tends to mean being true to the person you *really* are, despite pressure imposed by others. In other words, each individual has certain innate characteristics, and the goal of each individual should be to try to find out what those characteristics are and to develop them to their fullest. Individualism thus does not imply the ability to choose or change one's basic nature, but simply the right to stick to whatever one's basic nature was in the first place. Finally, the emphasis on individualism tends to be stronger in live-action films (often aimed at a slightly older teenage audience), while the endorsement of respect for the status quo tends to be stronger in the animated films, which are aimed at younger viewers.

Beauty and the Beast features traditional music, which reinforces the fairy-tale nature of the film and goes against a growing Disney tendency to try to give their films a slightly more contemporary air. But the music in the film is extremely effective and greatly helps to enhance the aura of magic that permeates the film. Indeed, magic, almost always a key ingredient in Disney children's film, is especially prominent here, which tends to convey the message that, while virtue might be rewarded, those rewards ultimately depend on forces that are beyond the control of mere individuals. Meanwhile, magically animated objects (including a candelabra, a teapot, and a clock—all of which turn out to be humans transformed by magic) play a very large role in the film, once again conveying the notion that objects can have magical powers and thus reinforcing a consumerist worship of commodities (while effacing the reality that these things can only come into existence through the agency of human labor).

This strong emphasis on magic continues in Disney's next major animated effort, *Aladdin* (1992), which followed *Beauty and the Beast* with still another hit—though one that has been roundly criticized for its depiction of Arabs as conniving, hook-nosed camel jockeys, while portraying the Arab cultures of the Middle East as savage and primitive. Indeed, whatever else one might say about *Aladdin*, it is inarguable that good and bad are racially coded in the film. Positive characters in the film invariably have entirely Aryan features, while the villains of the film are all given exaggerated features (such as large hook noses) that viewers can easily recognize as Arabic. One could, of course, argue that the film simply reflects ideas about Arabs and their culture that were already prevalent in American culture at the time. For me, however, this fact only makes the stereotypical depiction of Arabs in the film all the more troubling because it presents young viewers with attitudes they are likely to accept because they see these attitudes reinforced elsewhere.

The narrative of *Aladdin* is a simple one. The law of this backward Middle Eastern realm requires that the Sultan's daughter, Princess Jasmine (voiced by Linda Larkin, with singing by Lea Salonga), marry a prince, though she (being a typical Disney heroine) wants to marry for love. Meanwhile, Jafar, the Sultan's villainous Grand Vizier (Jonathan Freeman), plots both to win the hand of Jasmine and to usurp the Sultan's throne. Aladdin, for his part, is a poor "street rat," determined to show that he is nevertheless a man of merit. He then finds a magic lamp, thus becoming the master of the genie who has been trapped within. The genie transforms Aladdin into the dashing Prince Ali, who quickly wins Jasmine's heart. Problems with Jafar predictably ensue, but Aladdin eventually confesses his true identity, winning the respect of the Sultan, who thereby changes the law so that Jasmine and Aladdin can be wed. They then ride off together on a magic carpet.

At first glance, *Aladdin* might seem to be a true upward-mobility narrative, which would set it apart from the usual emphasis on staying in one's proper place. But the coding of the film (including the visual representation of Aladdin himself) makes it clear that Aladdin has a noble essence. After all, he is labeled early in the film as a "Diamond in the Rough" and is identified as a chosen one, the only person able to enter the magic cave from which the genie is retrieved in the first place. For his part, Jafar is clearly ignoble, both in appearance and action, so that, in the end, each person gets what he deserves based on his fundamental nature.

The poor-boy-makes-good motif that lies at the heart of *Aladdin* is a familiar American narrative, even if it is here translated from one of the Arab tales in *One Thousand and One Nights*. This Middle Eastern tale is filtered through the 1940 American film *The Thief of Baghdad*, which is probably a more direct source. Indeed, numerous aspects of the film (especially the attitudes of the main characters) are subtly Americanized, so that, while *Aladdin* may have announced the beginning of a decidedly multicultural phase in the production of Disney animated film, it also made clear that the central perspective of Disney films would remain resolutely white, middle class, and American.

Moreover, the film indicates the way in which "multicultural" for Disney often means merely "bicultural," with mainstream white American culture representing what might be called "normal" culture, while all nonwestern cultural perspectives are lumped into one exotic heap at the other pole.

This tendency to lump all nonwestern cultures together can perhaps best be seen in the sequence in the film in which Aladdin (posing as Prince Ali) takes Jasmine on a whirlwind tour of the ancient world. On this tour, they observe various wonders, including the Parthenon in Athens and the Sphinx in Egypt, though the latter is shown as still under construction. This latter motif allows for a gag in which a worker, startled by the tourists, accidentally chips off the nose of the Sphinx, though in point of fact the famously missing nose of this monument is believed to have been destroyed in the fourteenth century AD, while the Sphinx is believed to have been constructed in the third millennium BC. Add in the fact that the Parthenon was not constructed until the fifth century BC and it becomes clear that the film not only lumps all nonwestern cultures together, but also tends to efface history, viewing everything ancient as being of a piece.

Aladdin also marked a determination to make Disney's animated films hipper and more up-to-date, as a means of appealing to both increasingly sophisticated young viewers and the parents who would presumably be watching the films with their kids Thus, though still set in the distant past, the film uses much more modern music than its forerunners in Disney animated film, while also going for particularly hip (maybe too hip for young viewers even to understand) humor. Indeed, the genie discovered by Aladdin becomes pretty much the heart and soul of the film as the manic performance of Robin Williams (which includes a number of slightly off-color jokes) steals one scene after another. Disney put unprecedented emphasis on Williams's appearance in its promotion of the film, suggesting their understanding of the importance of his performance; this fact also served as something of a watershed that has led to a substantial increase in the use of high-profile Hollywood actors to provide the voices for animated characters in films.

Aladdin was followed by a string of unremarkable live-action films from Disney, including a 1994 live-action remake of *The Jungle Book*. But *Aladdin*'s huge box-office success also emboldened the Disney company to spend as they had never spent before in the production of their next animated features. *The Lion King*, released in the summer of 1994, had a production budget of nearly $80 million, well over twice that of *Aladdin*, but it returned nearly $800 million in worldwide box-office receipts, making it easily the highest-grossing animated film released to that time, both domestically and worldwide.[6] This was a film overtly designed to be *big*, employing, among other things, one of the most impressive arrays of voice talents ever utilized in an animated film, from James Earl Jones as the majestic King Mufasa, to Jeremy Irons (in a delightfully smarmy performance as the evil lion Scar, Mufasa's brother), to Matthew Broderick as the adult version of Mufasa's son, Simba. Even secondary characters are voiced by relatively well-known actors, such as Nathan Lane as Timon the Meerkat, Robert Guillaume as Rafiki the Mandrill, and Rowan Atkinson as Zazu the Hornbill. Meanwhile, two of the film's treacherous hyenas are voiced by Whoopi Goldberg and Cheech Marin, who give these villains a clearly ethnic slant (African American and Hispanic, respectively) that has drawn considerable criticism.

Though all Disney animated films are musicals to some extent, *The Lion King* may employ music more effectively than any other Disney animated film, which perhaps explains why it has also gone on to become a highly successful Broadway show. The music here is a bit hipper than the old-fashioned, romantic, nostalgia-laden tunes of a *Snow White*, which is only to be expected in a film whose major songs featured music written by pop icon Elton John and lyrics by Tim Rice (a longtime successful lyricist who wrote the lyrics for the 1971 rock opera *Jesus Christ Superstar*). John himself performs the Oscar-winning song "Can You Feel the Love Tonight," which plays over the film's ending credits and reinforces the typical happy Disney ending. The music, in fact, may be the most successful part of *The Lion King* and the biggest single reason for its great success. Benjamin, for example, enjoys the film (though I have serious reservations about it, as I will describe below), but he really likes the musical numbers more than any other aspect of the film and will happily watch these numbers over and over (especially his favorite, "Hakuna Matata"). He also sings the songs cheerfully to himself while playing elaborate high-imagination games with various toys.

If the songs of *The Lion King* are really more entertaining than the plot, it is also the case that the film has a *big* plot as well. Departing from the fairy- and folk-tale sources of most animated Disney films,

The Lion King is based on even older and more basic mythic material, in this case the wounded king myth (which also provides much of the background to works such as T. S. Eliot's classic modernist poem, *The Waste Land*). *The Lion King* also has some of the texture of Shakespearean tragedy, with *Hamlet* serving as a particularly obvious counterpart to the film—not to mention the fact that Timon and Pumbaa are reminiscent of the lower-class "mechanicals" who provide comic relief from the more weighty doings of royalty in so many of Shakespeare's plays.

As *The Lion King* begins, King Mufasa rules his African kingdom wisely and well; all of the other animals love and respect him, even those (such as the antelopes) whom Mufasa and the other lions kill and eat. It's all part of the circle of life, Mufasa tells Simba early on: the lions eat the antelopes, but when the lions die their bodies contribute to the growth of future grass, which the antelopes eat, and so on. Thus, though it is not emphasized (or even actually stated), there is at least a potentially positive ecological theme in the film that suggests the importance of the balance of nature. However, the principal political theme has to do with the machinations of the jealous Scar (aided by the dastardly hyenas) to try to take power from his brother. Scar ultimately engineers Mufasa's death and even manages to make the young Simba (voiced by Jonathan Taylor Thomas) feel responsible. He then convinces Simba to go into exile to avoid public humiliation, though he plans to have the hyenas murder the young lion on his way out of the kingdom. Simba escapes the murder attempt, but then nearly dies in the desert that borders the kingdom, to be rescued in the nick of time by Timon and Pumbaa, who take him in (feeling that having their own lion as an ally might be valuable) and teach him their personal, carefree philosophy of "Hakuna Matata." Simba grows to adulthood with the pair, sharing their worry-free lifestyle. In the meantime, with Scar and the hyenas in charge, Mufasa's former kingdom has become a blighted and barren wasteland, the natural balance having been upset.

After Simba learns of the state of the kingdom, he decides (with considerable reluctance) that it is his responsibility as his father's rightful heir to return to try to set things right. He returns to the kingdom and defeats Scar in one-on-one combat, after which the hyenas set upon their fallen leader and tear him to pieces. Simba assumes the throne and marries the young lioness who had been intended for him since they were cubs. As the film ends, the kingdom is once again becoming green and prosperous, the natural order of things having been restored. In a final flourish, Simba presents his newborn cub (seemingly a boy, though it turns out to be a girl in the 1998 straight-to-DVD sequel, *The Lion King II*) to his adoring subjects, providing assurances that the proper order of succession will continue after his reign.

Seemingly a simple story of good vs. evil, *The Lion King* certainly includes messages about responsibility and duty, but it has a power-fully reactionary subtext that, perhaps more than any other Disney film, touts the value of inheritance over accomplishment and of accepting one's lot over improving or changing one's place through merit and hard work. The film leaves no room for uncertainty that Simba is the rightful king because he was born the son of a king and anointed at birth, even though he has never demonstrated any aptitude for the position. Similarly, it goes out of its way to depict Scar as an unmitigated evil because he disturbs the natural order in almost every way imaginable. In the end, all is well because that order has been restored. Scar is dead, the hyenas have been put back in their place, and the rightful ruler is on the throne, with all of the other animals (even the ones who are likely soon to be eaten by Simba and his lion cohorts) accepting their roles as loyal subjects. Accepting one's des-tined fate (king or slave, predator or prey), after all, seems to be the principal message of this brilliantly well-made film.

Given its mythological resonances and the fact that it begs for com-parison with Shakespeare, *The Lion King* is Disney animated film at its most ambitious and magisterial, and (however problematic its poli-tics) the film achieves a certain sense of magnitude that Disney has failed to achieve in any of its subsequent animated films. For exam-ple, *Pocahontas* (1995), produced in parallel with *The Lion King* and viewed at the time by many at Disney as the more important film, is a relatively slight work in almost every way.

Pocahontas is a departure for a Disney animated feature in that it is based on a real historical figure, a young Powhatan girl (voiced here by Irene Bedard, with singing supplied by Judy Kuhn) who famously befriended English colonist John Smith (voiced in the film by Mel Gibson) during the building of Virginia's Jamestown settlement in 1607, furthering communication between the colonists and the Native Americans who inhabited the area. The film here goes to great pains to depict the Native Americans in a positive light; not only are they noble, honest, and trustworthy, but they live in great harmony with their natural surroundings. In short, they represent a virtual embodiment of Disney's long-standing glorification of the natural and the authentic. On the other hand, while Smith is portrayed positively, many of the English settlers are depicted as vicious schemers, bent on seeking profit at the expense of the tranquil Native American civilization that they interrupt. They have, in fact, been separated from nature by their greed, devoting themselves to a grasping, unnatural, and inauthentic quest for gold. Even the animation supports this cultural dichotomy. Reversing the trend seen in *Aladdin*, the Native Americans are drawn to appear noble and upstanding, while many of the settlers are caricatured, their warped visages reflecting their greedy natures.

For her part, Pocahontas is the daughter of a chief, which makes her essentially another in the long line of Disney princesses. She is depicted as happy and carefree, accompanied in her daily jaunts through nature by cute animal sidekicks that might have been very much at home in *Snow White* or *Sleeping Beauty*. Smith, meanwhile, is a typical hero, strong and brave, though ominously depicted as a great Indian fighter. As one crewmember notes when Smith boards the ship for America, "You can't fight Indians without John Smith!"

The colonists are led by one Governor Ratcliffe (David Ogden Stiers), who is depicted as particularly rapacious in his lust for gold and vicious in his condescension toward "savages" such as Pocahontas. He and the other colonists establish their credentials as enemies of nature early on when they decimate the local forest to build their fort. They are equally thoughtless in their dealings with the Native American inhabitants of that forest, though each side is highly suspicious of the other. In a story that resembles the real Smith's own (widely disputed) historical account, Smith is captured and nearly killed by the Native Americans, saved only by the intervention of Pocahontas, who subsequently befriends Smith and teaches him to respect nature. Pocahontas's father, Chief Powhatan (Russell Means, with singing by Jim Cummings), vows that any killing from this day forward will not be initiated by his people. As if in response, Ratcliffe soon afterward (in an episode with no historical basis) attempts to kill Pocahontas, who is saved by the intervention of Smith, while the English colonists mutiny against Ratcliffe. Smith himself is badly wounded, however, and is forced to return to England to seek medical treatment. Pocahontas, though clearly in love with Smith, stays behind with her people, and two Disney characters from different realms once again return to their own natural places. In the end, neither the English nor the budding capitalism that drives their colonial mission are really depicted as evil: the fault simply lies with a few bad individuals such as Ratcliffe.

By the time of *The Hunchback of Notre Dame* (1996), it was becoming clear that Disney, in an attempt to cash in as much as possible on the newly lucrative market for animated children's films, was becoming increasingly desperate for material. For example, in addition to their unlikely animated adaptation of this nineteenth-century French novel by Victor Hugo, Disney was by then producing, in their search for more product, a string of remakes and sequels, as well as distributing more and more films actually made by other studios (with Pixar as the leading example). In the case of *The Hunchback of Notre Dame*, Disney considerably sanitizes the source material (replacing the tragic conclusion of Hugo's original novel with a happy ending of triumphant celebration), but the material is nevertheless rather dark for a children's film. The music also seems pitched to a more adult audience and sounds more like Broadway show tunes than typical children's film music. In many ways, *Hunchback* is something of a mess that can't seem to decide what kind of film it wants to be, mixing dark, adult subject matter with wacky motifs (such as comic talking gargoyles) designed to make the film entertaining for children.

Whatever shortcomings it might have, *The Hunchback of Notre Dame* (helmed by the same creative team that had made *Beauty and the Beast*) is a daring effort that explores genuinely new territory in children's films. It is also one of the most overtly political films in the Disney oeuvre, containing a very clear critique of bigotry and oppression with its central focus not only on the persecution of the hunchback Quasimodo (voiced by Tom Hulce) but on the racist oppression of gypsies in the context of fifteenth-century Paris. The film's central villain, Minister of Justice Claude Frollo (Tony Jay), has dedicated himself to ridding Paris of gypsies altogether, a project he has been pursuing for many years. Indeed, the film opens twenty years before the time of the main action, when Frollo attacks and kills a gypsy woman, then nearly kills the baby she had been carrying in her arms. However, a kindly priest, the Archdeacon of Notre Dame (David Ogden Stiers), convinces him to spare the deformed child, which he subsequently hides away in the bell tower of the cathedral, raising the boy as his ward, but teaching the boy to regard himself as a monster and to shun human contact.

In the main plot of the film, Frollo recalls Captain Phoebus (Kevin Kline) from a military campaign in order to place the captain in charge of the campaign to drive the gypsies from Paris. Meanwhile, Frollo encounters the staggeringly beautiful gypsy street dancer Esmeralda (Demi Moore, with singing by Heidi Mollenhauer), who subsequently becomes the focus of his anti-gypsy hatred, partly because he clearly finds her so sexually alluring, arousing feelings in him that he would rather not have. Both Quasimodo and Phoebus find Esmeralda alluring as well, but the film makes it clear that the handsome Phoebus is the man meant for her. After a number of harrowing near-escapes, Phoebus, Esmeralda, and Quasimodo emerge triumphant, heroes of the people of Paris, while Frollo meets a horrific death.

In *Hercules* (1997), Disney turns to Greek myth for inspiration, though this film greatly modernizes the narrative, filtering it through contemporary popular culture and going to great lengths to spice up its mythic materials with wacky comedy and cheerfully anachronistic dialogue. The film also features a lively contemporary soundtrack, including several appearances by the Muses, employed as a chorus to further the telling of the story, in the guise of a black Motown girl-group reminiscent of the Supremes, with a dash of gospel thrown in for good measure. Indeed, the film announces early its intention to treat its mythic materials with lighthearted irreverence. This is a film designed for fun, not for paying respect to the cultural past, an attitude that can sometimes make it highly entertaining, but that participates in a particularly obvious way in the slow erosion of historical sense to which Disney's films have been contributing since *Snow White*.

Hercules himself is a clumsy but lovable lunk, struggling to come to grips with his superhuman strength, deriving his character more from Clark Kent than from traditional mythic accounts of the Hercules figure. Like Kal-el (Superman), he is sent to earth by his original parents, then adopted by kindly humans who raise him the best they can, keeping his superhuman powers a secret from the world. Ultimately, he has to struggle against the machinations of, you guessed it, an evil sorcerer, in this case Hades, god of the Underworld (voiced with charmingly comical smarminess by James Woods). Hades wants to usurp the place of Zeus, king of the Gods and father of Hercules, but to do so he must first get by Hercules, which he plans to do via a scheme to deprive Hercules of his superhuman strength by exploiting Hercules's love of the spunky human woman Megara (his version of Kryptonite). Hades fails, of course, because it is not his place to be king of the Gods. Hercules emerges triumphant, rescues Megara, and is restored to his rightful place on Mount Olympus. In a final romantic twist, however, Hercules gives up his divinity in order to become human and return to earth to be with Meg.

While *Hercules* still features a strong male character who rescues his beloved female from distress, the film ends with a progressive twist in that it is the male who must give up something in order to be with the female, instead of the other way around (as occurs most obviously in *The Little Mermaid*.) And Megara is certainly a stronger and more complex female character (through much of the film she is working, though under duress, in league with Hades) than the typical Disney princess. The film still implies, however, that Hercules was meant to be with Megara all along, so it does not really challenge the longstanding Disney advocacy for accepting one's natural role in life. Moreover, the lighthearted look and feel of the film tends to diminish any progressive message that the film might convey. The characters of *Hercules*, inspired by the designs of British caricaturist Gerald Scarfe, have a distinctive, comically exaggerated look, though some of them (especially Hades) may be a bit *too* exaggerated at times. And the completely anachronistic contemporary soundtrack once again announces the traditional Disney disregard for historical accuracy.

In 1998, Disney turned to Chinese legend for source material, thus continuing its efforts to scour the world's cultures for film fodder. *Mulan* also features an action-oriented female protagonist, and thus continues Disney's efforts in the 1990s to update their representation of women and girls, while making the film a sort of follow-up to *Pocahontas*. Gender is more to the foreground as an issue in *Mulan*, even if the critical depiction of patriarchal China tends to suggest that women in the West are treated more fairly. Meanwhile, an even larger than usual collection of anachronisms and historical inaccuracies not only continue Disney's traditional disregard for historicity but also tend to suggest that Chinese history is even less worthy of respect than is Western history.

The film, which focuses on an invasion of China by the Huns, also continues the racial coding that had been so problematic in films such as *Aladdin*. Thus, the evil Huns are not only depicted as savage and ruthless, but as being significantly darker than the Chinese, who here serve as the ethnic norm. In the subsequent mobilization to defend China, young Fa Mulan (Ming-Na, with singing by Lea Salonga) cuts off her long hair (even though Chinese women at the time would not have had longer hair than men) to disguise herself as a man so that she can fight to defend China—and to save her aging father from military service. She performs admirably, though the inclusion of a comic dragon—voiced by Eddie Murphy—as her sidekick is somewhat of a silly distraction from the story. In the end she is discovered to be a woman but is nevertheless declared a hero by the Emperor and invited to become a member of his council. She declines, however, returning to her properly feminine place at home with her father, with Captain Li Shang (B. D. Wong, singing by Donny Osmond), a man she met in the course of her military service, following close behind as her suitor. Mulan is thus safely re-enclosed in a traditional feminine role, even as her heroism is safely projected into an exotic fantasy world.

Disney next turned to one of the staples of twentieth-century American popular culture for material with its animated retelling of the Tarzan story. A huge success at the box office (raking in nearly $450 million worldwide), *Tarzan* (1999) is often considered to be the last film of the Disney renaissance, subsequent films declining in both commercial appeal and artistic ambition. Like *The Lion King*, *Tarzan* sidesteps uncomfortable issues such as colonialism and racism by depicting Africa as a land populated entirely by animals, with no black African humans anywhere in sight. Indeed, the makers of *Tarzan* seem to have had *The Lion King* in mind as a model in a number of ways, as when pop music icon Phil Collins was contracted to write the film's songs, seeking (unsuccessfully) to re-create the magic of Elton John's songs for *The Lion King*.

The conflict in *Tarzan*, however, is not between good and bad animals as in *The Lion King*, but between good gorillas (with Tarzan— voiced by Tony Goldwyn—among their number) and bad invading white humans. Some of the humans are virtuous, but most of them are villainous enemies of nature, intent on capturing gorillas so that they can be sold into captivity. The film is thus structured around the typical Disney opposition between the natural as good and the unnatural as bad, though it does show some flexibility in suggesting that, though Tarzan is biologically human, his natural place (given his upbringing) is among the apes. Thus, while there are some clear problems with the film's erasure of indigenous African humans, *Tarzan* is thus less purely essentialist in its definition of the natural and the authentic than are most Disney films. Of course, the white British woman Jane Porter (Minnie Driver), who meets and falls in love with Tarzan, in the course of the film also decides to live in Africa among the gorillas so that she can remain with Tarzan. The film thus once again suggests that the natural place for a woman is with her man, regardless of where that might be and regardless of her own origins.

The Emperor's New Groove (2000) continues Disney's multicultural trend of the 1990s. Its setting is an unnamed mountainous empire that is reminiscent of the Incan empire that reached the height of its power in the Andes region of what is now Peru in the fifteenth century AD, before being conquered by Spanish invaders in the sixteenth century. Indeed, numerous cultural, architectural, and topographic clues of the film link its fictional empire to the Incas. Perhaps the most obvious is that the emperor (voiced by comic actor David Spade) is named Kuzco; the Incas emerged around the twelfth century as a tribe in the Cuzco region of what is now southeastern Peru. However, *The Emperor's New Groove* has little interest in exploring Incan culture or history. Despite its seeming setting in the distant past, it is a radical departure from the Disney tradition of attempting to construct seemingly timeless tales. Instead, as the title indicates, this film goes all out for humor and hipness, presenting a lightweight tale that addresses few real issues. On the surface, the film goes against the tendency of Disney films to endorse the rule of hereditary monarchs by making the teenage Emperor Kuzco something of a clueless buffoon, too self-absorbed and self-indulgent to be anything like an effective ruler. He even remains pompous after accidentally being turned into a llama[7] early in the film (a guise in which he remains through most of the story) as the unintended side effect of an assassination attempt. And yet, the basic plot of the film involves an attempt by his advisor Yzma (Eartha Kitt) to use her powers as a sort of evil sorceress to usurp Kuzco's rule, an attempt that ultimately makes the shallow and superficial Kuzco into a victim and ultimately into a hero as he regains his rightful place on the throne in the tradition of all royal Disney protagonists. Granted, the film seems to suggest that the wisdom of common people—here embodied in the admirable figure of the lowly villager Pacha (John Goodman)—may outstrip that of

pompous rulers such as Kuzco, but Pacha's main contribution is to
help Kuzco defeat Yzma and regain his throne. The film entirely fore-
goes, for example, the possible route of having Pacha assume the
throne and lead the empire in a new and more democratic direction.
For his part, Kuzco presumably learns to care more about the feelings
of others (including commoners such as Pacha), though the only real
evidence of this is the fact that he rewards Pacha for helping him by
dropping his earlier plan to destroy Pacha's ancestral home in order to
build a palatial summer house (something along the lines of the Play-
boy Mansion) for himself on the same site.

Disney's most successful animated film of 2000 was *Dinosaur*,
which features some of the most impressively realistic animation ever
produced by Disney, made even more so by the use of lush live-action
backgrounds behind computer-animated prehistoric animals. The animation is good enough to suggest that Disney's in-house capabilities
might have come to rival Pixar's had the companies gone down different roads. But the storytelling is weak. Given its subject matter (the
lives of prehistoric animals), the film might have been vaguely educational, but the filmmakers decided to forego scientific accuracy, mis-
representing the appearances of several of the dinosaurs and lumping
together numerous animals from different periods or places without
regard for their actual origins. Apparently, Disney's tendency to treat
the historical past as a homogeneous stew from which to extract
ingredients extends to the prehistoric past as well. Most importantly,
the combination in *Dinosaur* of extremely realistic-looking visuals
(however scientifically inaccurate) with the fact that the animals can
talk and that they act in totally unrealistic (and essentially human)
ways makes this film annoying. Skylor has proclaimed it an atrocious
ripoff of *The Land Before Time*, and Benjamin just finds it plain boring. Kids do like dinosaurs, though, and the film was ultimately a hit:
the domestic box-office receipts barely recouped the film's reported
$130 million production budget, but big overseas business pushed the
worldwide gross to $350 million, roughly in line with most of the suc-
cessful works of the Disney renaissance—and roughly double the take
of either *The Emperor's New Groove* or the film that followed in
2001, *Atlantis: The Lost Empire*.

Atlantis: The Lost Empire is a work of retro science fiction, in many
ways reminiscent of the 1959 classic *Journey to the Center of the
Earth*, with a dash of Disney's live-action *20,000 Leagues Under the*

Sea (1954) thrown in for good measure. Here, bumbling would-be explorer Milo Thatch (Michael J. Fox) manages to win the support of mogul Preston B. Whitmore to mount a voyage in search of the legendary lost city of Atlantis, which Thatch believes he can find based on the journals of his own grandfather, a famous explorer and friend of Whitmore. The expedition, headed by Commander Lyle Tiberius Rourke (James Garner), includes a multicultural group of both men and women, somewhat in the mode of *Star Trek*. However, it differs from *Star Trek* in that several of the central characters are included mostly for comic relief, including demolition expert Vincenzo "Vinny" Santorini (voiced by Don Novello, better known to those of us of a certain age as Father Guido Sarducci), excavation expert Gaetan "The Mole" Moliére (voiced by Corey Burton in imitation of Peter Lorre), the redneck cook (a forerunner of Mater in *Cars*) Jebidiah "Cookie" Farnsworth (voiced by Jim Varney of Ernest P. Worrell fame), and the elderly, chain-smoking communications expert Wilhelmina Bertha Packard (Florence Stanley). Indeed, the crew is composed primarily of various stereotypical figures, and characterization is in general a weakness of the film. It does, however, involve a great deal of rousing action and some impressive visuals, perhaps due to the contributions of production designer Mike Mignola, a famed comic book artist known primarily as the creator of the *Hellboy* comics.

The plot of *Atlantis* is somewhat stereotypical as well. Predictably, the expedition does locate Atlantis, which turns out still to be thriving in an enclosed undersea realm. The society of Atlantis seems to be an odd combination of the modern and the ancient, driven by a combination of high technology and magic. But the discovery of the city turns sour when Rourke betrays the original intentions of the mission by attempting to steal (for his own financial gain) the mystical power source that enables Atlantis to survive, even though this theft will lead to the destruction of the city. Rourke's capitalist greed is, however, defeated by Thatch and the other crew members. Thatch remains behind to help his new love, Atlantis's Princess Kida (Cree Summer), rebuild the city, while the others return to the surface, agreeing to keep the discovery of Atlantis a secret to protect the city from future wealth-seekers from the surface. The message here is a fairly weak one, this being a film more about style than substance. However, aside from the typical Disney swipe at excessive greed (and apart from

Thatch's defection to Atlantis in the interest of true love), the film
once again delivers a rather segregationist moral. The two cultures
being so far apart, it is best, says the film, for the Atlanteans to remain
in Atlantis and for the surface-dwellers to remain on the surface.

Disney continued its foray into science fiction adventure with
Treasure Planet (2002), an animated remake of Disney's own *Treasure Island*, a live-action film from 1950 that was based on Robert
Louis Stevenson's 1883 novel of the same title. When this film took
in a little more than half the gross of the already unsuccessful *Atlantis*,
it was pretty clear that the Disney renaissance was in serious trouble,
even as the Pixar films were soaring to popular and critical success
and the first *Shrek* film had introduced a new DreamWorks franchise
that would ultimately eclipse even *The Lion King* at the box office.
Treasure Planet is a lightweight film that also indicates the extent to
which Disney had by this time given up on the idea that each of its
animal theatrical releases should convey heavy-duty educational
messages.

Still, by transforming this story of pirates seeking treasure on the
high seas into a story of outer-space adventure, *Treasure Planet* combines two of the long-standing interests of the Disney company: trans-
lating science fiction into children's entertainment and converting the
English literary tradition into child-oriented American pop culture.
The film certainly has its moments, and the decision to depict space
ships as looking exactly like nineteenth-century sailing vessels makes
for some interesting visuals. So does the decision to make the pirate
crew a multispecies group of aliens from various planets. This allows
for the imaginative representation of a variety of strange creatures,
somewhat along the lines of those in Pixar's *Monsters, Inc.*, which
had been released a year earlier. Still, while the basic premise is in-
triguing, *Treasure Planet* is a rather uninspired film that was pretty
much a disaster at the box office, especially in the U.S., where the
$140 million film took in only $38 million in gross receipts. The film
is largely a gimmick that conveys little in the way of a message accessible to children beyond the typical Disney glorification of individual
heroism. Regardless, the collapsing of the nineteenth-century seagoing adventure into science fiction serves as an acknowledgement of
the way earlier voyages of seagoing exploration have long been the
model for our visions of the exploration of outer space. It also conveys a subtle endorsement of ahistorical postmodern thinking: the

film treats the past as a treasure trove of images to be plundered for our present-day amusement—without any need to consider the original contexts of those images or the role they played in those contexts.

Disney stayed in the realm of science fiction with *Lilo & Stitch,* its principal film of 2002. This film also sticks with the typical Disney emphasis on individualism, with its focus on the orphaned Hawaiian girl Lilo (voiced by Daveigh Chase), a lonely Elvis-loving outsider who is considered weird by her schoolmates. Lilo lives with her twenty-one-year-old sister Nani (Tia Carrere), their parents having recently been killed in an auto accident. The two do the best they can, but their struggles to get along and get by have drawn the attention of the government, which sends social worker Cobra Bubbles (Ving Rhames), a former CIA agent, to keep tabs on the two and to determine whether Lilo needs to be removed from Nani's care for her own good. Nani, meanwhile, decides it would help Lilo to have a pet, so they go to the local animal shelter to adopt a dog. There, Lilo, always a sucker for the unusual, adopts Stitch (voiced by writer and codirector Chris Sanders), a creature who is posing as a dog. Stitch is actually a superstrong, superintelligent alien. He recently arrived on earth after fleeing captivity on his own planet, where he was produced by illegal genetic experiments conducted by the scientist Jumba (David Ogden Stiers). Meanwhile, he has been pursued to earth by Jumba and the alien agent Pleakley (Kevin McDonald), both bent on recapturing or even destroying Stitch, whom they know as Experiment 626.

This basic scenario leads to a considerable amount of mischief, while the Hawaiian setting allows for the introduction of significant local color, thus continuing the Disney gesture toward multiculturalism. But the bottom line is that Lilo finds a genuine soulmate in the fellow outcast Stitch, who for his part is transformed from a vicious agent of destruction into a loving (if still sometimes destructive) member of the household of Nani and Lilo, now newly cemented by his addition to their little family. Indeed, family is the key theme of this film, which (as in so many previous Disney films) features absent parents, but proves that parents are not necessary in order to have a family. Drawing upon the native Hawaiian concept of "ohana," the film suggests that families can come in different shapes and sizes, with a variety of makeups, as long as the members are loyal to one another.

Lilo & Stitch was a significant success, grossing more than $270 million worldwide (easily the most for a Disney animated film since

Dinosaur) and triggering a 2005 straight-to-DVD sequel as well as a Disney Channel animated television series. However, Disney followed it in 2003 with a deviation from its emphasis on science fiction in *Brother Bear* (2003), something of a follow-up to *Pocahontas* in its emphasis on Native American culture as more natural, spiritual, and authentic than Western culture. However, the main action of this film is set in the distant past (long before colonization, when woolly mammoths still roamed North America) and thus avoids any direct confrontation between modern Western and traditional Native American cultures. *Brother Bear* extends the emphasis of *Pocahontas* in that its Native American culture is more clearly depicted as being in tune not only with nature, but with the supernatural. The basic plot involves a young Inuit man, Kenai (voiced by Joaquin Phoenix), who kills a bear in anger because he believes the bear to be responsible for the death of his older brother Sitka (D. B. Sweeney). However, according to the dictates of Kenai's own culture, bears and other animals can be killed in self-defense or if needed for food or fur, but they should not be killed out of spite. Meanwhile, partly because of the nature of Inuit culture and (presumably) partly because this was a long time ago, before the onset of modernization and capitalist routinization, in the world of this film, the natural world and supernatural world exist in close proximity and sometimes overlap. In this case, the Spirits (including the spirit of Sitka) transform Kenai into a bear to teach him a lesson about living in harmony with nature and animals. Hater of bears that he is, Kenai is horrified by the change and devotes most of the rest of the film trying to find a way to become human again. In the meantime, though, he befriends a young bear cub, Koda (Jeremy Suarez), gradually realizing that the bear he killed earlier was Koda's mother. Eventually, Kenai is offered the opportunity to regain his humanity, but opts to remain a bear so that he can help take care of the orphaned Koda, thus making amends for his earlier inappropriate killing of Koda's mother. Thus, while Kenai does not, in typical Disney fashion, return to his original natural state, he does act to restore the natural order and the natural balance which had been upset by his earlier transgression. Moreover, by becoming a bear himself, Kenai is able to live in the ultimate natural state.

Home on the Range (2004) is a lighthearted Western that provides clear evidence that Disney had, by this time, abandoned once and for all the notion that each of its major theatrical releases should strive to be a timeless classic. *Home on the Range* can be fun, but it certainly lacks magnitude; it's an unashamed work of popular culture that goes for the quick laugh rather than any sense of larger purpose. It disavows both science fiction technology and magic (except to the extent that talking cows can be considered magical, but talking animals are, by the time of this film, merely conventional), adapting a predictable Western story to the context of children's animation. In the story, a group of three talking cows seek to apprehend a notorious rustler in order to collect the reward and save the small farm on which they all live from foreclosure. This story, however, is part of a larger one in which the rustler, Alameda Slim (voiced by Randy Quaid), turns out to be a big-time land baron engaged in a plot to drive ranches into bankruptcy by rustling their cattle so that he can then buy up the ranches at a discount. However, the film avoids any real exploration of themes involving capitalist exploitation or the routinization of the American West—as in such "waning of the West" films as *McCabe and Mrs. Miller* (1971) or *Heaven's Gate* (1980)—opting instead to go for sight gags, slapstick humor, and easy laughs. The result is good fun in places, but it's fairly pointless entertainment. Add that to the lackluster music and unremarkable animation, and it is not surprising that *Home on the Range* was the lowest grossing of Disney's major animated releases since the renaissance began with *The Little Mermaid.*

In *Chicken Little* (2005), Disney turned to all-out CGI animation, having announced that *Home on the Range* would be their last conventionally animated feature (though that decision has since been rescinded). Indeed, this was the first fully computer-generated Disney label film that was not produced by Pixar. Moreover, perhaps in keeping with this high-tech approach to animation, they also returned to science fiction, their favorite genre of the late renaissance, turning the traditional tale of Chicken Little into an alien invasion narrative. Actually, the well-known Chicken Little story (which evolved from an ancient Indian Buddhist fable) had been made by Disney into an animated short in 1943, but this full-length version takes the fable only as a starting point for launching into an up-to-date story (complete with a cool, rock music sound track) in which the falling sky famously announced by Chicken Little is actually a tile that came loose from an alien spacecraft. The result is a charming, funny, and highly entertaining film that makes a few points about friendship and father-and-son relationships, while also featuring the theme of respect for the downtrodden and the outcast that had been a Disney favorite at least since *Dumbo*. Here, the central outcast figure is Chicken Little himself (voiced by Zach Braff), who has become a laughingstock in his hometown—and even gained national infamy—because of his earlier declaration that the sky was falling, which led to a panic that nearly destroyed the town. Chicken Little's only friends are fellow outcasts such as the hugely fat pig Runt of the Litter (Steve Zahn), the aptly named Fish Out of Water (Dan Molina), and the ugly duckling Abby Mallard (Joan Cusack). All are members of the unpopular crowd in their school and receive considerable abuse at the hands of bullies Foxy Loxy (Amy Sedaris) and Goosey Loosey (Mark Walton).

Things take a turn for the better when Chicken Little (though almost accidentally) becomes the hero of his school's baseball team, allowing them to win a big championship game and thus helping the undersized chicken to follow in the footsteps of his father Buck "Ace" Cluck (Garry Marshall), a strapping rooster who had formerly been the school's biggest sports hero. Chicken Little's triumph is short lived, however. When still another piece of the sky falls on his head, he and his friends investigate and discover that the falling object was a tile from an alien craft. A subsequent series of misunderstandings leads to an all-out alien assault on the town in an attempt to rescue an alien infant whose parents believe it to have been kidnapped by the townspeople. Fortunately, Chicken Little is able to clear up the misunderstanding, return the alien infant to its parents, and save the town. He becomes a hero—and the subsequent protagonist of a big-budget Hollywood action film that portrays him as a courageous alien fighter.

The satire of Hollywood is here all in fun, of course, somewhat reminiscent of the ending of *Pee-wee's Big Adventure* (1985). Any other lessons that the film might convey are treated in a similarly lighthearted manner. One might note, however, that the misrepresentation of Chicken Little in this film-within-the-film is not that different from the liberties taken with the Chicken Little fable by *Chicken Little* itself. This ending thus serves as a sort of self-congratulatory declaration of the harmlessness of taking materials from the past and then warping them into whatever shape might make for good entertainment, continuing a troubling legacy of lack of respect for source materials that has been central to Disney films since *Snow White*. Here, however, the film at least acknowledges that it is playing fast and loose with its source material, thus avoiding what is probably the biggest problem with Disney's traditional treatment of source material—the fact that many young viewers will not realize what violence has been done to the original, and thus will take the Disney version as the authoritative one.

Chicken Little grossed $314 million worldwide, seemingly announcing a potential bounce back for Disney after the poor performance of *Home on the Range*. However, *The Wild* (2006) grossed almost exactly the same amount as *Home on the Range* (each made around $103 million worldwide), but was much more expensive to make at $150 million versus $110 for the earlier film, so was a bigger box-office disaster. In *The Wild*, a group of animals from the New York Zoo attempts to find their true selves in the wild, thus essentially rehashing the material of DreamWorks' *Madagascar*, released a year earlier, though *The Wild* had actually been in development well before the release of *Madagascar*. *The Wild* does contain some impressive computer animation, and its animal characters look almost real—even if they look like real stuffed animals rather than real live animals (making one wonder if they were designed specifically for potential co-marketing of stuffed-animal toys). Still, *Madagascar* is a better treatment of virtually the same material, making *The Wild* still another demonstration that Disney was no longer king of the animation world.

Meet the Robinsons (2007) is a rather lightweight, tongue-in-cheek time-travel adventure in which young Lewis Robinson, a boy inventor who has grown up in an orphanage, is spirited away via time machine into what turns out to be a glorious high-tech future. Numerous complications ensue, but Lewis ultimately discovers that this grand future is largely the result of the improvements to human life provided by his own inventions and that he, as Cornelius Robinson, his adopted name, is universally known as the "father of the future." He also finds that, in the future, Cornelius Robinson is the center of an extended and loving family and thus has precisely the sort of family connections that the orphan Lewis has always longed for. The bottom line is that he must overcome various difficulties in order to get back to the past so that he can make this future happen. He does, of course, so that the authentic timeline is restored. Indeed, despite the science fiction trappings, *Meet the Robinsons* is a fairly conventional Disney "real self" narrative in which young Lewis learns who he really is and discovers his true mission in life. To top it all off, the film ends with an on-screen quotation from Walt Disney that clearly makes Cornelius Robinson a figure of Disney: "Around here, we don't look backwards for very long. We keep moving forward, opening new doors and doing new things, because we're curious . . . and curiosity keeps leading us down new paths." This film thus emphasizes Disney's role as an innovator and visionary—as opposed to his counter-role as protector of tradition and guardian of convention. Disney himself wanted to have it both ways, but any given film generally has to focus on one aspect or the other. *Meet the Robinsons* opts for the innovation pole. Ironically, however, this film, a very modest success at $169 million in worldwide box office, again signaled that Disney proper was no longer the prime mover and shaker in the animated film business, a role that had now been ceded to its Pixar division (which had been acquired by Disney a year earlier), with DreamWorks remaining a major player as well, mainly because of the power of the *Shrek* and (to a lesser extent) *Madagascar* franchises.

Indeed, one of the most striking trends of the late Disney renaissance and beyond was the tendency for Disney films to be repeatedly scooped by their competitors, especially DreamWorks. The most glaring case is the release of *Madagascar* by DreamWorks a year before *The Wild*, but the tendency goes all the way back to the release of DreamWorks's *Antz* just weeks before the similarly themed Disney-Pixar release *A Bug's Life* in 1998. Similarly, DreamWorks released their South American film *The Road to El Dorado* in 2000, nine months before *The Emperor's New Groove*, while *Home on the Range* appeared two years after DreamWorks' much more serious (and successful) Western, *Spirit: Stallion of the Cimarron*.

If all this weren't enough, Disney itself followed *Meet the Robinsons* with the mostly live-action *Enchanted* (2007), which pokes a certain amount of lighthearted fun at the entire tradition of Disney animated films (especially those involving fairy-tale princesses), though it of course treats that tradition more respectfully than do the *Shrek* films. In *Enchanted*, Giselle, a Snow White-like fairy-tale princess (played by Amy Adams) suddenly finds herself transported from the animated world of Andalasia to real-world contemporary New York. The contrast between this new setting and her unrealistic expectations of what life is like lead to a considerable amount of comic confusion—and might even be taken as an admission of the unrealistic expectations fostered in little girls by traditional Disney films—except that everything (of course) works out in the end and Giselle does indeed find her true love, even if he is a cynical divorce lawyer (Patrick Dempsey) rather than the fairy-tale prince (James Marsden) for whom she had originally been intended in her animated world. Similarly, Disney's most recent animated film, *Bolt* (2008), includes some vague interrogation of the unrealistic images produced by children's television programming. But it ultimately descends into sentimentality, serving more than anything as a vehicle for Disney Channel diva Miley Cyrus (aka Hannah Montana), who provides the voice of a central character. Still, *Enchanted* and *Bolt* represent a real effort on the part of Disney to update their images (while retaining a certain amount of magic and nostalgia) rather than merely to recover their past glories; the films are certainly a step forward in that regard. Even so, Disney's most important post-renaissance step forward was the acquisition of Pixar, which has for some time now been the leading player in the animated film world.

—— 3 ——

Magic Goes High-Tech: Pixar and the Children's Film in the Age of Digital Reproduction

In the early days of film, audiences often attended screenings more to see the technological marvel of moving pictures than out of any interest in the particular films being shown. Over the years, audiences became less and less amazed by the very existence of movies, demanding more and more in the way of content and style. Yet an element of technological wizardry has always been crucial to film as a medium, especially in the post—*Star Wars* years when some of the most impressive achievements in the medium of film have involved advances in special effects, especially those generated by computers. Indeed, one of the most important fallouts from the entire *Star Wars* phenomenon was George Lucas's founding of Industrial Light and Magic (ILM) to develop the breakthrough special-effects technology that was necessary to make *Star Wars* a success. ILM then continued to push the special-effects envelope beyond *Star Wars*, remaining on the cutting edge of increasingly computer-dominated developments in special-effects technology.

ILM's computer graphics department fell on financial hard times in the mid-1980s and was eventually sold to Apple Computer guru Steve Jobs, who believed the group might be able to turn a profit by developing and marketing computer software and (especially) hardware for the government and medical community, with a potential secondary market for the use of movie studios (Disney was a key early customer) in creating computer-generated special effects. That business never really got off the ground, though the animated television commercials and short films made by the group (now known as Pixar) to generate extra income and demonstrate their technologies began to gain attention in their own right. The company continued to struggle, though a distribution deal with Disney kept them afloat until the release, in 1995, of *Toy Story*, the first fully computer-generated feature film. The rest, as they say, is history, and Pixar quickly became the leading player in the animated film business, each of its films becoming a major event and an instant classic.

At first glance, Pixar's films appear distinctively different from traditional Disney films, partly because of the foregrounding of technology, rather than the typical Disney emphasis on magic. To date, in fact, there are no Pixar films that feature magic or the supernatural, unless one counts the monsters of *Monsters, Inc.* as somehow supernatural—or, of course, unless one counts talking animals, superheroes, or animated toys as supernatural, but these are by now such film conventions that they merely suggest narrative convenience, rather than magical intervention. There are, however, numerous ways in which Pixar films have consistently tended to convey an ideology that is rather similar to the mainstream ideology of Disney films, especially in their emphasis on the importance of naturalness and authenticity.

Toy Story is a revolutionary film, historically comparable, in many ways, to *Snow White and the Seven Dwarfs* in the way it introduced an entirely new form to feature film. In recognition of this fact, John Lasseter, the film's director, was given a Special Achievement Academy Award for the film. Importantly, *Toy Story* is also an extremely warm, charming, and sentimental film that easily overcomes any concerns that an entirely computer-generated film might somehow seem cold and mechanical—or that *Toy Story* itself might turn out to be a mere technological curiosity. Some of the film's warmth comes from the lovability of the characters, enhanced by the voice performances of well-known actors Tom Hanks and Tim Allen in the roles of the film's central toy characters, Woody (a talking cowboy doll) and Buzz Lightyear (a spaceman action figure), respectively. Some of the warmth comes from Randy Newman's Oscar-nominated soundtrack, including the song "You've Got a Friend in Me," which also won an Oscar nomination for Best Song. In addition, a key secret to the success of *Toy Story* is in its storytelling (it also won an Oscar nomination for its screenplay, written by, among others, Joss Whedon, who would soon become a legend in his own time for his creation of tele-vision's *Buffy the Vampire Slayer*).

Ultimately, though, *Toy Story* (like all Pixar films) is all about the animation and about the ability of Pixar's animators to produce impressive, convincing computer-generated visuals that are full of warmth and humor. As one might expect in such a technologically-driven product, each Pixar film is more impressive in its animation than the one before, yet *Toy Story* still holds up well, perhaps because its animation of anthropomorphized toys is relatively unambitious. The basic plot is simple as well. The film stipulates that toys are secretly sentient, and the plot is actuated when a young boy named Andy (voiced by John Morris) has a birthday, triggering anxiety among his current toys that Andy might receive new toys as presents that he likes better than his old toys. And their fears seem to be realized when Andy's favorite gift turns out to be a fancy Buzz Lightyear figure, apparently a product inspired by a children's television program.

Buzz Lightyear comes complete with lots of bells and whistles to keep Andy's interest. When Andy is not around, however, Buzz turns out to be not only cocky and self-centered, but convinced that he actually is *the* Buzz Lightyear rather than a mere toy replica. Woody, displaced as Andy's favorite toy, plots to get rid of the interloper, setting into motion a train of events that eventually finds both Woody and Buzz lost and then found by Andy's neighbor, the vicious Sid (Erik von Detten), whose favorite activity is torturing and destroying toys in various gruesome ways. Aided by Sid's own mangled toys, Woody and Buzz finally learn to work together and to escape, then to catch up (via an exciting chase scene) to Andy, who just happens on this day to be moving away to a new home.

As Newman's key song indicates, *Toy Story* deals centrally with the theme of friendship, especially that which is eventually established between Woody and Buzz. As with so many Disney films before, meanwhile, the film also deals with authenticity: crucial to the film's successful conclusion is Buzz's discovery and final acceptance of who (or what) he really is. Meanwhile, the film also deals with the issue of obsolescence of commodities, somewhat as *The Brave Little Toaster* had done before. However, the obsolescence suggested here becomes particularly poignant because we are dealing with children's beloved toys. Among other things, the obsolescence of toys can be taken as a marker of the fleeting nature of childhood itself. Toys become obsolete not just because they are replaced by newer, more technologically sophisticated toys, but also because children grow older, enter new phases, change interests, and start to be amused by different things.

Of course, *Toy Story* gives this potentially sad narrative an upbeat twist by suggesting that Andy's old toys don't really become obsolete upon the arrival of Buzz Lightyear, with the concomitant suggestion that we can all maintain a part of our childhood selves even as we grow older. Not only does Andy still love Woody as the film ends, but his collection of toys includes a number of classics (e.g., Mr. Potato Head, plastic toy soldiers[1]) that have been around for decades— at least since I (and Pixar principals such as Lasseter, who are of my generation) were children. *Toy Story* thus delivers the comforting message that the joys (and toys) of the past can be preserved even in the light of ongoing technological innovation.

This message applies to the world of film as well. After all, the narrative in *Toy Story* of the transition in toy technology from the charming but rather simple Woody to the fancy, high-tech Buzz can also be taken as an allegory of the history of children's animated film—and particularly of the transition from Disney to Pixar. The message seems to be the reassuring one (aimed perhaps at both the film's audiences and Disney executives) that, just as there will still be a place in Andy's heart for lovable old Woody after *Toy Story*, so too will there still be a place in children's film for the kind of films that Disney has traditionally made. Meanwhile, Buzz's journey of discovery can also be taken as a self-deprecating gesture on the part of Pixar, acknowledging that, hey, it's just a movie: the technology is impressive, but not as impressive as a cure for cancer or a new, more efficient electric engine that would solve the oil crisis.

On a more somber note, the charmingly personified toys of *Toy Story* would seem a virtual dramatization of the fascination with manufactured objects that Marx referred to as the "commodity fetish." Moreover, given the vulnerability and suggestibility of small children (Benjamin wants virtually every toy in the film), there is a clear problem with a film that celebrates the lovability of toys. In the kind of contradiction that frequently appears in Disney films, *Toy Story* celebrates consumerism (which requires the continual buying of new things) even as it also shows support for the idea of keeping and valuing one's old things.

Given the lucrative market in film-related toys and other merchandise, one cannot help but wonder if one element in the development of *Toy Story* was not a recognition that a film whose major characters are toys was ideal for co-marketing purposes. An extensive line of toys related to the film was, in fact, manufactured under license by Thinkway Toys, which had already produced a number of toys related to Disney films (beginning with *The Little Mermaid*) and which has continued to market Pixar-related merchandise ever since, including most recently an extensive line of robot toys based on characters from *WALL-E* (2008).

In fact, with the possible exception of *Ratatouille,* all Pixar films through *WALL-E* seem unusually well suited for co-marketing purposes, though the second Pixar film, *A Bug's Life* (1998, again directed by Lasseter), is less so than most. All of the characters of *A Bug's Life* are insects (mostly ants), which would seem a rather novel idea had the film not been scooped as it was by DreamWorks' *Antz*. These two films would ultimately be joined by Warner's *The Ant Bully* (2006) to form a sort of trilogy of ant films, though ants (noted for their lack of individuality) would at first seem to be fairly unpromising as characters for American films, which tend to emphasize individualism so heavily. Granted, there is a long tradition in individualist dystopian fiction of using the conformist societies of communal insects such as ants and bees as satirical stand-ins for human society, but none of the ant movies emphasize this connection enough for children to get the point, even if *Antz* does come close. Moreover, *A Bug's Life* was the only one of these three films to be a big box-office hit, and that perhaps more for the Pixar-Disney brand recognition and marketing machinery than for the qualities of the film itself.

A Bug's Life may, in fact, be the least interesting of the Pixar films produced to date. It focuses on a colony of ants that has come under the domination of a local gang of grasshoppers, led by the vicious Hopper (voiced by Kevin Spacey), who force the ants to work to gather food for the grasshoppers, who are thus spared the need for physical labor. The film can thus be seen as a very loose transcription of Aesop's fable "The Ant and the Grasshopper" (adapted—and sanitized—as a Disney animated short entitled "The Grasshopper and the Ants" in 1934), here updated through the modern gangster genre.

A Bug's Life features the unlikely narrative expedient of an individualist inventor ant, Flik (Dave Foley), whose attempts to make the ants' lives easier through technology meet mostly with disdain from his fellow ants. The main events of the plot are set in motion when Flik's efforts inadvertently lead to the loss of the food supply that has been gathered by the ants to pay tribute to the grasshoppers, causing a crisis in which the ants seem doomed to suffer violent retribution from the thuggish grasshoppers. So Flik sets out on a journey from the insular colony to the outside world, hoping to hire mercenaries to protect the colony from the grasshoppers. Through a series of misunderstandings, he actually hires and brings back a troupe of circus bugs, the colorful members of which provide an assemblage of interesting secondary characters somewhat analogous to the cast of supporting toys in *Toy Story*. It all works out, however, partly because the ingenious Flik designs an artificial bird that is used to help battle the invading grasshoppers—though the vile Hopper actually meets his horrific death at the beak of a real bird, which snags him and takes him back to her nest to feed to her hungry babies.

Ultimately, the ants defeat the grasshoppers through sheer force of numbers, rallying together to support Flik in his struggle against Hopper. The film thus delivers a message about the power of collective action and even potentially yields a radical class-oriented political message, with the ants playing the role of the exploited proletariat and the grasshoppers playing the role of the bourgeoisie, who feed on the labor of the workers without doing any productive work of their own. The ant victory thus becomes a virtual workers' revolution— except, of course, that the film itself is not at all interested in delivering this message, instead focusing on the very mainstream American story of the lone individual (Flik) who makes good and saves the day, delivering independence to the ants (who maintain their own royalist internal political structure). The political issues raised by *A Bug's Life* are thus unlikely to deliver an effective radical message to young viewers, though they do make for some interesting dialogue with the other ant movies, as I will discuss in the next chapter.

Toy Story 2 (1999), again directed by Lasseter, is a direct sequel to *Toy Story* and shows relatively little in the way of technical advancement beyond Pixar's first feature film. In fact, at this point, Pixar's third film already being a sequel to its first, the innovative potential of the company might have seemed seriously in doubt. *Toy Story 2*, though, was again a megahit at the box office (grossing over $480 million at the worldwide box office, over $100 million more than either *Toy Story* or *A Bug's Life*), so the company's financial future seemed secure. Meanwhile, the direct connection between *Toy Story* and *Toy Story 2* provided a strong basis for the beginnings of the intertextual relationships that would eventually evolve among all of the Pixar films. Each of them features numerous clever allusions to its predecessors, the identification of which becomes a sort of insiders' game for aficionados of the films, though they are generally accessible even to alert younger viewers. (In fact, Benjamin and Skylor both probably notice more of them than I do.)

Toy Story 2 treats virtually the same topics as *Toy Story* (and features the same central voice cast), though it explores the theme of toy obsolescence in a much more detailed and sophisticated way. Here, Woody falls into the hands of a sinister toy-store owner, Al McWhiggin (Wayne Knight), somewhat of a successor to Elmo St. Peters of *The Brave Little Toaster*. McWhiggin is no true lover of toys, but instead regards them merely as commodities from which he can make a profit. Indeed, he has for some time been gathering a collection of vintage toys to sell to a Japanese museum for a huge sum. These toys are all related to a popular 1950s children's television show (clearly based on *Howdy Doody*) in which Woody had been the star character, though (in a motif resembling the Buzz Lightyear plot of *Toy Story*), the show had lost popularity and abruptly been canceled after the 1957 launch of Sputnik caused children to switch their interest from cowboy toys to space toys.[2] It turns out, however, that Woody himself, now an extremely rare and valuable toy, has been the only item missing from the collection. His acquisition thus clears the way for McWhiggin's big windfall.

Woody himself is stunned to learn of his heritage and of his financial value—and pleased, among other things, to be reunited with his trusty horse, Bullseye. Meanwhile, he staunchly opposes the commodification of toys (and, by extension, childhood), arguing that toys are intended to provide joy to children, not profits to collectors. On the other hand, this simple opposition is complicated by the fact that one of the other toys, Woody's feminine counterpart, the cowgirl Jessie (Joan Cusack), points out that she had once been the beloved plaything of a little girl, but then cast aside when the girl grew older and developed other interests. Jessie, therefore, is perfectly happy to contemplate a future life as a museum piece, where she will presumably remain of interest for a much more extended time. The theme of

obsolescence of toys is thus here intertwined with the theme of commodification of toys in a fairly complex way—and in one that potentially addresses a number of issues regarding the decline of historical
sense in our postmodern era. The museum motif, for example, provides a particularly interesting entry point for a reading of the film
through the optic of Jameson's vision of postmodernism as reducing
the historical past to a museumlike spectacle in which images can be
viewed (and reused) unmoored from their original historical contexts.

As one might expect, however, *Toy Story 2* retreats from any
detailed exploration of these issues, opting instead for a fairly simplis-
tic, conventional, and sentimental resolution that ignores the reality of
the film itself (as a high-profile, big-profit commodity accompanied
by extensive co-marketing of both cowboy and spaceman toys) in
these issues. Thus, Woody's view prevails, and he convinces Jessie to
join him and Bullseye in going back to live with Andy (and Andy's
younger sister, who might also enjoy Jessie), where they can become
an integral part of Andy's childhood fun, enjoying it to the utmost for
however long it lasts. Childhood itself, the message seems to be,
should be a happy time, the enjoyment of which should not be marred
by the fact that it is inevitably temporary. The question of what will
happen to Woody and his cohorts after Andy grows older is left open.
Meanwhile, the old Disney theme of being what one was supposed to
be is seemingly reinforced once again: toys were meant to be played
with by kids, not encased in museum displays. Again, however, the
film ignores the fact that toys are, in fact, designed and manufactured
for the principal purpose of generating corporate profits, whatever
fun children might have with the toys being merely a means toward
that end.

The two *Toy Story* films (*Toy Story 3* is slated to appear in June
2010) engage the Western genre and, to a lesser extent, science fiction, while *A Bug's Life* draws in important ways on the gangster
genre, along with the circus (and circus films, including several subtle
allusions to *Dumbo*). In *Monsters, Inc.* (2001), Pixar turned to the hor-
ror/monster movie genre, seemingly a stretch for a children's film.
Monster movies had long been aimed primarily at teenage audiences,
although some (such as *Gremlins*) had sought to bring in younger
viewers as well. *Monsters, Inc.*, directed by Pete Docter and written
by Andrew Stanton and Daniel Gerson, is at first glance a film that
carries a potentially powerful (and even radical) political message.

Like most Pixar films, it is based on the notion of an alternative world or reality, the "Monster World" that exists in parallel with our own "Human World." The premise of the film is that the energy needed to power the Monster World and its main city of Monstropolis is derived from the screams of human children. Monstropolis is much like a slightly retro human city except for the nature of the inhabitants, though this change itself creates a context in which numerous aspects of our own society (such as the prevalence of advertising slogans) are satirized from a defamiliarized perspective. Most importantly, power generation in the Monster World is the responsibility of corporate giant Monsters, Inc., which continually sends specially trained monster agents into the human world (emerging from closets on the other side) to frighten (though never actually to harm) human children and collect the energy from their screams for processing into electricity and other forms of power. One might, thus, summarize the message of the film as a suggestion that monstrous corporate interests (especially energy companies) derive their resources from the brutal exploitation of the weak and the helpless (such as children).

On the other hand, this message is greatly mitigated by a number of factors. For one thing, the entire film is presented as a running joke that effectively defuses any of its potentially anticapitalist critique. More than anything, the premise seems designed primarily to provide Pixar's computer animators with an opportunity to design and animate a variety of whimsically weird monsters. Indeed, no two monsters in the Monster World seem to be quite alike, so that the strange appearances of the monsters serve as a sort of lighthearted visual dramatization of the ethos of individualism. Moreover, the jokey nature of the film does not undermine this individualist message as thoroughly as it undermines the potentially anticapitalist message because so many elements of the plot of the film also convey an individualist ethos. In particular, the plot of the film centers on the efforts of superstar child frightener Sully (voiced by John Goodman) and his sidekick Mike Wazowski (Billy Crystal) to save a small human girl, Boo (Mary Gibbs), after she is accidentally allowed to enter the Monster World. These efforts are made necessary because the official propaganda of the Monster World has demonized human children to the point that all of the monsters believe the mantra that "There is nothing more toxic or deadly than a human child." Sully and Mike, after they realize that Boo is not really dangerous, thus go against the full force of both official power and received wisdom in their society in order to do the right thing and protect the child.

The film thus celebrates individuals who are willing to go against the grain of popular opinion in order to make the right choices and do the right thing, which places it very much in the tradition of Disney's children's films. Even the film's critique of capitalism, which ultimately centers on an individualist response against conformism, is fairly well in line with the Disney tradition, though the Pixar film perhaps focuses a bit more on the media and on the official manipulation of public opinion than would be typical of a Disney film. Perhaps the most innovative aspect of *Monsters, Inc.* is its treatment of genre: based on the monster movie, the film gains most of its energy from reversing the conventions of that important genre, making monsters the central characters and making a small human child a terrifying invader from another dimension. In this sense, the film resembles the immensely successful *Shrek*, which was released five months earlier but which likely exercised little direct influence, Pixar films typically being several years in the making. *Shrek*, however, is far more subversive in its play with genre, especially as the principal target of its generic parody is the Disney fairy-tale film, thus situating that film in direct opposition to perhaps the single most important strand in American children's film. *Monsters, Inc.*, on the other hand, travesties a genre that has long been considered marginal already and that has certainly played only a small role in children's film. Indeed, the generic reversals of *Monsters, Inc.* actually serve to make the film less subversive. The sympathetic treatment of monsters such as Sully and Mike, even though they go against the grain of their society, deflects attention away from the monstrous activities of the corporation for which they work. Its activities are anyway ultimately attributed to the rogue CEO, Mr. Waternoose (James Coburn), rather than to a flaw in the corporate system itself.

Andrew Stanton's *Finding Nemo* (2003), with its evocation of an absolutely convincing underwater animated world, represents Pixar's most impressive advancement in animation technology since the original *Toy Story*. It is also Pixar's most overtly sentimental film to date, drawing upon its central theme of a devoted father braving innumerable obstacles in an attempt to rescue his kidnapped son to produce what is by a wide margin Pixar's most commercially successful film so far. *Finding Nemo* grossed $340 million in domestic box-office receipts and a staggering $865 million worldwide, placing it above *The Lion King* and above two of the three *Shrek* films, surpassed only by *Shrek 2* as an animated box-office hit. *Finding Nemo* is also reportedly the top-selling DVD of all time. It won the 2003 Academy Award for Best Animated Feature, thus becoming the first Pixar film to win that award, which was first given in 2001.

Finding Nemo begins with a rather risky opening sequence in which a clownfish named Marlin (voiced by Albert Brooks) sets up housekeeping in a sea anemone with his new mate, who subsequently lays hundreds of eggs, only to be eaten, along with all but one of the eggs, by an attacking barracuda. Nemo (voiced by Alexander Gould) soon emerges from the remaining egg, though with one damaged flipper, apparently as a result of the barracuda attack. As a result of both the attack and the injured flipper, Marlin then becomes a particularly protective bachelor father, hoping to shield his son from any further trauma or violence, but thereby threatening to impoverish Nemo's experience of life as well.

This violent and even shocking beginning provides important background to the remainder of the film, motivating Marlin's overprotective behavior, though there is obviously a danger that it might be disturbing or even terrifying to children. Still, there is substantial precedent in the Disney tradition for such scenes, with the killing of Bambi's mother being the most obvious example, though the most direct precedent might be the killing of the mother dinosaur at the beginning of *The Land Before Time* (1988), a non-Disney product. Meanwhile, the remainder of *Finding Nemo*, though it contains a number of perilous scenes, is pretty much free of carnage, while chock-full of enough comedic and heartwarming moments (including a quintessentially happy ending) to more than make up for the violent beginning.

The main plot of *Finding Nemo* begins when young Nemo, overcoming Marlin's anxiety and consternation, ventures out of the anemone to start to school. On his very first day at school, Nemo rebels against Marlin's suffocating overprotectiveness, venturing out into the open sea, only to be immediately captured by a diver, seemingly verifying his father's fearful attitude. Nemo is then taken to a Sydney (Australia) dentist's office, where he joins other fish in the dentist's fish tank. Marlin then spends the rest of the film in a heroic transoceanic quest to rescue his son, despite the fact that clownfish are a relatively reclusive species who tend not to venture far from their anemone homes. Then again, the very fact that Marlin remains a male goes against clownfish nature: clownfish (all of which are born male) live in small family-like units in which there is only one (adult) female. If the female dies, the dominant male then becomes the female of the group. It is fairly easy to see why Pixar opted not to include this particular aspect of clownfish physiology in the film.

The visually impressive underwater animation of *Finding Nemo* (which goes so far beyond that of predecessors such as *The Little Mermaid* or even a slightly later work such as DreamWorks' 2004 *Shark Tale*) is certainly a key to the film's success. But it is also the case that the film is unusually successful in anthropomorphizing its animal characters, even though fish are by nature far less like human beings than are the dogs, cats, and the other mammalian characters that are typically featured in animated films. Indeed, Stanton and the other filmmakers at Pixar play very fast and loose with nature in *Finding Nemo*, showing no hesitation to give their fish and other sea creatures entirely human personalities and inclinations and managing to do so in unusually convincing fashion.

Despite the fact that its major characters are all fish, *Finding Nemo* has some of the most charming and endearing characters in the entire pantheon of children's film. Due partly to Brooks's voiceover performance and partly to the heroic quest in which he is engaged, Marlin himself is an extremely sympathetic character, despite being neurotic and overprotective. He is joined in his quest by Dory (Ellen DeGeneres), a regal tang fish who suffers from short-term memory loss, leading to a number of entertaining comedic moments along the journey, though one could argue that it is inappropriate to derive humor from her infirmity (just as it may be inappropriate to derive humor from Marlin's neuroses). Meanwhile, Nemo himself provides a prominent and sympathetic figure with which children viewing the film can presumably identify.

Apart from these central characters, *Finding Nemo* also has a particularly effective cast of supporting characters, even for a Pixar film (in which the supporting casts are typically unusually good). Marlin and Dory encounter a number of these secondary characters in their quest to find Nemo, including most memorably a group of sharks, led by the large and frightening great white Bruce (Australian comedian Barry Humphries), who are attempting to swear off the eating of other fish and thus to establish a new and more benevolent image for sharks as a whole. Marlin and Dory are invited to a hilarious Alcoholics Anonymous—style meeting in which Bruce and his friends attempt to provide support to one another in breaking their fish addictions. Unfortunately, Dory accidentally receives a bloody nose in the midst of the meeting, and the smell of blood in the water sends Bruce into a frenzy in which he nearly devours Marlin and Dory, who ultimately escape only because a nearby minefield is accidentally set off, causing Bruce and the other sharks to flee the subsequent explosions.

Also particularly charming are a group of surfer-dude sea turtles (led by the 150-year-old Crush, voiced by Stanton himself) who help Marlin and Dory ride the east Australian current to Sydney. Some of the film's most effective comic moments involve a flock of voracious sea gulls who inhabit the Sydney harbor, attempting to eat everything in sight, including Marlin and Dory when they arrive there. The two are saved by another secondary character, the pelican Nigel (Geoffrey Rush), who, having heard the spreading legend surrounding Marlin's quest for Nemo, takes the two to the dentist's office to seek Nemo, only to find that Nemo has apparently been killed. The most important secondary characters in *Finding Nemo* are the denizens of the fish tank in that office. This colorful group includes the starfish Peach (Allison Janney), the self-inflating procupinefish Bloat (Brad Garrett), the yellow tang Bubbles (Stephen Root), and a germophobic Royal Gramma (Austin Pendleton). Ultimately, however, the most important member of the Tank Gang is a tough Moorish Idol fish named Gill (Willem Dafoe), who serves as the leader of the gang. Like Nemo, Gill has a damaged flipper; unlike Nemo, he has never let that infirmity limit him in his actions. Gill teaches Nemo to strive to be strong and independent and to overcome his infirmity, thus providing positive lessons that the overprotective Marlin had failed to supply.

In the end, Nemo is fine, of course. He and Marlin are reunited, both having presumably learned valuable lessons that will enrich their lives in the future and allow them both to pursue a less circumscribed existence. And Dory stays with them as well, having realized that she and her problematic memory seem to function better when they are around Marlin, who will now become her interspecies love. Romantic love thus joins fatherly love in the film as a force basic enough and powerful enough to overcome other natural impulses, such as the tendency to mate within one's own species—though this aspect of the

film is not really pursued and the exact nature of the future relationship between Marlin and Dory (which has thus far been platonic) is
left ambiguous.

In addition to its technical advances in animation, *Finding Nemo*
would seem to be something of a breakthrough in that, despite its
seemingly simple and sentimental family-related narrative, it appears
to go very much against the grain of Disney tradition: in order to find
Nemo, Marlin must behave in a way that is entirely unnatural both for
him as an individual and for clownfish as a species, striking out into
the open sea instead of remaining in the protective environs of his
anemone. Ostensibly, he thus must become something other than what
he is naturally meant to be. On the other hand, what the film really
seems to say is simply that fatherhood is more basic than any of Marlin's other characteristics and that his innate love for his son is a more
powerful natural impulse than is the impulse to stay safely at home in
his anemone. In the film's other example of characters attempting to
overcome their basic natures, Bruce and the other sharks come off as
comic buffoons, their quest to change their natural inclinations
depicted as merely silly.

Finding Nemo made it clear that Pixar was here to stay and that the
company was far more versatile than their first few films suggested.
In *The Incredibles* (2004) the company moved in still another entirely
new direction, adapting the superhero narrative to children's animated
film. *The Incredibles* was also something of a departure in that it was
the first Pixar film to be directed by an outsider, rather than one of the
Pixar principals. *The Incredibles* was helmed by former Disney animator Brad Bird, who had worked extensively in animated television
(especially on *The Simpsons*) and who had directed the animated film
The Iron Giant (1999). Indeed, *The Incredibles* was apparently Bird's
brainchild and thus the first Pixar film to have been pitched to them
by an outsider rather than developed in-house.

The Incredibles engages in a fairly sophisticated dialogue with the
superhero tradition, while tossing in important elements from science
fiction and Cold War spy films such as the James Bond sequence—
especially in the music, which is so dramatically different from that
of the earlier Pixar films. The film's central characters are a family of
superheroes who form a superhero team somewhat in the mold of
Marvel Comics' Fantastic Four. They are led by the superstrong and
virtually indestructible Mr. Incredible (voiced by Craig T. Nelson)

and his wife, Mrs. Incredible, the former Elastigirl (Holly Hunter), whose super elastic body can stretch into virtually any shape. Their children Violet and Dash (voiced by Sarah Vowell and Spencer Fox, respectively), are "supers" as well: Dash can move at incredible rapid speeds, while Violet can become invisible and project force fields. The baby of the family, little Jack-Jack (voiced by Eli Fucile and Maeve Andrews) is ostensibly an ordinary human, though he turns out at the end of the film to have multiple superpowers.

The premise of the film (following such updates of the superhero genre as Alan Moore's 1986–1987 graphic novel *Watchmen*) is that public outcries against the activities of superheroes have essentially caused them to be outlawed. The Incredibles thus join the government's Superhero Relocation Program and now live in the guise of a typical suburban family. Mr. Incredible is anonymous as Bob Parr, an ordinary insurance adjuster, while Mrs. Incredible poses as Helen Parr, an ordinary housewife. Their children attend public school as regular children. Unfortunately, this humdrum existence proves increasingly unsatisfying to Mr. Incredible, even as evil forces are afoot in the world that will require the intervention of superheroes. These forces are operating under the control of Syndrome (Jason Lee), a Bond-style supervillain, the former Buddy Pine, who had years earlier been spurned in his efforts to use his talents as an inventor of clever gadgets to become Mr. Incredible's sidekick, though Buddy himself lacks actual super powers.

The bulk of *The Incredibles* consists of a series of action sequences involving the battles of the Incredibles against Syndrome and his various high-tech devices, including powerful, destructive robots known as Omnidroids. Many of these sequences, especially the ones at Syndrome's island stronghold, are highly reminiscent of the Bond movies, while drawing (as do the Bond movies) a significant amount of imagery from the realm of science fiction. *The Incredibles* thus pulls from a number of different genres, though the same might be said of superhero narratives in general. Meanwhile, this postmodern mixing of genres is accompanied by a mixing of time periods as well. Even apart from the science fiction hardware, the technologies routinely available to the characters within the film would mark its setting as the present time (or even near future); meanwhile the Bond elements have an inherently 1960s flavor to them, while other elements (such as the depiction of the Parrs' home life) seem derived from the 1950s.

Indeed, the Incredibles themselves tend to seem more like 1950s or early 1960s superheroes than contemporary ones.

Syndrome's plan is to unleash a killer robot that no one can stop except Syndrome himself (because he secretly controls it), thus propelling him to superhero status at last. Of course, the robot goes out of control, but, by combining their innate super powers with courage and resourcefulness (and with an unexpected final assist from Jack-Jack, whose multiple powers begin to manifest at last), the Incredibles manage to win the day and save their city. Unfortunately, just as all seems well (and after life has seemingly returned to normal for the Parrs), a new threat emerges from beneath the streets of the city in the form of the Underminer, a new supervillain, voiced by John Ratzenberger. The film then ends, seemingly setting the stage for a sequel, though more than anything this ending seems merely to be a pastiche of the endings of superhero narratives in general, especially those in comic books, which often end with such cliffhangers.

The appearance of Ratzenberger (who appears as voice talent in all Pixar films, usually in a very small role) is a key example of the way in which each Pixar film works in allusions to earlier Pixar films, building up an intertextual connection among the films. Such allusions can be part of the fun of watching these films, identifying them becoming a sort of game. But the familial relations among Pixar films that are set up by such allusions also serve as a sort of branding device that strengthens the Pixar name, which itself has considerable market value. By the time of *The Incredibles*, in fact, Pixar had probably supplanted Disney as the most marketable name in children's film, or maybe even in film as a whole. Each Pixar film now draws a huge audience simply because it is a Pixar film, regardless of the nature of the film, which is something no other studio can really say, including its parent, Disney.

The very fact that Pixar has become such a marketing (and co-marketing) juggernaut, not to mention the fact that it is now a wholly owned subsidiary of Disney, is certainly worth pondering in considering the potential political implications of any Pixar film. In the case of *The Incredibles*, there is a certain amount of gentle satire of the routinization of life under modern capitalism in the scenes of his life as Bob Parr. This is especially true in the scenes set at the insurance company, where Parr's weasely boss, Gilbert Huph (Wallace Shawn), makes it clear that the company is in the business of squeezing money out of their policyholders, not helping them. But *The Incredibles* is not really interested in pursuing this kind of critique, which is presented as a sort of burlesque, cynically suggesting that everyone already knows how rapacious insurance companies are, but that there's really nothing to be done. The scenes in the Parr home can also be taken as a gentle satire of the banality of suburban life (or perhaps a vague pastiche of television sitcoms about suburban life), but conditions in the home are not that bad: they're just ordinary, which is the problem. After all, the Parrs/Incredibles are not ordinary folk. They are supers, stipulated to be innately superior to ordinary humans, even if the rabble that constitutes ordinary humanity does not appreciate them. Young Dash is particularly troubled by the insistence of his parents that he maintain their cover and not appear extraordinary, even though he knows that he is. In one of the film's key moments, Dash complains that he is not allowed to use the powers that make him special. "Everyone's special," replies his mother, trotting out a key cliché of Americanism, to which Dash retorts, "Which is another way of saying no one is."

Ostensibly, then, *The Incredibles* can be taken as a critique of socially enforced conformism, in which the truly gifted are forced to sink back to the level of the masses to avoid persecution and just to get by. In this sense, the film is again very much in the Disney vein (though it was the last Pixar film released *before* the Disney buyout): ultimately, the world is saved because the Incredibles throw off the mantle of conformity and become their true (and truly special) selves, using the abilities that were naturally given to them. Unfortunately, *The Incredibles* is plagued by potentially right-wing political implications that are built into the premises of the superhero genre itself, whatever the intentions of the filmmakers might have been. The Incredibles come very close to being supermen in the Nazi (or Nietzschean) sense, innately better than ordinary people, who are, conversely, treated somewhat contemptuously in the film as a crowd of ignorant rabble.[3] We are all created equal, but some of us are more equal than others. In this light, Mr. Incredible's rather insensitive rejection of young Buddy Pine because Buddy is not a natural superman takes on ominous tones.[4]

Pixar again switched directions with its next film. Lasseter (with an assist from longtime Pixar associate Joe Ranft) returned to the helm in *Cars* (2006), a film whose characters are anthropomorphic automobiles who inhabit a world without human beings. Pixar's most American film, *Cars* is a sort of homage to America's car culture in general, with a nostalgic look back at the days of driving on scenic highways in the days before interstates and a nod toward NASCAR racing culture as well.[5] Indeed, the film premiered at Lowe's Motor Speedway in Concord, North Carolina, playing up the NASCAR link. The cars of the film function surprisingly well as characters, and children seem to have no difficulty with the premise—which is, of course, once again ideal for merchandising purposes, allowing for the marketing of a wide range of toy cars and related products. In fact, merchandising for this film (toys, clothing, bedding, etc.) reached the billion-dollar mark, a new record for a Pixar film. But the characterization in this film is particularly heavy-handed, and virtually every character represents some sort of cultural stereotype, suggesting that car characters might not lend themselves well to subtle gradations in personality and temperament.

The central character of *Cars* is brash young race car Lightning McQueen (voiced by Owen Wilson), who is a rookie star on the Piston Cup stock racing circuit.[6] Indeed, going into the last race of the season, McQueen is tied in the Piston Cup points standings with perennial champ Strip "The King" Weathers (voiced by Richard Petty and modeled on Petty's blue 1970 Plymouth Superbird) and perennial runner-up Chick Hicks (voiced by Michael Keaton). Improbably, the three tie for first in the last race of the season, leaving them equal in the points standings and necessitating a runoff race scheduled for one week later in California to determine the Piston Cup winner. The cars all then set out on the cross-country trek to the West Coast, but on the way McQueen is separated from the Mack Super-Liner truck (voiced by Ratzenberger) that is carrying him and his equipment and ends up stranded in the remote Western town of Radiator Springs, once a key stop on Route 66 but now much off the beaten path because the interstate does not go through it.

Having accidentally torn up the highway that runs through Radiator Springs, McQueen is arrested and ordered to fix the road before he can proceed on his journey. The pompous McQueen is horrified by the prospect not only of the physical labor involved, but of spending time with the hicks in this backwoods town that he regards as "Hillbilly Hell." Eventually, of course, he discovers that the denizens of Radiator Springs are not as stupid as he first thought, something along the lines of city-slicker-comes-to-respect-local-yokels films such as *Doc Hollywood* (1991), a film to which *Cars* in fact bears more than a passing resemblance. During his stay in Radiator Springs, McQueen becomes enamored of Sally (Bonnie Hunt), a Porsche Carrera who runs a near-deserted motel in the town but who had been a big-time Los Angeles lawyer before moving to Radiator Springs to seek a simpler and more meaningful life and to enjoy the striking beauty of the surrounding countryside. In addition, McQueen discovers that town doctor and judge Doc Hudson (Paul Newman, in his last film role) had actually been a legendary race car (The Fabulous Hudson Hornet) decades earlier, but had had his career cut short by an accident, after which he was shoved aside by the racing world to make way for newer models.

Other locals in the town with whom McQueen interacts (but does not get to know well) include the local Sheriff (a 1949 Mercury Club Coupe, voiced by Michael Wallis); Ramon, a lowrider Chevy Impala (Cheech Marin) devoted to the fancy painting and detailing of cars who serves as the film's Hispanic character; Flo (Jennifer Lewis), an African American who runs the town's drive-in restaurant/gas station; and Lizzie (Katherine Helmond), the aging 1923 Model T Ford who basically satirizes the memory lapses of old people. Other characters occur in pairs, including the excessively (and stereotypically) emotional Italian duo of the Fiat Luigi (Tony Shalhoub) and the custom forklift Guido (Guido Quaroni), who run the local tire store, and the love-hate pair of Sarge (Paul Dooley), an extremely patriotic military jeep who runs the local army surplus store, and Fillmore (George Carlin), an aging hippie (a VW bus, of course) who represents the local counterculture and makes his own organic fuel.

However, the most important of the locals in Radiator Springs is probably Mater (voiced by comedian Larry the Cable Guy), a beat-up, rusted tow truck that serves as the film's token redneck. Mater is a good-hearted but simpleminded soul, and it is perhaps from him that McQueen presumably learns the most important (if clichéd) lessons about loyalty, friendship, and respecting others for who they are. After all, if he learns to respect Sally and Doc it is partly because they aren't small-towners at all, but have had sophisticated experience of the outside world. Mater, however, really *is* a sort of hillbilly and really is simpleminded. He and McQueen become friends largely because he idolizes the famous race car, while McQueen in turn treats

Mater with a significant amount of condescension, even to the end, when he has presumably learned to genuinely care about the tow truck.

The stereotypical characterization of Mater as a dumb redneck is one of the most problematic aspects of *Cars*, especially as it is merely the most obvious of the film's many examples of ethnic and cultural stereotyping. Mater is treated as lovable and well-intentioned (though somewhat sadistic in his treatment of "subhuman" vehicles such as the cow-tractors that populate the farms around the town), but he is both ignorant and stupid. As Jim Goad has argued, "rednecks" and "white trash" have often been represented in this way in recent American culture, coming to be the last remaining American social group against whom it is acceptable to employ sweeping negative stereotypes, making clear that racism in America is quite often more than a simple case of ethnic prejudice. In this case, there is a cultural and class-based prejudice at work as well, rednecks presumably being poor, uneducated, and working class. As voiced by Larry the Cable Guy,[7] Mater is definitely a Southerner, though he lives out west, but it is also important to note that he is the only major character in the film who is a legitimate working vehicle, so that one might argue that he is the film's only major working-class character, illustrating the way in which prejudice against rednecks might actually be a transposed form of contempt for the working class.[8]

During his week in Radiator Springs, McQueen, formerly a fiercely independent loner, learns the importance of getting support from others and supporting others in turn. He also learns (from Sally) the value of taking time in life to smell the roses, while learning from Doc not to jump to conclusions about others (and not to devote himself uncritically to the racing game). Despite it all, though, he does make it to California in time for the race, followed by a contingent of cars from Radiator Springs who serve (admirably) as his pit crew. However, the once-selfish McQueen ultimately sacrifices a sure victory in the runoff race in order to help the noble King limp across the finish line after the old champ is badly damaged in an accident caused by the malicious Chick Hicks (mirroring the earlier accident suffered by Doc). McQueen declines a lucrative new sponsorship deal from the Dinoco oil company (which had appeared in the *Toy Story* films), deciding to stay instead with the small-time (somewhat embarrassing) sponsors who had allowed him to get his start in Piston Cup racing.

McQueen even moves his racing headquarters to Radiator Springs, which will presumably not only allow him to spend more time with his newfound friends, but also stimulate the local economy in such a way to allow the town to return to its glory days of the 1950s—though there is no suggestion that this change might allow the town to update itself to the twenty-first century.

This sweet, rather old-fashioned ending is very much in tune with the overall tenor of the film, which is in many ways even more nostalgic than most Disney and Pixar films. If the film is an homage to car culture, for example, it is an homage to the car culture of the 1950s and even before, when scenic routes such as Route 66 were the only way to travel cross-country in the U.S. And the film's overt endorsement of small-town values participates in a long line of such endorsements in American culture (think Mayberry), most of which tend to locate their idyllic small towns in an idealized past. Such nostalgic representations of small-town life are, in fact, so ingrained in American popular culture that they would seem to be virtual paradigms of Americanness (and thus capitalism), except for the fact that capitalism is a fundamentally urban-centered phenomenon devoted to innovation, making small-town nostalgia the virtual antithesis of capitalism.

Of course, Christianity (with which Pixar films carefully avoid any engagement) might also seem the antithesis of capitalism, but that has not stopped the capitalist system from using Christianity as a key tool of ideological manipulation during its rise to global hegemony in the past several hundred years. A similar point might be made about small-town nostalgia, the promotion of which in American popular culture might seem anticapitalist, but which in fact also diverts attention from some of the more unappetizing aspects of American culture (such as an almost total lack of respect for tradition), making capitalism seem much warmer and fuzzier than it really is. Meanwhile, the endorsement of old-time, small-town values in *Cars* also seems to conflict with Pixar's own high-tech reputation, but it can also be seen in this sense as an attempt to moderate that reputation and to ensure that Pixar will not come to be seen as so technological that it begins to lack humanity and warmth.

Cars seems in its endorsement of small-town values and in McQueen's rejection of Dinoco sponsorship to convey a fairly clear and seemingly anticapitalist message that tradition is more important than innovation and that people (even when they are cars) are more important than money. It may also be significant in this context that the company sponsoring the villainous Chick Hicks is called Hostile Takeover Bank, thus aligning some of the more predatory practices of capitalist corporate culture with the ruthless, cheating antics of Hicks. On the other hand, this sponsorship is really more of a gag than a critique, a one-liner ostensibly meant for the amusement of adults that is not likely to teach children about the rapaciousness of capitalism. Meanwhile, although McQueen rejects Dinoco's sponsorship (which seems a positive move, given the negative reputation of large oil companies), it is also the case that Dinoco, as represented by their CEO, the Cadillac Coupe de Ville Tex Dinoco (voiced by Humpy Wheeler), is presented as a sympathetic and honorable character who also makes Dinoco seem somewhat like a family-owned business rather than a ruthless corporation. Meanwhile, McQueen's original sponsors, the Rust-Eze brothers Rusty and Dusty, are still running a profit-seeking capitalist enterprise—and one that clearly employs misleading advertising in its attempts to make old rusty cars believe that they will be like Lightning McQueen if only they use Rust-Eze bumper ointment.[9] While *Cars* does clearly identify this advertising as false, it also treats it essentially as a joke, with no real criticism seemingly intended, the implication presumably being that anyone stupid enough or gullible enough to believe such advertising deserves what they get. They may have a point in some cases, but the fact remains that Pixar is in the business of making money off the fantasies of children, who are inherently gullible and who not only identify with the characters in the films when they see them in theaters, but can also spend a significant amount of time and money on DVDs and toys that help them to continue to experience their identification with the film's characters far beyond the time spent in the theater. Given this aspect of Pixar's business, one cannot expect them to be too critical of capitalist marketing practices. The small amount of critique of greed and corruption might be as much as anyone could possibly expect. Still, we should be aware of the profit motivation behind Pixar's filmmaking, which is so often presented simply as a quest for quality and innovation, damn the bottom line.

Indeed, the careful packaging of Pixar's image (which began well before the Disney takeover) has been one of the hallmarks of the company's history, leading in recent years to the creation of a slickly produced celebratory 2007 documentary entitled "The Pixar Story" (included on the DVD version of *WALL-E*). Made by Leslie Iwerks (granddaughter of Ub Iwerks, Walt Disney's original partner and longtime associate), the film is self-promoted with the declaration, "An Award-Winning Filmmaker Tells the Riveting Story of the Innovative Company That Revolutionized Hollywood." And it's a good story, too, quintessentially American, a rags-to-riches tale fueled by breakthrough technology and dedication to hard work.[10] Of course, this sort of image-making was perfected years ago by Disney, and many of the public relations techniques employed by Pixar were probably learned from the older and larger company. However, the differences between the contents of Disney's classic self-marketing and Pixar's newer campaign are quite telling: Disney placed great emphasis on the wholesomeness of their product (personified by Uncle Walt himself) and on the ways in which their films stood as bastions against arrant modernization, regardless of how innovative they might be. Pixar essentially reverses this mix, sending forth the message that their films are the embodiments of American know-how and high-tech innovation, regardless of how wholesome they might be. And the difference can clearly be seen in the two companies' best-known marketing images, Disney represented by Walt's own personal (if falsified) signature and Pixar represented by a Luxo lamp of the kind typically found on the desks of engineers (and featured in one of the company's first demo shorts).

But as the Pixar oeuvre grows, it also becomes harder to characterize their output in a simple way. Pixar's next film, *Ratatouille* (2007), was the second Pixar film to have been directed by Brad Bird, but in many ways it could not have been more different from *The Incredibles*. In fact, *Ratatouille* is a bold and daring film that is different from everything that came before it (from Pixar or anyone else), even if it ultimately descends into some fairly conventional sentimentality.

The basic concept of *Ratatouille* could not seem less promising for a children's film. Basically, it is the story of a French rat who travels to Paris and then becomes one of the top chefs in that city of haute cuisine. Thus, apart from the unappetizing prospect of a rat working in a restaurant kitchen, the film has the problem that young viewers might not have much interest in the world of fine cooking. To make matters worse, the film features little in the way of catchy music and sports no big-name voice actors in the major roles. No worries, though: *Ratatouille* might appeal to a slightly older audience than most of the previous Pixar films, but it is highly entertaining and its rodent protagonist (after all, rodent protagonists are not exactly new in the Disney universe) is thoroughly charming, both because the preposterous plot actually works and because of the typically superb Pixar animation.

When Remy, the rat protagonist (voiced by comedian Patton Oswalt), comes to Paris, he has long harbored the unlikely dream of being a chef, buoyed by his fascination with one Gusteau (Brad Garrett), a top chef famed not only for running his own five-star restaurant but also for authoring the best-selling volume *Anyone Can Cook*. Remy, in fact, winds up in Gusteau's own restaurant, though the famous chef has by this time died and the reputation of the restaurant, under the guidance of Skinner (Ian Holm), Gusteau's smarmy successor, has begun to decline. Meanwhile, Remy arrives just after young Linguini (Lou Romano) has started work in the restaurant in a menial clean-up role. Linguini and Remy are thus, in many ways, natural allies, both occupying lowly positions in the strictly hierarchical world of haute cuisine. Indeed, they do become allies, with Remy learning essentially to control Linguini like a puppet so that the latter can cook. Remy's skill and inventiveness help Linguini to become an immediate success, building a growing reputation as an up-and-coming chef and drawing the jealous ire of the seemingly untalented Skinner. Skinner's jealousy becomes even greater when he learns that Linguini (unbeknownst to Linguini himself) is actually the son of Gusteau and stands to inherit the restaurant, the ownership of which would have otherwise passed to Skinner. Skinner attempts to undo Linguini, especially after he realizes that Linguini is in league with a rat. Nevertheless, Linguini seems headed for success, but on a crucial evening when influential food critic Anton Ego (Peter O'Toole) visits the restaurant, Linguini's entire kitchen staff—except for his love interest (and female chef) Colette (Janeane Garofalo)—deserts him when they learn about Remy. Remy, though, calls in his entire rat clan to work in the kitchen, meanwhile whipping up (via Linguini) a batch of ratatouille to serve to the haughty Ego. The dish, traditional peasant cuisine in France, seems an unlikely choice to serve to such a patron, but it turns out to be a big hit, its hearty taste reminding Ego favorably of the food served him by his mother during his own modest upbringing.

Ego writes a glowing review and the restaurant seems headed for success—while the film seems headed for a contrived and stereotypical happy ending. Bird and Pixar still have one final twist in store, though, which saves the ending of the film from seeming entirely contrived. Word gets out about the rats in the kitchen, and Gusteau's is forced to close by the health department. Then, in one last gesture in favor of democratization, Linguini, Colette, and the rats set up shop in a modest bistro, which features one dining area for humans and a separate one for rats.

At first glance, *Ratatouille* would seem to be an extended celebration of the lowly and the outcast, a designation that would surely apply to the film's rats (the ultimate wretched of the earth), but also to Linguini. It also seems to celebrate collective action, both in the teamwork between Remy and Linguini and in the way the rats work together to rescue Linguini on the night of Ego's visit. Meanwhile, the film critiques elitism and pretentiousness of the kind often associated with the world of French haute cuisine. The film also provides a critique of capitalist profit-mongering by favorably opposing the art of cooking (pursued for the sheer joy of creativity) to the business of cooking (pursued for profit). In particular, it depicts Skinner as a businessman more interested in making money than making fine food. Thus, as opposed to Gusteau, for whom cooking was an art, Skinner reduces cooking to mass production, endorsing an extensive line of frozen-food products that are designed to cash in on the Gusteau name. Finally, the film even inserts a critique of sexism in one diatribe in which Colette (anything but the typically demure Disney princess type) complains of how hard it is for a woman to get an opportunity in the male-dominated world of professional cooking.

To this extent, *Ratatouille* is surely the most progressive of the Pixar films—and one of the most progressive American children's films of all time. However, there are a number of contradictions that prevent the film from becoming an all-out statement in favor of leftist egalitarianism. For example, Colette's feminist anger is treated as comically exaggerated, and it is important to note that, within the film, she remains subsidiary to Linguini and circumscribed within the orbit of his masculine desire. Meanwhile, collective action in the film is presented not in political terms, but personal ones. Linguini and Remy overcome their differences to work together as a matter of friendship; the rats band together not from class-based solidarity but from family loyalty. Tellingly, late in the film, Ego (who should know, given his own humble origins) treats us to a handy explication of Gusteau's "anyone can cook" dictum, noting it doesn't mean that anyone can be a great artist, but simply that a great artist can come from anywhere. If this interpretation is correct (and the film seems to endorse it), then Gusteau's motto is not as egalitarian as it sounds; in fact, it can be taken as an elitist/individualist declaration of the importance of inherent individual talent, which can trump all else. Viewed this way, *Ratatouille* becomes a rather traditional Disney film that values personal relationships over political alliances and treats inherent merit (and inherited position) as preferable to a status earned by effort (honest or otherwise). Thus, Remy may be born a rat, but he is born a special rat with innate cooking abilities; meanwhile, Linguini may be entirely without talent, but he is treated as the unquestionably rightful heir (according to the paternalistic bourgeois property system) to Gusteau's restaurant, despite the fact that Skinner has worked long and hard to get to the position he occupies as the film begins. Linguini, though he can't actually cook, is an aristocrat of cooking whose rightful place is to head a restaurant; Skinner, though he can cook, is a mere commoner. Finally, there is much to be said of the cooperation between rats and humans that underwrites the favorable outcome of the film and that can be taken as a statement against racism. However, though this can't-we-all-just-get-along solidarity extends to sharing the bistro at the end of the film, the fact remains that rats and humans remain segregated within the bistro, occupying their respective separate dining areas, somewhat in the mode of Disney's Fox and Hound.

Even the obvious critique of capitalism in *Ratatouille* is a fairly orthodox Disney theme, Disney films having long been critical of the capitalist tendency to turn any and all aspects of life into regimented, routinized, profit-making enterprises (even as the Disney company itself was scrambled to squeeze every ounce of profit out of its major properties). Further, while *Ratatouille* clearly prefers art to commerce, the fact also remains that its critique of the commodification of cooking seems aimed more at Skinner's personal villainy than at the capitalist system itself. After all, the effrontery with which he sullies Gusteau's name by using it to hawk frozen burritos suggests a lack of respect for the art of cooking that helps to make him an unattractive figure, even if a film genuinely interested in egalitarianism might have at least explored the possibility that Skinner's marketing projects represent a form of democratization in themselves by producing foods that are both attractive and affordable to the masses.

Indeed, the film's lack of any sympathy for Skinner may be one of *Ratatouille*'s major shortcomings, especially as this lack is reinforced by a stereotypical visual representation of the chef as short, swarthy, and ugly, continuing the longtime Disney tradition of equating conventional Western physical beauty with moral purity. Granted, such sympathy would have introduced a moral complexity that is traditionally not to be found in children's films. From *Snow White* and *The Wizard of Oz* onward, such films have tended to rely on strict black-and-white oppositions between good heroes and evil villains. Even recent, seemingly subversive films such as the *Shrek* sequence largely retain such oppositions, even if they switch the roles, making a troll the hero, while traditional Disney heroes such as Prince Charming and the Fairy Godmother become villains. The representation of Skinner in *Ratatouille* might have offered opportunities for some genuine complexity. One could, for example, make a case that he, having presumably served an appropriate apprenticeship, deserves to be Gusteau's successor far more than does Linguini, whose only claim to the position is the accident of his birth and the fact that he effectively—and dishonestly—fakes the ability to cook. And, by any real standards, one can hardly fault Skinner for wanting to keep rats out of his kitchen, even though the film seems to treat his opposition to the rats as a key mark of his villainy.

WALL-E (2008), directed by *Finding Nemo*'s Stanton, is perhaps the most complex and innovative of all the Pixar films. Though still a charming film for children, it is a genuine work of science fiction cinema that participates in a number of science fiction subgenres, including most obviously the typically dark subgenres of the postapocalyptic narrative and the dystopian narrative. These two subgenres are also among the most satirical and political of all science fiction forms, and *WALL-E* certainly touches on a number of potentially serious political issues. The film envisions a future earth that has been rendered uninhabitable by an environmental collapse in which most of the earth's surface seems to have been covered by garbage, causing the remnants of the human race to take up residence in gigantic spaceships.[11] The film thus suggests quite clearly that this environmental collapse has been triggered by excessive consumerism, a suggestion that is reinforced by the fact that the collapse seems to have followed the rise to global hegemony of the Buy N Large (aka BNL) megacorporation, which dominates every industry at the time of the collapse, including functions formerly reserved for the government. It is, in fact, this corporation that administers the plan to move humanity into space, meanwhile constructing a fleet of robots designed to clean up the earth in humanity's absence, projecting that the cleanup will take five years, after which humans can return to the planet. The film is set 700 years after humanity's departure from earth, by which time it is clear that BNL's original plan has gone badly awry. Humanity still lives in space, while the fleet of cleanup robots seems to have worn out and ceased to function, except for one lone robot (the WALL-E of the title, an acronym for "Waste Allocation Load Lifter—Earth Class"). This robot still labors away alone in an abandoned city (unidentified, but vaguely similar to New York), crushing trash into cubes that it then stacks into huge towers, waiting to be picked up and incinerated by other equipment that no longer functions.

The humans in space still send periodic probes back to earth to check on conditions there, seeking in particular to find signs of plant life that would suggest that life is now sustainable on the planet. Otherwise, however, so much time has passed that the human race seems to have lost most of its memory of Earth, having learned to live a passive life of total luxury in the glistening and sterile environment of the spaceships, all their needs being met by a fleet of service robots. Humans, in fact, have become so accustomed to this service that they have lost the ability to walk, moving about instead on automated recliners. Their bodies have become fat and bloblike, with atrophied limbs. In short, humans have lost much of their humanity, and this supposedly perfect environment is clearly meant to be regarded as a dystopia. The WALL-E robot back on Earth, meanwhile, has evolved as well, over time apparently having gained not only intelligence, but a certain personality, becoming humanlike even as the humans in space become robotlike.[12] WALL-E still goes about its appointed task (keeping itself going by cannibalizing defunct WALL-E units for spare parts), but it seems to have become sentimental and even nostalgic. It has adopted a pet cockroach (cockroaches are, in a nod to their legendary toughness, apparently the only living creatures to have survived on Earth) and has started a collection of trinkets found among the garbage it gathers. Further, it repeatedly watches an old VHS tape of the 1969 film *Hello, Dolly!*, being particularly mesmerized by certain musical sequences and romantic moments in the film.

WALL-E's routine existence is interrupted when a ship arrives bearing a sleek white levitating robot known as EVE (Extraterrestrial Vegetation Evaluator), sent to earth to seek evidence of plant life. Having been rendered hopelessly romantic by repeated viewings of *Hello, Dolly!*, WALL-E (coded throughout the film as masculine) immediately falls in love with the new arrival (coded as feminine), though EVE is initially all business and spurns his advances. As luck would have it, though, WALL-E quickly becomes part of her business when he reveals that he has recently found a growing plant amid the city's garbage. EVE grabs the plant, stores it in a cavity in her body, then summons the probe ship back to take her to the mothership, which happens to be the *Axiom*, flagship of the BNL fleet. She is loaded on the ship, which takes off with WALL-E clinging to its exterior, not wanting to lose his new love. The two arrive on the *Axiom*, which eventually returns to Earth to start life there anew, after an extended sequence in which the ship's soulless autopilot robot (AUTO) attempts to prevent the return because it has been programmed to do so and because it, unlike WALL-E, lacks the imagination to go beyond its programming.

The basic scenario of *WALL-E* offers a number of opportunities for environmentalist and anticonsumerist commentary. Many conservative critics have charged the film with having a left-wing anticapitalist agenda. Yet, most of the films warnings are simple common sense, and makers of the film seem largely uninterested in the film's potential as a political statement, placing much more emphasis on the love story between WALL-E and EVE and indeed backing away from a full exploration of the political implications of the film's scenario. In fact, some commentators have seen the film as irresponsible precisely because it does not follow up on these implications or provide any sort of suggestion for preventing an environmental catastrophe such as the one depicted in the film, while even providing a contrived happy ending in which the two lovers are together, humanity has returned to Earth, and all appears well.[13] Meanwhile, any anticonsumerist critique in the film is rendered problematic by the fact that the film itself was produced by a megacorporation and has now grossed more than half a billion dollars in worldwide box-office receipts. This success has been accompanied by Pixar/Disney's usual massive merchandising campaign, with a special emphasis on toy versions of the film's loveable robots (who are, of course, perfect models for such toys).

It is certainly the case that, read seriously as a science fiction satire, *WALL-E* has a number of problems. It never really tells us anything of substance about conditions on Earth outside the one city in which WALL-E works, and it seems to forget that there is supposed to be a whole fleet of space habitats, showing us only the *Axiom*. Meanwhile, the humans on the *Axiom* are caricatures, their atrophied condition a bit too extreme to be believable, especially as there are scenes in the film involving live human actors, the first to appear in a Pixar film.[14] Indeed, *WALL-E* is significantly less concerned with believability than is typical of the best science fiction, being perfectly willing to go beyond the bounds of credibility in order to further its narrative. For example, the remnants of civilization on earth seem to have decayed surprisingly little in 700 years: scraps of newspaper still blow about in the wind, perfectly readable, while the ancient videotape of *Hello, Dolly!* still plays beautifully, whereas real videotapes have a life span of ten years or so before serious degradation begins, even if handled well (as opposed to WALL-E's tape, which is kept in a toaster, with no case).

Hello, Dolly!, of course, is important to the overall feel of *WALL-E*, serving as a perfect symbol of the film's postmodern nostalgia. One of the songs from *Hello, Dolly!*, "Put on Your Sunday Clothes," even serves as the opening theme for *WALL-E*–and seems to be WALL-E's favorite, as he has copied it onto his own internal recorder so that he can play it as he works collecting trash, a function which is enhanced by the fact that WALL-E's copy is on videotape, even though in reality it would have to be stored on a digital medium (such as DVD) to survive so long. After all, not only is *Hello, Dolly!* a film from an earlier time (relative both to the making and the setting of *WALL-E*), but the story of *Hello, Dolly!* was already from an earlier time in 1969, being set in 1890. Of course, from a perspective of more than 700 years in the future, 1890 and 1969 might be considered roughly contemporaneous, both serving as emblems of the pre-BNL past, nostalgically presented here as a romantic time when, among other things, the city of New York was a glistening place of adventure rather than a dismal trash-heap.

WALL-E's lack of verisimilitude might be taken as a sign of its weakness as a science fiction narrative, but the film is in fact less a science fiction narrative than a pastiche of a science fiction narrative, working in as many familiar motifs from previous science fiction films (both in terms of general images and ideas and specific references to individual films) as it possibly can. Some of these references are fairly subtle, as when the voice of the *Axiom*'s ship's computer is supplied by science fiction icon Sigourney Weaver. Others are more obvious; *2001: A Space Odyssey* is a particularly important referent. Many aspects of the *Axiom* segments of *WALL-E* recall that film, including the fact that the *Axiom* itself is often visually reminiscent of the spaceship *Discovery* in *2001*, while AUTO is reminiscent of the HAL-9000 computer from that film. Especially obvious is the way that, when the ship's captain, B. Mcrea (voiced by Jeff Garlin), rises from his automated chair and takes his first steps (thus signaling a declaration of independence from machines), these steps are accompanied by the stirring music of Richard Strauss's *Also Sprach Zarathustra*, used so memorably in *2001*. WALL-E himself, meanwhile, recalls any number of earlier science fiction robots. For example, he looks a great deal like the robot Number 5 from the 1986 film *Short Circuit* and has some of that robot's personality, though his personality is also similar to the well-known R2-D2 droid from the *Star Wars* films.[15] (WALL-E is also oddly reminiscent of E.T., a fact that I had not noticed until Benjamin, aficionado of science fiction films that he is, pointed it out to me.)

WALL-E's failure to adhere to science fiction seriousness can also be taken as a sign of the film's postmodern generic hybridity. It is not *just* science fiction, but also romantic comedy; it is not *just* political satire for adults, but also an animated feature for children. Indeed, while *WALL-E* seems aimed at a more mature audience than any other Pixar film, it is important to remember that the film is also designed to appeal to children. In fact, it seems reasonable to assume that it is designed to appeal *primarily* to children, who can understand more of the film than one might at first suspect. Having read a great deal about the film before its release, I went to see it in the theater with Skylor only, leaving Benjamin behind because I didn't think it would hold his attention. After I had seen it, I still felt the same way, though I was pretty sure that he would like the first thirty minutes, which feature WALL-E going about his rounds, then responding to EVE's arrival prior to their departure for the *Axiom*. After all, it is a well-known fact that kids love cute robots, and WALL-E himself is nothing if not cute. I was a bit surprised, however, at the extent to which Benjamin took to the film once we got it on DVD, though the first thirty minutes are indeed his favorite part. Among other things, watching the film with Benjamin and Skylor (along with a number of others, especially *Lilo & Stitch*), I came to appreciate how easily even small children can recognize and understand science fiction motifs. That attests, I think, to their extensive exposure to such motifs and to the prominent role played by science fiction in our contemporary mediascape, including the legacy of children's science fiction films from Disney and others.

Whatever its shortcomings as a work of science fiction, *WALL-E* can be considered a breakthrough in the genre simply because its animation is so good that it points toward a future in which CGI can be used more and more effectively (and ubiquitously) in science fiction films. Filmmakers will be free to explore any territory that they can imagine, confident that these imaginary worlds can be created on film via computer. The film could thus conceivably signal the beginning of a science fiction renaissance comparable to that triggered by *Star Wars* back in 1977. It would certainly be welcome, considering that science fiction film has been in a pretty sad state so far in the twenty-first century. *WALL-E* is a tour de force of computer animation of science fictional worlds, a fact that can easily be discerned by comparing the scenes on the *Axiom*, say, to the spaceship scenes in something like *Lilo & Stitch*. But the most impressive animation in *WALL-E* appears in those first dazzling thirty minutes, which look almost real and which are mesmerizing even with virtually no dialogue. WALL-E himself is a masterpiece, down to the detailed and realistic treatment of the reflections that can be seen in his glass-lensed eyes.

The sheer technical virtuosity of *WALL-E* is, of course, part of its ultimately (and oddly) optimistic message, suggesting that technology can overcome any and all obstacles. In addition, as with all Pixar films, technical virtuosity is largely the point: even in a film with such overtly political content, the filmmakers seem virtually oblivious to this content: director Stanton has claimed to have been amazed that so many people have read environmentalist and anticonsumerist messages into what for him was simply a story about a lonely robot. The romanticized treatment of this theme, including the central plot of the love story between WALL-E and EVE, is a bit silly if read straight, of course, but it's also pure Hollywood. Meanwhile, much of this film, however inventive, is pure Disney as well. When the humans return to earth, they are resuming their natural place, in classic Disney fashion, while many of the dystopian conditions aboard the *Axiom* can be interpreted as the result of the fact that the humans there are living in an unnatural state. WALL-E, of course, represents a potential complication to the traditional Disney celebration of the natural and the authentic. As a mass-produced machine, he would seem to be unnatural by definition, but his gradual evolution of intelligence and personality can be interpreted as a move toward the natural, which seems very Disneyesque, though marking a different trajectory from that of classic Disney heroes, except perhaps Pinocchio. However, WALL-E's dogged pursuit, through seven centuries, of his programmed trash compacting task suggests that he never fully overcomes his initial status as a machine. Further, this aspect of WALL-E's supposed personality casts doubt on the authenticity of his romantic relationship with EVE. After all, WALL-E's tendency to act in a programmed manner, taken in conjunction with his proclivity for repeated viewing of *Hello, Dolly!*, potentially suggests that he has simply been programmed by that film to act in a romantic fashion. By extension, this motif can be taken as a critique of the power of popular culture in general (especially film) to program audiences to act in specific ways. Of course, there is little chance that children viewing *WALL-E* will take it as a warning against such interpolation by popular culture and little reason to believe that Stanton or anyone else at Pixar intended such a critique. If anything, the fact that WALL-E is so enamored of *Hello, Dolly!* is presented as part of his charm and part of what makes him human, suggesting that romantic Hollywood fare increases our humanity rather than programming us to act in sentimental and romantic ways. Thus, *WALL-E* becomes simply an example of Hollywood sentimentality, rather than a critique of it. The whole phenomenon of film-linked merchandising (with the inevitable tie-ins to McDonald's Happy Meals and other high-profile venues) makes it clear that, from at least the 1930s, with Disney's extensive co-marketing of Mickey Mouse, children's films have been designed to help children develop the kind of consumerist mentality upon which the U.S. economy crucially depends. Meanwhile, the prominent presence of *Hello, Dolly!* in *WALL-E* points toward the possibility that, if children's films are in some ways designed to teach children to become ideal consumers, much of this project also involves training them to be consumers of Hollywood film itself—which then, of course, continues consumerist training throughout adulthood.

Among other things, this project is enhanced by the fact that so many children's films are in fact genre films, with science fiction being an especially prominent genre. Pixar's latest effort, *Up* (2009), is essentially an entry in the adventure film genre, a sort of eccentric, children's version of the *Indiana Jones* films, with a dash of *The Lost World* thrown in for good measure. Perhaps even more than with *WALL-E*, there is room seriously to question whether *Up* is a children's film at all, given the number of serious issues with which it deals. The first segment of the film relates the touching love story between two characters named Carl and Ellie, who meet in childhood, find that they share a similar interest in adventure, then fall in love and marry, living happily together (despite the disappointment of not being able to have children or of being unable to pursue their most colorful dreams of adventure). Finally, Ellie dies, leaving the elderly Carl alone in the home where they shared their life together, growing cranky and bitter. All of this takes only a few minutes and is related essentially in the manner of a silent film, without dialogue. It's a little masterpiece of its own kind, though I'm not really sure how much of it smaller children will fully grasp or appreciate. Benjamin seemed pretty oblivious to this segment, and definitely started to squirm in his seat.

Most of the plot of *Up* involves the efforts of the widowed Carl (voiced by Edward Asner) to pursue the central dream of adventure he and Ellie had shared through their time together: to travel to remote Paradise Falls in South America, where once-famous adventurer Charles Muntz—the childhood hero of both Carl and Ellie—had supposedly recovered the skeleton of a giant bird, a member of a previously unknown species. Experts declared the skeleton a fraud, prompting Muntz to return to Paradise Falls to try to recover a live specimen of the bird. Muntz was never to be heard from again. Through the unlikely expedient of attaching a vast array of helium-filled balloons to his house, Carl lifts off and indeed flies to Paradise Falls, with a pudgy Asian boy named Russell (Jordan Nagai) tagging along as a stowaway. In the rainforest near the falls, they encounter Muntz (voiced by Christopher Plummer), now deranged by the continuing failure of his quest to catch one of the exotic birds. Carl and Russell are nearly done in by Muntz and his army of trained talking dogs, but survive with the help of one of the dogs and one of the giant birds, eventually returning to civilization aboard Muntz's huge airship. Carl, meanwhile, has not only fulfilled the dream of seeing Paradise Falls, but has (more importantly) overcome his bitterness. He has bonded with Russell and the dog, but, more importantly, he has realized that the everyday adventure he had shared with Ellie, despite the disappointments, was more rare and precious than any exotic trip into the wilderness could ever be.

Up includes a number of stunning visuals (sometimes enhanced by the Disney 3-D process, though the 3-D seems pretty unnecessary here) as well as enough wacky animal characters to entertain younger children who might not appreciate the film's overall message about pursuing one's dreams but also making sure one is careful to realize when dreams have been fulfilled. Meanwhile, the focus on the love story between Carl and Ellie (supplemented by the bonding among Carl, the boy, and the dog) continues Pixar's slide into Hollywood romanticism, making the film a direct follow-up to *WALL-E*. All in all, it's a complex and beautiful film, even if it tends to verge on cliché and even if it sometimes seems cobbled together from bits and pieces of films we've seen before. Younger children, of course, might not have seen those films before, though they are likely to see them again; for these children the main import of the film might be to prepare them to receive such films in a predictable manner in the future.

Up is a decided departure for Pixar in that it seems to offer unusually meager opportunities for co-marketing, especially of toys. It is also less ostentatious than most Pixar films in directing attention to the technical quality of its animation, unless one counts the excellent use of 3-D. In fact, all in all, the film, while lacking appeals to fairytale magic, is something of a throwback to the classic Disney films in that it depends more on sentimentality than virtuosity for its effects. Indeed, *Up* seems to be something of a retreat from perhaps the most important breakthrough made by Pixar (enabled by a growing cynicism in the American population at large): the way in which Pixar has so openly presented their films as high-tech commodities, as opposed to Disney's traditional strategy of marketing their films as exceptions that resist the general commodification of American culture. Much of this change has to do with context, of course: Pixar's films appear in the midst of a well-developed postmodernist culture in which the commodification of culture has become an accepted (and seemingly irresistible) fact, while Disney's classic films were released at a time when it was still possible to imagine alternatives to commodification. The landscape of the children's film business has changed dramatically as well. Children's film has become a much more lucrative enterprise than it was in the half century of Disney hegemony from the 1930s to the 1980s. As a consequence, there is now much more competition and there are now many more players in the field. But Pixar remains the centerpiece of the children's film industry, having scored hit after hit and having won four of the eight Oscars for Best Animated Feature that have been given through 2009. No film made by Disney proper has won that award, but Pixar's success means that Disney, now a huge and powerful multifaceted media corporation, remains the leading player in the children's film industry.

——4——

The Contemporary Challenge to Disney: Dreamworks and Others

Having scored major hits with *Jaws* (1975) and *Close Encounters of the Third Kind* (1977), a young up-and-coming director by the name of Steven Spielberg had an even bigger smash with *Raiders of the Lost Ark* (1981), a tongue-in-cheek action-adventure that also seemed aimed at a somewhat younger audience than Spielberg's earlier films. With the release of *E.T. the Extra-Terrestrial* (1982), Spielberg scored another megahit (and produced another classic of popular cinema). He also continued the trend toward young target audiences in what was the first of his films that one might legitimately consider a children's film, though it certainly deals with issues that seem appropriate for a somewhat older audience than the core audience of Disney's animated films. Of Spielberg's subsequent directorial efforts, only the ill-fated *Hook* (1991), a live-action update of *Peter Pan*, could really be considered a children's film. But, through his work as a producer and through his participation as a founding partner of DreamWorks, Spielberg would go on to become a force in American children's films exceeded only by Walt Disney himself (with John Lasseter perhaps now gaining ground from the rear).

Of course, dating back at least to *The Wizard of Oz*, there have been important children's films that were not made or distributed by Disney or Pixar, though it is certainly the case that Disney's ongoing dominance in this arena, regardless of changing conditions within the industry and within society as a whole, has been one of the most remarkable phenomena in American cultural history. As a marker of this dominance, in the American Film Institute's 2008 listing of the top ten animated films of all time, the top five films are all Disney films (with *Snow White* at the top of the list); the next five include two Disney films, two Pixar films, and *Shrek*.

The hugely successful *E.T.*, with its story of a lovable alien that presumably teaches tolerance for the Other, came at a time when Disney's films had been particularly unremarkable for some time. *E.T.* itself was by a wide margin the top-grossing film of 1982. When adjusted for inflation it is still the fourth highest-grossing film and the top-grossing children's film of all time, though it is a complex work that includes a number of adult themes that make its categorization as a children's film a bit problematic. Still, the film suggested a huge market for films accessible to children, though one that would not be fully tapped until the Disney renaissance of the early 1990s. Thus, the other most notable children's film of 1982 was Don Bluth's *The Secret of NIMH* (jointly distributed by MGM and United Artists), a beautifully animated talking-animal feature that has continued to have something of an audience over the years, but was not a huge hit at the time. Disney itself didn't even produce a children's film in 1982, releasing only *Tron*, a science fiction film still remembered for its cutting-edge special effects, but one that brought in less than one-tenth the gross of *E.T.* There was clearly a vacuum in the world of children's film in the early 1980s. In fact, Disney didn't release another children's film until *The Black Cauldron* in 1985, and even that was considerably darker than Disney's classic films had been. Meanwhile, Spielberg and his production company Amblin Entertainment did more than anyone to fill the void, producing a string of films that included *Gremlins* (1984), *Goonies* (1985), *Back to the Future* (1985), *Young Sherlock Holmes* (1985), and *Harry and the Hendersons* (1987), all of which were aimed at youthful audiences, though less at younger children than the classic Disney films had been. Then again, the film business is a complex one that involves a number of alliances, even among rivals. Thus, one of Spielberg's and Amblin's most interesting productions of the 1980s was *Who Framed Roger Rabbit* (1988), produced in conjunction with Disney and distributed by Disney's Touchstone Pictures unit (on the premise that the faux noir subject matter of this innovative mixture of live action and animation was a bit too mature to carry the Disney logo).

In the same year as *Who Framed Roger Rabbit*, Spielberg and Amblin produced *The Land Before Time*, distributed by Universal (as most Amblin films had been) and directed by Bluth, a former Disney animator who had by this time developed a considerable reputation for his meticulous attention to detail in animation. The animation of *The Land Before Time* is actually unremarkable, though effective, but its story of a group of young dinosaurs traveling cross-country in search of the Great Valley, where food is plentiful and all dinosaurs live together in peace[1], proved a big hit with kids (Benjamin loves it), not only propelling the film to box-office success but triggering a whole franchise that has included a dozen straight-to-video feature-length sequels and a television series that now airs on Time-Warner's Cartoon Network in the U.S.

The year after *Who Framed Roger Rabbit* and *The Land Before Time*, Disney would make its big comeback with *The Little Mermaid*, reclaiming the lead in the field of animated children's films, though that dominance would never again be as complete as it had been in the glory days from *Snow White* to *The Jungle Book* (produced during the life of Walt Disney). It was not, in fact, until after Disney's death that children's films produced by companies other than Disney began to make a significant impact, and then only in a piecemeal fashion. As early as 1968, *Chitty Chitty Bang Bang*, a British-produced film (distributed in the U.S. by United Artists), was a key hit that openly poached on Disney territory. A film vaguely in the mode of *Mary Poppins, Chitty Chitty Bang Bang* starred Dick Van Dyke and featured songs by the Sherman brothers, just as *Mary Poppins* had done. Other challenges to Disney's control of the children's film industry arose here and there, largely through adaptations of well-known children's books. For example, 1971 saw the release of *Willy Wonka and the Chocolate Factory* (distributed by Paramount Pictures), a somewhat sanitized film version of the 1964 novel *Charlie and the Chocolate Factory* by Roald Dahl (who had, incidentally, coscripted *Chitty Chitty Bang Bang*).

One of the most important non-Disney films of the early post-Walt years was the animated film *Charlotte's Web* (1973), also distributed by Paramount. This film has proved an enduring favorite over time and was the first animated film from a company other than Disney for which that statement could be made. One of several attempts of the successful animated television production company Hanna-Barbera to break into the theatrical film business, *Charlotte's Web* was the first theatrical film produced by Hanna-Barbera that was not a spin-off of one of their television series, though it did not turn out to be the beginning of big things for the company in feature film. Animated in a simple style that is more reminiscent of Hanna-Barbera's television series than of the Disney animated classics, *Charlotte's Web* also represented a significant departure from the Disney tradition in terms of content. Based on the acclaimed 1952 children's novel by E. B. White, the talking-animal film was originally only a moderate critical and commercial success, but over the years it has gained a following and now ranks as something of a classic of children's film, becoming one of the best-selling video titles of the 1990s.[2] The film follows the book rather closely in terms of plot, though White was apparently unhappy with the adaptation, largely because it is a musical whose songs frequently interrupt the narrative. In any case, the film details the story of Wilbur (voiced by Henry Gibson), a runt pig that is nearly killed at birth by farmer John Arable (John Stephenson) because it is deemed too small to survive. Arable's daughter Fern (Pamelyn Ferdin) intervenes and agrees to raise the pig herself. She successfully does so, until it is too big to stay with her and has to be sold to her uncle Homer Zuckerman (Bob Holt), who lives on a neighboring farm. Initially distraught at the move, Wilbur settles in well in Zuckerman's big red barn, especially after he finds a friend in barn spider Charlotte A. Cavatica (Debbie Reynolds).

Unfortunately, matters take a dark turn when Wilbur learns that it is the usual fate of a spring pig like himself to be slaughtered late in the fall, possibly to be eaten as part of Christmas dinner. Charlotte, however, swears that she will save Wilbur from this fate and begins weaving words (beginning with "SOME PIG") into her webs to try to send the message that Wilbur is a special animal who should be spared. These web messages gain considerable attention and eventually make a crucial contribution to Wilbur's winning of a special award at the County Fair, a distinction that spares him from slaughter and gains him a place in Zuckerman's barn for the remainder of his natural life. Charlotte's natural life, however, runs out while they are at the fair, just after she deposits her egg sac, which Wilbur carries back to the farm and protects until the young spiders hatch the next spring. The spiders then go out into the world to seek lives of their own, except for three runts too small to venture forth. These stay in the barn with Wilbur, who helps them grow to adulthood.

The potential critique of the meat industry in *Charlotte's Web* is muted by the happy outcome for Wilbur, as well as by the focus on a small family farm, which places Wilbur's potential slaughter outside the realm of the commercial meatpacking industry. Instead, the central message of this charming film concerns the importance of friendship and the acceptance of difference: Wilbur becomes a great success despite starting out as a lowly runt, while Charlotte becomes his greatest friend despite her own lowly status as a barn spider. Indeed, this film well illustrates the tendency of American children's film to sanction acceptance of the Other and to celebrate the potential achievements of the lowly and the different. Even Disney's films convey such messages, though they tend to frame them within a preserve-the-natural-order imperative that is pretty much missing from *Charlotte's Web*. In this sense, such films provide direct support to the official rhetoric of American society, even as they convey a much more leftist and humanitarian attitude than has traditionally been mainstream practice in the U.S. Indeed, at least in children's films made since the 1960s, one could argue that children's film leans significantly to the left of the actual midpoint of American social and political attitudes—not because Hollywood is dominated by leftists who seek to subvert our children but because, deep down, we know that these attitudes are the proper ones to have for decent-thinking human beings and we want our children to be good people (at least until they reach college age and need to settle down to start becoming good wage-earners).

Charlotte's Web hardly ushered in a new age of animated film. In 1994, however, *Charlotte's Web* surprisingly became the top-selling video title of the year, presaging the major box-office hit *Babe*, a vaguely similar Australian film produced in the following year. The success of such films led to the production of a live-action adaptation of *Charlotte's Web* in 2006, produced by Paramount, Nickelodeon Pictures, and Walden Media, and distributed in the U.S. by Paramount. Among other things, this film thus represents part of the effort of the television cable entity Nickelodeon (owned, like Paramount, by the corporate media giant Viacom and the principal competitor to Disney's battery of cable channels) to break into the feature film business. This project began with *Harriet the Spy* (1996) and has included several films based on Nickelodeon's television programs as well as some coproductions with DreamWorks, including the big-budget box-office disappointment *Lemony Snicket's A Series of Unfortunate Events* (2004) and the recent *Hotel for Dogs* (2009). None of the Nickelodeon films have made major impact or changed the landscape of children's film.

However, in addition to the special case of DreamWorks, to which I will return at the end of this chapter, several other non-Disney phenomena have made important contributions to American cinema. One instance, for example, involves the films of Tim Burton, the former Disney animator who has, over the years, been involved in a number of projects (some with participation by Disney itself) that might be characterized as children's film, though the characterization is problematic in his case. In addition, the commercial success of the films of the Disney renaissance in the 1990s has spurred a number of existing major studios to make the leap into the children's film business, though with mixed results. Disney-Pixar remains the 500-pound gorilla in the room, but at least it is no longer the only animal in the zoo.

TIM BURTON

Though sometimes involving the participation of Disney, the films of Tim Burton might in many ways be considered an alternative to Disney in the realm of children's film. In his brief stint with Disney, Burton produced such short films as *Vincent* (1982) and *Frankenweenie* (1984), a full-length version of which he is, as of this writing, working on (again for Disney), animated in stop-motion. *Vincent* was an animated short about a little boy who is obsessed with the ghoulish world of Vincent Price films. In the film, the boy's morbid fascination with death eventually leads him simply to collapse and die, at least in his own mind. Predictably, Burton encountered considerable resistance concerning this film from Disney, which wanted to supply a happy ending. The live-action *Frankenweenie* does have a happy ending, though one so contrived that it seems to mock the imposition of happy endings, and the film as a whole was just as problematic from a Disney perspective. *Frankenweenie* retells the Frankenstein story (especially as refracted through the James Whale film of the Frankenstein story) in the setting of modern suburban America, with the monster replaced by a household dog, Sparky. When the dog is hit and killed by a car, its owner, schoolboy Victor Frankenstein (Barret Oliver), is plunged into despair. Using information gleaned from his school

science class, young Victor brings the dog back to life. But its subsequent strange appearance (it has been roughly stitched back together
and has a bolt in its neck) causes the neighbors to hate and fear it,
eventually leading them to become a mob in the mold of the villagers
of the original *Frankenstein* film, then to drive the dog to a second
death. In the process, however, Sparky saves the life of Victor, leading the neighbors to realize that they have misjudged the animal. They
then circle him with their automobiles and jumpstart him back to life
by wiring their car batteries to the bolt in his neck.

Not surprisingly, Burton's career with Disney was short-lived.
Frankenweenie was not even released by the studio in the United
States and became available to the public in its full version only as an
extra feature in the DVD release of *The Nightmare before Christmas*
(1993), about which I'll write more later. Meanwhile, Burton departed
Disney after *Frankenweenie*, but that film drew the attention of Paul
Reubens, who was looking for a director for a feature film based on
his Pee-wee Herman character. *Pee-wee's Big Adventure* (1985) then
launched Burton's career as a director of feature films, many of which
might be described as adult films masquerading as children's films—
except that children tend to find them highly entertaining as well.
Pee-wee's Big Adventure was one of Adam's favorites as a child,
while Skylor is particularly fond of another Frankenstein-inspired
Burton film (filtered through the optic of the fairy tale), *Edward Scissorhands* (1990). Other films in this category include *Beetlejuice*
(1988) and *Charlie and the Chocolate Factory* (2005), a masterpiece
of postmodern image-making that tries to remain truer to Dahl's original vision than had the earlier *Willy Wonka and the Chocolate Factory*.[3] Even Burton's decidedly gothic *Batman* (1989) and *Batman
Returns* (1991) have had a considerable audience among young viewers, though some of Burton's films, such as *Sweeney Todd: The
Demon Barber of Fleet Street* (2007), are decidedly not suitable for
most children. By contrast, in addition to *Frankenweenie*, Burton's
current projects include a remake of *Alice in Wonderland* (for Disney), slated for release in 2010 and providing clear evidence that Burton's seemingly eccentric films have failed to escape the gravitational
pull of Disney.

The Nightmare before Christmas is of special note in this regard.
Though directed by Henry Selick, the film was based on a concept
by Burton and produced by Burton. *Nightmare* is a truly original

stop-motion animated musical that looks and sounds like nothing else. It begins with the basic concept that all holidays emerge into our world from worlds of their own and proceeds from there to imagine what might happen if the inhabitants of Halloween Town got bored with their own holiday and attempted to conscript Christmas for their own use. The resulting conflation of holidays that are so radically different makes for some amusing moments, but the plot of the film is really beside the point. This film, like most Burton films, is all about the images it conveys, though in this case the music (written, as with most Burton films, by Danny Elfman) is also especially important. Variations on a few basic sounds are deftly woven into the soundtrack, helping to create the film's unique atmosphere of the bright-spirited macabre. After seeing the film, Benjamin (who always responds strongly to good movie music) went around the house for days singing lines from the rousing opening song, "This Is Halloween." Elfman himself supplies the singing voice of Jack Skellington, the Pumpkin King, a Halloween Town leader who inadvertently discovers Christmas, then tries to conscript it for his own. The real star of the film, though, is the animation of the panoply of bizarre and monstrous figures constituting the population of Halloween Town. In this, the film is something of a predecessor to *Monsters, Inc.*, but the Pixar film actually pales in visual inventiveness beside *The Nightmare before Christmas*.

In the end, Jack and the other denizens of Halloween Town return to doing what they do best (Halloween), while Christmas (here treated as an entirely secular holiday) is turned back over to its rightful producer, Santa Claus. Thus, at first glance, *Nightmare* is essentially a sheer spectacle that carries little in the way of obvious message, other than the vague (and, ultimately, Disneyesque) suggestion that one should stay in one's own natural place. Indeed, the film was made in conjunction with Burton's former employers at Disney, which released the film to theaters under its Touchstone Pictures label because it felt that the look and subject matter of the film were too dark and scary to carry the Disney brand name. Over the years, though, *Nightmare* has become such a cult favorite (proving attractive and not particularly disturbing to even very small children) that Disney has finally embraced the film as its own, releasing a new, elaborately packaged collector's edition DVD in 2008 under the Disney imprint.

A closer look, however, shows that *The Nightmare before Christmas* contains potential layers of complexity that are decidedly non-Disney. For one thing, the contrast between Halloween Town and Christmas Town suggests contradictions in American (and Western) religious observances that go beyond simple cultural richness. The values commonly expressed in these two holidays as currently celebrated in our society are incompatible. If the obvious answer to this contradiction is that our culture has clearly given priority to the values of Christmas, it is also the case that one of the most striking things about *The Nightmare before Christmas* is that (despite Jack's fascination with the newly discovered Christmas) the characters and overall culture of Halloween Town are far richer and more interesting than those of Christmas Town. Without Halloween Town this would have been a boring film indeed. Christmas Town may be pure and clean (and no one there, we are told, is dead), but it is also sterile, monotonous, and boring. Halloween Town is dirty, decaying, and teeming with oodles of gross creatures (many of them dead), but it has a vitality and a diversity that is entirely lacking in Christmas Town. The latter has the blandness of "Jingle Bells"; the former has the spectacular energy and charm of "This Is Halloween" and the other songs from Elfman's soundtrack. The film thus presents a potentially carnivalesque challenge that reverses the official priorities of Western society.

Burton also produced Selick's *James and the Giant Peach* (1996), based on Dahl's controversial 1961 children's book of the same title (which many felt was, like much of Dahl's work, entirely unsuitable for children, partly because of its prominent use of the theme of child abuse). *James* is again a visually inventive work, fairly true to Dahl's original novel (and thus somewhat darker thematically than most children's films). However, Randy Newman's music seems flat and uninspired compared to the Elfman music of *The Nightmare before Christmas*, and *James* is ultimately a less interesting film, though it is highly entertaining. Further, its open representation of the greed and viciousness of the evil aunts who take James in after his parents are killed by a seemingly supernatural rhinoceros carries some potential criticism of the social systems that are in place for the care of orphaned children, while its positive treatment of the downtrodden James and the brave insects who befriend him in the film has progressive potential as well. Finally, the film's ultimate conclusion, in which James is wrested from the control of the aunts and allowed to live with the insects in his own home, runs directly counter to the Disney tradition of suggesting that it is best for everyone to remain in his or her conventional place.[4]

The real follow-up to *The Nightmare before Christmas*, with its stop-motion animation of macabre characters and rousing musical accompaniment, is *The Corpse Bride* (2005), directed by Burton himself, with help from Mike Johnson. Elfman again provides the original score and songs in a film marked by stirring music and captivating visuals. If *The Corpse Bride* seems less inventive than *The Nightmare before Christmas*, it is largely because it has that film as a predecessor. Benjamin saw *The Corpse Bride* before *The Nightmare before Christmas* and was absolutely blown away by the look of the film, so different from anything he had seen before. When he discovered *Nightmare*, however, it quickly became one of his favorites of all time, again partly because of the visuals, but especially because of the music, which is even more entrancing than the music of *The Corpse Bride*, though the latter does include one production number featuring a chorus line of skeletons that Benjamin can watch over and over.

TWENTIETH CENTURY FOX

One of the first major studio responses to the success of the Disney renaissance at the beginning of the 1990s was the distribution, by Fox, of the Australian-produced *FernGully: The Last Rainforest* (1992). An overtly environmentalist film, based on the *Fern Gully* stories of Diana Young, *FernGully* focuses on the theme of the destruction of the earth's rainforests. In this case the rainforest is located near Mount Warning, on the northern coast of Australia, but the theme is global and the specific location is not particularly emphasized. Indeed, the voice actors in the film are mostly American and no Australian accents are featured. The film is quite clear in its identification of the destruction of the rainforest as a crime against nature, though it is somewhat vague in its explanation of the dire consequences of rainforest destruction and it addresses the economic impetus behind this destruction hardly at all. Further, the urgent real-world issues featured in the film are presented within a supernatural plot featuring fairies and an evil spirit, as well as a number of talking animals, which might make the film more entertaining to children but probably also obscures the environmentalist message by displacing it into an unreal world.

The film focuses on FernGully, a particularly rich area within the rainforest that serves as the home of a magical tree spirit, Magi Lune (voiced by Grace Zabriskie), who many years earlier had saved the area from the ravages of the evil spirit Hexxus (voiced by Tim Curry with an over-the-top spirit of menace) by entrapping the villain within an enchanted tree, but only after all humans had fled the area. Subsequently, the animals of the rainforest have lived in peace and harmony with their natural surroundings, believing humans to have been rendered extinct by Hexxus's earlier assault. The central character of the film is one Chrysta (Samantha Mathis), a young fairy who is training (halfheartedly) to succeed the aging Magi Lune as the guardian of the forest. The tranquil life of the denizens of FernGully is initially interrupted by the arrival of Batty Koda (Robin Williams), a somewhat deranged bat that has been rendered so due to the results of gruesome experiments conducted on him by human scientists. This character thus not only offers Williams a chance to enact his trademark hyperactive zaniness, but also introduces the secondary theme of animal experimentation, though with a light touch that presents this potentially horrifying motif as essentially humorous.[5] Indeed, the song "Batty Rap," in which Batty relates his experiences in the laboratory, was specifically censored in the final released version of the film in order to make those experiences seem less frightening to children.[6] The film does very little to suggest that the same sort of mentality that enables such experimentation on animals is also central to the lack of respect for nature that has led to the ongoing destruction of the world's rainforest (and environment as a whole). Individual viewers can, of course, supply such links in their own readings of the film, but I suspect that children would be unlikely to make this interpretive move without considerable urging from parents.

The peaceful forest is then disrupted much more seriously when human loggers arrive at the rainforest with their monstrous "leveller," a machine that saws down and cuts up trees en masse. In the process, the loggers cut down the enchanted tree and free the evil Hexxus, who takes control of the leveller and heads straight for FernGully, hoping for revenge against Magi Lune. Ultimately, Hexxus is defeated and FernGully is saved, so that the film ends on an upbeat note that diminishes the urgency of its environmentalist message. All in all, the film seems to suggest that some heroic figure will surely ride to the rescue and save the planet, no matter what threats are heaped upon it. In addition, the magical elements of the film contribute to the exotic and almost otherworldly feel to the setting of the film, which tends to make its message seem less relevant to everyday life in the United States. Finally, the fact that most of the true evil in the film is attributed to Hexxus rather than to human profit seekers displaces the real blame for environmental destruction from its real perpetrators onto nonexistent supernatural perpetrators, further diluting the political message. As Ian Wojcik-Andrews argues, "*FernGully* is a disturbing film, because the words and images it uses to discuss the destruction of the environment do not actually critique the ideological systems causing the environmental destruction" (133). But the film does at least make an effort and it could probably make a positive contribution in conjunction with other films delivering similar messages.[7]

FernGully was, in fact, followed one year later by *Once Upon a Forest*, another film with environmentalist themes that was distributed by Fox, though this time produced by Hanna-Barbera. This film dispenses with magic, but still employs the time-honored children's film precedent of cute talking animals to convey themes concerning the threat of human development to the natural habitats of animals. Here, a poisonous gas spill ravages one animal community, while a construction project threatens the wetlands that provide homes for a community of birds. As in Disney films such as *Bambi*, the focus of *Once Upon a Forest* is entirely on animals, while human beings are treated as strange, faceless, alien threats. The film delivers a clear message that pollution is bad and nature is good, but (even more than with *FernGully*) the film avoids any real engagement with the issues involved. It opts instead to focus on a plot that involves (successful) efforts to save one small badger whose lungs are badly damaged in the poisonous gas spill. Meanwhile, the success of these efforts ironically involves the ability of a group of animal "children" to build a flying machine based on the designs of their mentor, the old badger Cornelius, thus presumably setting the animals on the same road of technological development that has threatened their habitats in the first place.

It may be telling that both *FernGully* and *Once Upon a Forest*, though they appeared in the midst of the heyday of the Disney-led renaissance in animated film, were flops at the box office, suggesting a poor market for their environmentalist themes, though it is also the case that the two films (especially the latter) are undistinguished in their animation and storytelling. Meanwhile, Fox's effort to break into the newly lucrative animated film market eventually led it to found its own animation unit, Fox Animation Studios, under the leadership of Gary Goldman and Bluth. This ill-fated studio, however, released only two features to theaters (both directed by Bluth and Goldman): *Anastasia* (1997), a modest success, and *Titan A.E.* (2000), pretty much a box-office disaster that led to the dismantling of Fox's animation unit as then constituted.

In the meantime, however, Fox had acquired the high-tech Blue Sky Studios in an attempt to produce CGI-animated films in competition with the likes of Pixar. Fox—Blue Sky has produced a series of moderately successful films that have provided some serious competition for Disney-Pixar, even if they have not quite matched the success of that company's films. The first of these, *Ice Age* (2002), is a talking-animal film with the gimmick that it is set in the distant past (during the last ice age, which peaked roughly 20,000 years ago and ended around 12,000 years ago). This premise allows the film to feature a number of quirky and exotic creatures who are either members of extinct species (such as mammoths, saber-toothed cats, and dodos) or the ancestors of today's animals, even though 12,000–20,000 years would not be nearly enough time for the evolutionary changes suggested by the film to have occurred. Kids, of course, are not bothered by such details, though the visual jokes played with evolution in the film could be a bit troubling in today's embattled climate, when religious extremists have for some time been agitating to undermine the teaching of evolution in public schools, despite the overwhelming physical evidence that makes evolution a fact accepted by all reputable scientists. At least the filmmakers avoided the temptation to include dinosaurs (which had been long extinct) in the film, though dinosaurs are in fact introduced (but with an explanation) in the film's second sequel. Meanwhile, the placement of the film in the last ice age means that human characters can be introduced as well, though the focus is very much on the animals.

Directed by Chris Wedge (a cofounder of Blue Sky who had worked as an effects animator on *Tron* early in his career), *Ice Age* is essentially a variant on the buddy/road picture that focuses on the growing bonds of friendship among an interspecies group of mammals. The central character of *Ice Age* is a mammoth named Manny (voiced by Ray Romano), a good-hearted but somewhat irascible loner who finally learns to think of himself as a member of a community after he is joined by the sloth Sid (John Leguizamo) and the saber-toothed cat, or Smilodon, Diego (Denis Leary). These three gradually come to think of themselves as a sort of family in the course of a journey that begins when they rescue a human baby that has been separated from its tribe due to an attack by Diego's pack of cats on the human village. Most of the plot of the film involves the efforts of the group to overtake the migrating humans, all the while being shadowed by the pack of cats, which still seeks to recover and kill the baby. The pack and its leader, Soto (Goran Visnjik), has identified the humans as its mortal enemies thanks to the recent success of the humans in hunting both the cats and the large prey that the cats depend upon for food. Through most of this journey, Diego is actually working with the other cats, planning to lead Manny and the rest of the group into an ambush. Not too surprisingly, his bonding with the other members of the group leads him to switch his allegiance and help to rescue them in the end, enabling the safe return of the baby to its father and his tribe.

Since the cats (as cats so often are in animated film) are treated as the unequivocal villains of the piece, while the defenders of the baby are naturally coded as the good guys, the film seems to have no ambivalence about simultaneously endorsing both the solidarity of Manny and his ragtag group and Diego's betrayal of his own tribe. In fact, *Ice Age* leaves relatively little room for ambivalence or ambiguity of any kind. Meanwhile, one might note that the bonds formed among the members of Manny's group are unnatural and that Diego's defection goes particularly against his nature as a predator, so that the film does go against the typical glorification of the natural, the original, and the authentic that is so prevalent in Disney films. However, the film really makes no point of this issue, and there is no indication that the subversion of this Disney trope was conscious or intentional. *Ice Age* is a simple film, simply animated (one might even say crudely, if charmingly, animated, in comparison with the Pixar films); it is seemingly devoted to telling its story of friendship within the context of a quest narrative and a good vs. evil conflict, all tied together with a series of slapstick sight gags. The film relies for its appeal mainly on its array of charming creatures, the eccentricities of which tend to reinforce an individualist ideology; in some cases, for example, different members of the same species seem to have different evolutionary eccentricities, as when two prehistoric rhinoceroses who attack Sid (but are driven off by Manny) have completely different, bizarre nose-horn formations. In addition, the members of the film's central group are all in one way or another loners and outcasts who initially either lack a community to which to belong or (as in the case of Diego) don't really fit in with the other members of their existing community. Of course, the central characters eventually form their own alternative community, and *Ice Age* really wants to have it both ways, emphasizing the individualism of its characters while at the same time having the central characters form a community in which their individual eccentricities can be tolerated and accepted. But this, of course, is American capitalist ideology par excellence: be yourself, be different, but don't be *too* different—you still have to be a cog in a gear, even if you have a choice of gears. Or, in consumerist parlance, buy whatever you want: just buy! Regardless, I see no evidence that *Ice Age* is consciously designed to convey this capitalist message; rather, my guess is that the filmmakers (like most Americans) have themselves absorbed this message so thoroughly that they convey it automatically and unconsciously, unable to conceive of an alternative.

If the ultimate success of Manny and his group seems to be an all-American underdog-makes-good story, it is also the case that the real underdog in the film is the saber-toothed squirrel[8] Scrat (voiced by Wedge himself), who plays no actual role in the plot, but essentially stars in his own film-within-a-film that involves his incessant efforts to garner an elusive acorn. Scrat chases this acorn with total futility, exposing himself to a preposterous amount of slapstick violence as he does so—much in the way that Wile E. Coyote chased the Road Runner to no avail in *Looney Tunes* cartoons. Like the coyote, however, Scrat is a resilient and entirely cartoonish figure who survives all this violence with no apparent damage, ready to move on to his next mishap.

Made for $59 million, *Ice Age* pulled in $383 million in worldwide box-office receipts, which proved just how charming its offbeat animal characters could be. This huge commercial success also paved the way for the inevitable sequel, *Ice Age: The Meltdown* (2006), which built on the brand recognition of the first film to take in $652 million in global box office, on a production budget of $80 million. Directed by Carlos Saldanha (who had assisted Wedge with the direction of *Ice Age*), this film was thus more commercially successful than any Pixar film except *Finding Nemo*, though in fact it's a relatively pointless film in the sense that it's pretty much the same film with the same characters as the first film. Granted, the sequel dispenses with human characters, but they were never really all that important to begin with. It still features Manny, Sid, and Diego, now having spent more time together and thinking of themselves even more solidly as a family. And it still features the group on a cross-country quest, this time just to find a safe place to live given that the icy environs in which they have formerly resided are now thawing thanks to the impending end of the ice age, threatening to cause cataclysmic floods. And they are still dogged on their journey by dangerous predators, this time by aquatic super-reptiles (presumably leftover from the dinosaur era) who had long been frozen in ice, but have now been released and revived by the thaw. But, of course, the animal heroes overcome all obstacles and make it to safety. Meanwhile, Scrat the squirrel again provides comic relief, here playing an even larger role due to his popularity in the first film (though again his misadventures are essentially unrelated to the main plot). In fact, Scrat himself gets frozen in ice in this film, waking in our own time to continue his ill-fated pursuit of the acorn unabated.[9]

If all of this sounds like more of the same, that might explain why both I and my kids sometimes have trouble remembering which specific scenes occur in which of the two films. The theme of individualism, however, is given something of a new twist in the second film when Manny realizes that he hasn't seen another mammoth in quite a while and begins to suspect that he might be the last living member of his species. This suspicion understandably has Manny feeling lonely, but then he meets Ellie (Queen Latifah), who might just be the last living female mammoth. Unfortunately, this discovery is complicated by the unlikely fact that Ellie was raised from infancy by a family of opposums, two of whom, Crash and Eddie (Seann William Scott and Josh Peck), still live with her as her brothers. The three join Manny, Sid, and Diego on their quest to find a new home, with both the acrobatic antics of Crash and Eddie and the self-misrecognition of Ellie providing considerable comedy along the way.

Eventually, Manny is able to convince Ellie that she is really a mammoth, which paves the way for the two to get together and perhaps perpetuate their species for at least one more generation, despite their rocky courtship. Indeed, the two seem poised to remain a couple even after they discover a large mammoth herd at the end of the film, bringing great relief to Manny and reinforcing the theme of both films that individualism is a good thing, but one that is best pursued in a group setting. Meanwhile, the great global success of the film (it took in more than twice as much abroad as in the U.S.) suggests that this message, like the wacky animals that helped to deliver it, had broad international appeal.

In between the first two *Ice Age* films, Fox—Blue Sky switched from funny animals to funny machines with the release of *Robots* (2005), again directed by the team of Wedge and Saldanha. An interesting film that deals with a number of overtly political issues, *Robots* still managed to be a reasonable success at the box office, taking in approximately $260 million, split nearly evenly between the U.S. and the rest of the world. For an American children's film, *Robots* deals particularly directly with the theme of class, initially focusing on a poor working-class family of robots (the father is a lowly dishwasher in a restaurant) who acquire a new baby (the delivery occurs by truck, in a box), then gradually raise it as best they can given their meager means, which require them to fit it with numerous used and hand-me-down replacement parts as it grows older. Despite his lowly origins, however, this young robot, Rodney Copperbottom (Ewan McGregor), has big ideas. In particular, Rodney hopes to become a successful inventor like his hero, the famed inventor Bigweld (Mel Brooks), who has used his own talent for inventing to found a major corporation, Bigweld Industries, whose gates (like Bigweld's mind) are always open to new inventors with new ideas. Given his background, Rodney is particularly attracted by Bigweld's egalitarian slogan, which he feels speaks directly to him: "Whether a 'bot is made of new parts, old parts, or spare parts, you can shine no matter what you're made of."

Showing a definite talent, but finding his prospects limited in his hometown, young Rodney decides to head for Robot City to take his latest invention to Bigweld Industries, hoping to make his fortune and help himself to "be somebody." On the way he meets the comically dysfunctional robot Fender (Robin Williams), who provides much of

the film's humor. However, when Rodney arrives at Bigweld Industries, he is shocked to discover that conditions there are much
changed. In a sort of corporate coup, Bigweld has been pushed aside
(now spending his time assembling domino arrays), and the company
has been taken over by the sinister Ratchet (Greg Kinnear). Under the
behind-the-scenes manipulation of his even more sinister mother, Madame Gasket (Jim Broadbent), Ratchet has not only canceled the
company's open-door policy, but has instituted a new corporate policy, based on the maximization of profit for the company, rather than
the maximization of opportunity for all. Feeling that Bigweld's attitudes encouraged robots to be happy with themselves as they were,
Ratchet announces a new corporate strategy (reminiscent of corporate
marketing strategies in our own world) of encouraging consumers to
feel that they need to be better—via the products offered by Bigweld
Industries. Declaring that the company is in the business of "sucking
every loose penny out of Mr. and Mrs. Average Knucklehead,"
Ratchet institutes a policy of withholding spare parts from the market
so that customers will be forced to buy more expensive upgrades. He
also supports this policy with a new corporate slogan: "Why be you
when you can be new?" While the company's customers are being
exploited, their workers are exploited also, as Madame Gasket over-
sees the institution of slave-like working conditions on the company's
assembly lines. Finally, in an even more sinister move, broken robots
who can't afford an upgrade are gathered by the company to be
melted down for recycling. Buy or die.

Rodney thus arrives in Robot City at a particularly bad time, and is
predictably rebuffed in his attempts to sell his invention to the company. Spurned, he falls in with Fender and a group of broken-down
robot rejects. He then strikes a blow against the new policies of Bigweld Industries by using his talents as an inventor to repair broken
robots even without the availability of conventional spare parts. Eventually, Rodney and his friends enlist the aid of Bigweld himself in carrying out a successful revolt against Ratchet and Gasket, reinstituting
the company's earlier, more democratic policies.

Based on the plot alone, *Robots* reads largely like an extended critique of the exploitative and rapacious policies of corporate capitalism, though it is a bit difficult to take the critique seriously given the
prominence of Fender's antics in the film, as well as the importance
of various forms of juvenile humor, such as fart jokes. Worse, the film

attributes the evils of the revamped Bigweld Industries not to the profit-driven pressures of the capitalist system itself, but to the particular vileness of Gasket and Ratchet, presented here as aberrations within the capitalist system, not as typical representatives of it.

In *Dr. Seuss' Horton Hears a Who!* (2008), Fox—Blue Sky turned for inspiration to the work of one of the most beloved authors in the history of children's literature, highlighting the source by including the name of the author (the pen name of Theodor Geisel). Based on the 1954 children's illustrated book *Horton Hears a Who!*, the film thus had a certain amount of built-in nostalgia appeal in that both parents and grandparents could remember the book from their own childhoods. It also featured the voice of Jim Carrey as the elephant protagonist, providing a further tie-in to Carrey's earlier performance as the Grinch in the highly successful 2000 live-action film adapation, *Dr. Seuss' How the Grinch Stole Christmas*. That casting, though, might be part of the problem with this lackluster film. Carrey's antics aren't quite appropriate to Seuss's original character, and the film as a whole is never able to capture the charm of Seuss's original book, perhaps because the effort to update the story with a variety of hip pop-cultural references detracts more than it adds. Still, the film was a moderate commercial success, and it does include some highly amusing sequences, as when Horton (who seems not to understand how bulky he is) crosses, with great difficulty, a rickety rope bridge over a yawning chasm.

Horton Hears a Who! involves the discovery by the elephant of the title that a speck of dust that floats by him in the air is inhabited by tiny people, who must be saved from certain catastrophe by Horton's efforts, even though his fellow animals scoff at the notion that the speck is inhabited. The most obvious political message in the film concerns the acceptance of others, as Horton's mantra ("a person's a person, no matter how small") helps the other animals in his world learn to acknowledge and respect the residents of Whoville, despite their small-sized otherness. Meanwhile, this message is multiply delivered, as the other animals learn to accept Horton's eccentricities as well, while the people of Whoville learn to respect their oddball mayor (voiced by Steve Carell). In addition, the fact that all of the citizens of Whoville must band together in order to make enough noise in order to be noticed by the animals of Horton's world potentially delivers a message about the power of collective action, though this motif is carefully moderated in the film (and the original book) by an individualist add-on in which the final success of this effort is determined by the addition of one final tiny individual to the mix. This moderation was probably to be expected in 1954, when any suggestion of support for collective action might have brought charges of communist sympathizing, though such individualist gestures remain central to children's film in the early twenty-first century. The message about acceptance of the Other in *Horton Hears a Who!* remains useful today, even though it was probably even more needed in the peak Cold War period when the book was published than when the film was released, by which time it was a cliché of children's film.

The story of an impending apocalypse in the tiny town of Whoville has all sorts of political potential that is never really developed in the film. This motif again must have had a special resonance for readers in the 1950s, saturated as their world was by fears of nuclear disaster. Of course, our own world is still endangered by nuclear weapons, though the possibility of a total ecological collapse now seems more pressing. Unfortunately, as hard as the film tries to update the book with cool pop-cultural references, it does essentially nothing with the potential of this story to address environmental concerns. In this, *Horton Hears a Who!* is very much in line with the other recent children's animated films distributed by Fox, which have similarly tended to concentrate on entertaining and amusing animation, with little interest in political commentary.

WARNER BROTHERS

Through their *Merrie Melodies* and *Looney Tunes* series, Warner Brothers provided the principal competition to Disney's animated shorts of the 1930s. Indeed, Warner Brothers, through the popularity of signature *Looney Tunes* characters such as Bugs Bunny and Daffy Duck, eventually emerged as the dominant force in this area, especially after World War II, when Disney concentrated more on feature-length films and placed less and less emphasis on animation as a whole. However, though Warner has of course remained a major player in the feature film arena, the company has never really been a major force in the realm of children's film. Indeed, if Disney's children's films (especially the animated ones) over the years have been distinguished by a remarkably consistent and coherent corporate vision, Warner has often seemed to show a complete lack of such vision. Through most of their history, Warner's involvement in children's film has been somewhat secondary, such as their coproduction (with Amblin) of the *Gremlins* films or their distribution of the German-produced *NeverEnding Story* (1984) in the 1980s, or their cobbling together of previously released shorts into feature-film form in *Bugs Bunny's Third Movie: 1001 Rabbit Tales* (1982).

Other attempts to employ the *Looney Tunes* characters in feature films have included such efforts as *Space Jam* (1996) and *Looney Tunes: Back in Action* (2003), both of which mix live actors with the animated. This is somewhat in the mode of the 1988 Disney-Amblin coproduction *Who Framed Roger Rabbit*, to which Warner also contributed several *Looney Tunes* characters, thus allowing them to interact on the same screen with the classic Disney animated characters (such as Mickey Mouse) for the first time ever. *Space Jam* was a commercial success, though it really serves more as a vehicle for basketball superstar Michael Jordan, part of the one-man media barrage through which Jordan shrewdly parlayed his preternatural athletic ability and charismatic likeability into what was probably the most successful commercial endorsement career in history. In fact, *Space Jam* itself actually grew out of a television commercial, first aired during the 1993 Super Bowl, in which Jordan and a group of *Looney Tunes* characters played basketball against a team of Martians. *Space Jam* is pretty much the same idea, as Jordan leads a team of *Looney Tunes* characters to victory over a team of aliens who have stolen their basketball abilities from various NBA stars (who also appear in the film, befuddled by the sudden loss of their abilities). By winning the game, Jordan wins back the stolen abilities for his fellow basketballers, while also winning the freedom of the *Looney Tunes* characters, who otherwise would have been conscripted to serve as attractions for an outer-space amusement park. By highlighting Jordan's individual ability (and virtue), *Space Jam*, like Jordan's huge oeuvre of TV commercials, is essentially a celebration of individualism, touting Jordan as perhaps the most capable individual of all. However, the individualist ethos that the film conveys to children is of the decidedly ambivalent type that is typical of capitalist ideology: by featuring Jordan, the film reminds viewers of how much one individual can accomplish, but by featuring someone so obviously out of the ordinary, the film also reminds individual viewers of their own limitations, so that they, as individuals, do not aspire to achieve too much.

Essentially an attempt to translate the zany energy of the *Looney Tunes* shorts directly to feature film, *Looney Tunes: Back in Action* seemed mainly to prove that this energy was best suited to the short form. A box-office disaster, the film was also panned by many critics and serves largely to indicate the lack of vision with which Warner has repeatedly failed to understand the genre of feature-length children's films. A classic example is *The Iron Giant* (1999), perhaps Warner's finest children's film but one that was again a box-office flop thanks largely to Warner's inept marketing of the film. Luckily the film has lived on in the DVD world and has gained a growing following among fans and critics.[10]

The Iron Giant was the first feature-length directorial effort of former Disney animator (and future Pixar director) Brad Bird, best known at the time for his work on the *Simpsons* television series. The film is based (fairly loosely) on the 1968 illustrated children's novel *The Iron Man*, by the prominent British poet Ted Hughes. Set in 1957, *The Iron Giant* is a variation on the 1950s alien invasion film, filtered through more recent benevolent invader films such as *E.T. the Extra-Terrestrial*. Here, a giant metal-eating robot from outer space lands on earth (near the small, aptly named town of Rockwell, Maine—as in Norman Rockwell, the official artist of small-town Americana, with perhaps a side reference to Roswell, New Mexico, as well). The mission of this robot is never made entirely clear in the film, partly because the robot itself loses all memory of its mission after it is shocked into unconsciousness when it tries to indulge its hunger for metal by eating a local power plant. Indeed, the robot is apparently saved from total destruction only by the intervention of a local boy, Hogarth Hughes (voiced by Eli Marienthal), who manages to shut off the power before the giant is entirely destroyed. Hogarth then befriends the robot as it attempts to regain the memory of its mission and to gain a better understanding of the strange society within which it now finds itself. Hogarth is helped in this task by local sculptor Dean McCoppin (Harry Connick, Jr.), who conveniently owns a junkyard that serves as a source of materials for his art but that also provides food for the metal-eating robot.

Reported sightings of the landing of the original spacecraft bring government investigator Kent Mansley (Christopher MacDonald) to

Rockwell, on the suspicion that the landing might be part of a communist invasion attempt. Mansley's unscrupulous (and ultimately cowardly) actions place him (and, to an extent, the U.S. government) in a negative light, while the innocent boy Hogarth and the uncorrupted hipster artist McCoppin become the heroes of the film. Ultimately, however, it is the Iron Giant itself that performs the most heroic deed, sacrificing itself to avert a nuclear missile that has been launched (on the misguided order of Mansley) at the town of Rockwell in an effort to destroy the robot. As the film ends, however, there are signs that the remarkably resilient robot, scattered in pieces across the face of the earth, is already engaged in the process of reassembling itself.

The Iron Giant recalls such classics of 1950s science fiction film as *The Day the Earth Stood Still* (1951) in its depiction of a paranoid (and violent) response to a seemingly friendly visitor from outer space, a motif that forms a part of the film's larger critique of the tendency to fear and even hate anyone or anything that appears strange or different. Mansley himself actually embodies this attitude more than do the inhabitants of Rockwell, suggesting that such paranoia cannot be attributed to the naiveté of the locals but instead arises from official government attitudes during the Cold War. Mansley himself acknowledges that he has no idea of the robot's origins or purpose. However, (after noting in a paranoid fashion that "Everyone wants what we have, everyone!") he declares, "All I know is we didn't build it, and that's reason enough to assume the worst and blow it to kingdom come!" On the other hand, the robot is huge, powerful, and dangerous, armed with an array of immensely destructive weapons. Within the film, it only uses these weapons defensively, primarily employing them to neutralize the attacks made upon him by U.S. military forces. At one point, however, he nearly kills Hogarth when the boy playfully points a toy gun at him. Indeed, the robot seems to have a strong aversion to guns or weapons of any kind, an attitude reinforced in a *Bambi*-like early scene in which it witnesses the killing of a harmless deer by two local hunters. However, it is also possible that the robot has been sent on a mission to attempt to avert earth's escalating arms race—either to prevent the people of earth from destroying themselves or (somewhat in the spirit of the robot Gort from *The Day the Earth Stood Still*) to prevent earthlings from eventually developing the capability to take their destructive capabilities into space.

The clearest political message of *The Iron Giant* is its rejection of xenophobia and its plea to try to understand the point of view of the Other. Thus, the giant itself, scorned by most of the humans in Rockwell as a threatening alien presence, ultimately saves the town. Meanwhile, this theme is further reinforced by the fact that those who are willing to accept and support the robot, despite its difference, are a child and an artist—themselves outsiders to the mainstream society of Rockwell. However, the more interesting point made by the film may be in the subtle way it challenges the Disney convention of celebrating the genuine and the natural. The admirable robot, after all, is a manufactured object, presumably programmed by its makers and therefore having no natural identity. Beyond that, however, Hogarth urges the robot to learn to make its own decisions and to be the kind of being it wishes to be, whatever its initial programming and mission. In particular, the robot, having been especially reminded of the horrors of guns in the earlier killing of the deer, struggles with the growing realization that it seems to be a powerful killing machine in its own right. Hogarth tells it, "It's bad to kill. Guns kill. And you don't have to be a gun. You are what you choose to be."[11] The robot, accordingly, opts to eschew violence, despite the fact that it was designed with an extensive capability for destruction. Thus, the film declares that true individualism does not entail the simple discovery and acting out of one's true nature, but instead the personal choice of an ethical course of behavior in any given situation. Further, the film suggests that such choices can, in some cases, involve fundamental changes in one's personal makeup. Meanwhile, use of the robot in this context suggests that the Disney characters who merely act out their true natures are in fact behaving like robots or preprogrammed automatons, incapable of free will or free choice.

In a dialogue that is completely missing from the original novel on which the film is based, *The Iron Giant* uses a genre (the alien invasion narrative) that often served as a key expression of the Cold War paranoia of the 1950s to satirize that paranoia, though such satire could already be found in such 1950s films as *The Day the Earth Stood Still*. *The Iron Giant* makes for a particularly interesting comparison with such films of the 1950s as *Invaders from Mars* (1953), in which a young boy is initially the only human who is aware that sinister invaders from Mars are gradually taking over and controlling the bodies of the adult authority figures around him. The 1950s science fiction film that perhaps makes for the most direct comparison with *The Iron Giant* is *Tobor the Great* (1954), a children's film that also features the boy-and-his-robot theme. Here, however, the robot is American made (designed to serve as a pilot for spacecraft, thus avoiding the need to risk human pilots) and serves the primary purpose in the film of helping to defeat sinister Soviet spies who want to steal our secrets. *Tobor the Great* thus merely reinforces the anticommunist paranoia of its time, just as *the Iron Giant* (made several years after the end of the Cold War) challenges that paranoia.

Another interesting example of an animated film distributed with little success by Warner was *The Ant Bully* (2006), produced by Tom Hanks and Gary Goetzman's Play-Tone production company. *The Ant Bully* features excellent computer-generated animation, an A-list voice cast, and a good-enough (if not all that original) story with a positive message, yet it went nowhere at the box office, taking in a paltry $55 million worldwide off of a $50 million production budget. Part of the problem was that the film was bizarrely panned by right-wing critics as crude communist propaganda, proving that Cold War paranoia was alive and well. But part of the problem was also that Warner never did much in the way of marketing to counter this mischaracterization of the film, which does, granted, suggest that it is good to play well with others (what an outrage!), but whose main message is that one should treat others with respect and accept their differences. The latter is, indeed, one of the central tenets of communism, but it is also central to most Western notions of ethical behavior.

The Ant Bully focuses on the travails of young Lucas Nickle (Zach Tyler Eisen), a lonely, bespectacled grade-school outcast who is constantly set upon by the local bully, who points out that he can do anything he wants to Lucas because he is big and Lucas is small. On the same premise, the humiliated Lucas takes out his frustrations on the ants who have a colony in his yard, earning him the nickname of "The Destroyer" among the anthropomorphic ants. However, the ants strike back as the ant wizard Zoc (Nicolas Cage) develops a potion that reduces Lucas down to ant size, plunging the boy into a new world of unfamiliar perspectives. We've seen this kind of size-based defamiliarization before, in films from *The Incredible Shrinking Man* (1957) to Disney's *Honey, I Shrunk the Kids* (1989), but not since *Gulliver's Travels* has it been used to explore the workings of an alternative society as effectively as in *The Ant Bully*. Given their chance for revenge, the ants opt for mercy, choosing to educate tiny Lucas rather than exterminate him, on the orders of their ethereal queen (voiced by Meryl Streep). The ants bow to the queen's wishes (and her monarchic power seems to be the biggest flaw in the political organization of the ant society, especially as that power seems almost religious, rather than political, a fact that shows how silly the characterization of the film as communist propaganda really is).

Still, there is considerable disagreement among the ants concerning Lucas's fate, and it is here that we first come to understand that these animated ants are not nearly so blindly devoted to their roles in the community or lacking in individualism as real-world ants are purported to be. Indeed, when Lucas is sentenced to work as an ant works so that he can learn the value of the labor that he has been destroying with his pranks, he comes to understand that each of these ants is a unique individual, from the kindly Hova (Julia Roberts) who maternally supports him in every way she can, to the comically macho Fugax (Bruce Campbell, in the film's liveliest voice performance). He learns that the lives of the ants are hard and dangerous, but that they are enriched by the mutual support that they all enjoy, despite their individual differences, which are not merely tolerated, but cherished. It is possible, Lucas learns, for each individual to be special and still to work together with others for the good of all, rather than simply to compete against others for personal gain.

Lucas gradually bonds with the ants (though some aspects of their culture are initially disgusting to him) and helps them to overcome various difficulties, such as an attack by their enemies, the wasps. Ultimately, though, even the ants and wasps work together when they are faced with an even more ominous threat in the form of the human exterminator Stan Beals (Paul Giamatti). The sinister Beals is considerably cruder and more vicious than he really needed to be (taking excessive pleasure in killing bugs in all sorts of horrible ways), which may also be a weakness of the film, especially as he is the film's only working-class human character, thus conveying (again in a very noncommunist fashion) negative, class-based stereotypes. Beals, however, is defeated through the combined efforts of Lucas, the ants, and the wasps, who manage to administer a small dosage of the shrinking potion to the exterminator, who is reduced to the size of a small child and sent fleeing on a tricycle.

Ultimately, Lucas returns to his normal size (which is still small for a ten-year-old), whereupon he is once again confronted by the bully. Employing the lessons he learned among the ants, Lucas convinces the bully's gang (the members of which are also small and subject to abuse by the bully) to join with him in a group effort. Together, they easily defeat the bully and send him screaming for his mommy. In short, this is not a film that urges children to extinguish their individuality in the interest of the group, as some critics charged. Instead, it is a film that promotes individualism of the finest sort, the kind that means not only exploring one's own individuality, but also respecting the individuality of others. If anything, critics who saw this film as promoting communism serve simply as an appalling reminder of the state of American society in the early twenty-first century, when any promotion of cooperation with others is automatically taken by many as a bad thing.

Warner had its greatest success as a distributor of children's animated films with *Happy Feet* (2006), an Australian-produced film that features some of the most impressively realistic animation ever created. *Happy Feet* won the 2006 Academy Award for Best Animated Feature and still stands (after the 2008 awards) as the only film to win that award that wasn't made and/or distributed by Disney-Pixar or DreamWorks. Individualism is once again at the center of the narrative as the film's central character, a young emperor penguin named Mumble (voiced by Elijah Wood), finds himself very much at odds with the conformist mentality of his penguin society in frigid Antarctica, only to use his unique viewpoint to save his fellow penguins from starvation due to the excessive fishing of the waters surrounding Antarctica by humans. The film clearly celebrates Mumble's status as a unique individual, though it also indicates quite clearly that his unusual nature is the result of a birth defect caused by the fact that his father dropped him onto the frozen surface of Antarctica while he was still in his egg. This defect causes Mumble to be unable to sing in the way that penguins usually sing to announce their individual identities; instead, Mumble expresses his individuality through tap dancing (thus the title of the film), a practice that draws the ire of the sour-faced elders of his clan.

Already something of an outcast within his own kind, Mumble is unable to generate support for his plan to investigate the causes of the fish shortage that threatens the penguins' survival. Indeed, the tribal elder Noah (Hugo Weaving) even blames the shortage on Mumble's unconventional behavior, claiming that the young penguin's dancing has drawn the ire of the gods. Mumble eventually becomes an exile. Rejected even by his formerly supportive father, Mumble goes off on his own to try to learn about the aliens he believes may be stealing the fish, accompanied on his journey by a group of smaller adelie penguins (the Amigos) who have befriended him, finding his dancing abilities impressive rather than appalling. However, knowing the trip is dangerous, Mumble declines the offer of Gloria (Brittany Murphy), the young female penguin (an unusually gifted singer whose singing meshes well with Mumble's dancing) with whom Mumble has long been in love.

After a series of harrowing escapes (and lots of comic relief supplied by the Amigos and by Lovelace, a pompous rockhopper penguin) Mumble realizes that humans are to blame for the fish shortage and even manages to call the attention of humans worldwide to the plight of the penguins in Antarctica, an effort that will presumably lead eventually to a solution to the fish crisis. *Happy Feet* thus delivers a reasonably effective environmentalist message, though it may well be that it suggests that environmental problems are much easier to solve than they really are. In the meantime, *Happy Feet* is a highly entertaining film (it was Benjamin's favorite for months back when he was two, though he seems to be a bit tired of it now) that combines truly impressive, Pixar-quality animation with a number of rousing musical numbers and even especially effective track music. Benjamin especially loves a scene in which the emperor penguins dive playfully off an ice cliff into the ocean while the Beach Boys' "Do It Again" plays in the background.[12] Robin Williams turns in his usual peripatetic voiceover performance in a dual role as Lovelace and as Ramón, leader of the Amigos. Murphy's musical performances as Gloria (especially in her high-energy rendition of "Boogie Wonderland") are especially notable, but others are effective as well, as when Mumble's future parents enact the usual singing ritual of mating penguins by singing well-known popular songs. Thus, the father, Memphis (essentially a penguin Elvis impersonator, voiced by Hugh Jackman) sings "Heartbreak Hotel," to which the mother, Norma Jean (a penguin Marilyn Monroe, voiced by Nicole Kidman) responds with her rendition of Prince's "Kiss," eventually joined in duet by Memphis, sealing the deal that leads to Mumble's birth.

All of this engagement with American popular culture from the 1950s onward provides points of identification for parents, but also serves as a sort of endorsement of the past half-century of American culture as the official soundtrack to the individualism touted by the film. Mumble, after all, is pretty much Dumbo, and his adventures convey the same message as the adventures of Dumbo and so many other outcasts who become heroes. But figures such as Mumble and Dumbo have unusual talents that allow them to succeed. In a sense they are superheroes, and their heroism (like that in *The Incredibles*) conveys a very limited, don't-try-this-at-home form of individualism. Everyone may be special, but not just anyone can do what Mumble and Dumbo do.

DREAMWORKS

Jeffrey Katzenberg left Disney in 1994 with considerable rancor (and with $280 million won in a lawsuit against Disney for his treatment there). Subsequently, he banded together with music industry mogul David Geffen and superstar director and producer Steven Spielberg to form DreamWorks SKG, a new state-of-the-art movie studio that would also be active in the production of music, television programming, and video games. Aided by a $500 million investment from Microsoft cofounder Paul Allen, DreamWorks was flush with cash and overflowing with talent and seemed to have an extremely bright future as it sought to inject some new energy into the Hollywood film industry. And the company did meet with considerable success, such as the winning of three consecutive Best Picture Oscars in 1999, 2000, and 2001. However, some of its most ambitious plans (such as the building of a vast studio campus that would include elaborate on-site housing for many of the principals) never came into the being, and the company was plagued by financial struggles almost from the beginning. By the end of 2005, the company had agreed to sell off its live-action operations to Viacom-Paramount, though DreamWorks Animation was spun off into a separate, independent entity.

Daniel Kimmel concludes his study of the demise of the once-promising company, written just after the sale to Paramount, that "for all practical purposes, the DreamWorks story is over. But the story of DreamWorks Animation may be just beginning" (206).[13] From my point of view, it is certainly DreamWorks Animation that has been the most important part of the company. Indeed, despite occasional successes such as *Happy Feet* or the *Ice Age* films, DreamWorks Animation has remained, since its entry into the field in late 1998 with *Antz*, the most important rival to Disney-Pixar's dominance of the children's animated film business. This rivalry was very much by design. DreamWorks entered the fray with a direct challenge to Disney-Pixar, releasing the computer-animated *Antz* in October 1998, the month before the release of *A Bug's Life*. The company then immediately followed in December with the release of the traditionally animated *The Prince of Egypt*, thus quickly staking a claim to be a major player in animated film.

Antz immediately announced the intention of DreamWorks to produce films that were hipper, smarter, and less sentimental than the traditional Disney animated film, aimed at an audience of children assumed to be more intelligent and sophisticated than Disney had apparently long assumed children to be. *Antz* features political intrigue, graphic violence, and even mild obscenities, all of which won the film a PG rating—but also helps to make the film more entertaining to adults, as do the numerous pop-cultural references with which the film is sprinkled. The casting of Woody Allen to voice the main character was also an inspired move, especially given that this character, known simply as Z, is largely the same one that Allen had played in so many of his own films: a neurotic, vaguely intellectual worker ant who wants to be somebody special but who feels insignificant amid the sea of forces that surround him.

Z, designated from birth to be a worker ant and never given any choice in the matter, feels that he is completely unsuited to the role, a situation that opens up an opportunity for the film to explore a number of political issues, most of them surrounding the opposition between individualism and totalitarian conformism. Actually, the political situation in the ant colony of the film is more complex than this simple polar opposition. As the film begins, Z's individualism is opposed to traditional ant-style conformism; the colony is essentially an enlightened monarchy, ruled by a queen who is relatively benevolent, but who also expects all of the ants in the colony to fill their assigned roles without question. However, the sinister General Mandible (Gene Hackman) is plotting a coup that will replace the monarchy with what would essentially be a fascist dictatorship, with himself at the helm. In so doing, Mandible coldly plans to wipe out a large percentage of the colony's population, which he regards (echoing the Nazi rhetoric of racial superiority) to be weaker elements who need to be destroyed in order to make way for his new world.

Ant physiology being what it is, Mandible will still need a queen for his new colony, so he attempts to force Princess Bala (Sharon Stone), the heir apparent, to be his queen. First, however, he contrives to send all of the military units that are loyal to the current queen off on a suicide mission to attack a nearby termite colony. Z, having traded places for a day with Weaver, a soldier ant (voice by Sylvester Stallone), finds himself caught up in the mission, then ends up being the only one to survive the ensuing battle, thus returning to the colony as a hero, which makes him a threat to Mandible's plans. This and the fact that he survived the battle through cowardice rather than heroism eventually lead him to flee the colony, taking Bala with him as a hostage, though he has also developed romantic feelings for her. He takes her with him in search of the fabled Insectopia, which turns out to be a picnic ground where treats for insects are indeed plentiful, but so are the dangers. Bala, meanwhile, is furious with him for kidnapping her.

Ultimately, however, all works out well. Z and Bala return to the colony and manage to defeat Mandible's nefarious scheme, with the help of Weaver and Cutter (Christopher Walken), Mandible's former right-hand man. The old social order has still been shattered, but it will now be replaced by a new era of democracy, rather than fascism. The lowly worker Z even wins the hand of Bala in marriage, signifying the egalitarianism of this new society, in which all will be treated as equals but respected as unique individuals. In short, *Antz* is a fairly straightforward celebration of the values of Western liberal democracy, mediated only slightly by a class egalitarianism that goes beyond that of any real-life capitalist democracy.

Even this slightly left-of-center nod is something, of course, and *Antz* definitely departs from the Disney tradition of urging children to believe that true individualism means being who you were born to be in the first place. After all, Z was born to be a lowly worker, but has evolved to a point where that role no longer really suits him, and he is able to find a different place in the order of things that suits him better. And if that development requires that the entire social order be changed, then so much the better, because the film thus provides a reminder that true happiness is not always a matter of separate individuals achieving their dreams: it can also require collective action to enact genuine social change. Meanwhile, the misadventure in Insectopia delivers the message that, in order to improve society, one must work for change rather than simply hope to find ready-made solutions.

If *Antz* was thus in many ways a clear step forward for children's film, *The Prince of Egypt* seems a definite step backward. The film relates the biblical story of Moses, including his upbringing in the court of Egypt's pharaoh and his eventual departure to lead his people, the Jews, out of Egyptian slavery. It's a fairly straightforward account, taken from the book of Exodus, and presents Moses as a chosen one, selected for his fate by forces higher than himself. In short, by becoming the leader of his people he is simply doing what God has always intended him to do, almost back in the Disney mode of doing what comes naturally, except that Disney has typically avoided overtly religious themes in its films. And with good reason. *The Prince of Egypt*, though beautifully animated and though it includes a few colorful flourishes thrown in for the entertainment of children, is not really a good children's film, partly because its source material was itself not intended for children. Moreover, films such as *The Prince of Egypt*, which are so closely tied to one particular religious perspective, find themselves caught in a double bind. On the one hand, parents (like myself) who do not share the Judaeo-Christian perspective of the film, might find it awkward to explain to children that many people take the film's story seriously, despite the fact that it may be a mere fiction. On the other hand, parents who do share the film's religious perspective might fear that the placement of this narrative within the context of a children's film might lead children to assume that it is a mere fiction, rather than the historical fact that such parents believe the story to be.

All in all, *The Prince of Egypt* was probably a bad idea, and the film certainly diminished the start to which DreamWorks was off with *Antz*, one of the finest children's films of the 1990s. However, *The Prince of Egypt* actually grossed more than *Antz* worldwide, partly because *Antz* was hurt by its head-to-head competition with the lighter and sillier (and thus perhaps more entertaining to younger children) *A Bug's Life*. DreamWorks then followed in 2000 with another conventionally animated film, *The Road to El Dorado*, an even worse idea for a film; it effaces the reality of the holocaust initiated by the

European conquest of America, making the genocidal hunt for treasure in America into a comic romp. Though it makes a few nods toward respect for other cultures, *The Road to El Dorado* is a forgettable film that treats a highly volatile subject in an entirely irresponsible way. A brief appearance by the conquistador Cortez makes him a villain, but the film's protagonists are Europeans who just happen to be loveable rogues bent on looting a Native American city of its treasures, which in the film seems okay because the Native American society is so benighted (and so devoted to superstition and backwards religious practices such as human sacrifice) that it wouldn't be able to make good use of the treasure anyway. I've never shown *El Dorado* to Benjamin, and I don't plan to; Skylor saw it once, but luckily didn't like it.

Also in 2000, DreamWorks released another traditionally animated, Bible-based snoozer, *Joseph: King of Dreams*, though this one at least went straight to video. In short, after the great start with *Antz*, DreamWorks had released three straight duds, and one might have assumed that the company didn't have much of a future in the animated film business. Their next two films weren't much more promising. *Sinbad: Legend of the Seven Seas* (2003) is about as uninteresting (and was equally unsuccessful at the box office, losing so much money that it nearly bankrupted the company) as *The Road to El Dorado*. *Spirit: Stallion of the Cimarron* (2002) is much more interesting, but didn't do much better commercially. Here, a wild stallion roams free on the American prairie, only to be captured and taken to a fort run by the U.S. cavalry, where he is abused and brutalized in an attempt to break his wild spirit. The attempt is unsuccessful, however, and he escapes with the help of an Indian brave who has also been taken captive at the fort. Much of the film consists of a contrast between the treatment received by Spirit at the hands of the white cavalry on the one hand and the much more humane Native Americans on the other hand. At one point, the cavalry even launches a murderous (and seemingly unmotivated assault) on the Indian village to which Spirit has been taken, making it more than clear that, in this film, the white invaders are the villains, while the peaceful Indians are the victims. This politically progressive point, however, is somewhat muted by the film's happy ending, in which Spirit seems to have almost single-handedly stopped white expansion into the West, averting the extension of a railway into his native stomping grounds and returning to live free and wild with his original herd. The film thus effaces the historical reality of the ultimate taming of the West, which wiped out the homelands of Spirit, his fellow wild mustangs, and the Native Americans he has befriended.

Spirit includes a few narrative innovations as well, such as the fact that, in the actual scenes of the film, Spirit and his fellow animals cannot talk, though they are still supplied with very human emotions and motivations and though Spirit does in fact supply a voiceover narration (voiced by Matt Damon) to accompany much of the action. In any case, the conventionally animated films from DreamWorks never did have much success, which might explain why the company has now moved exclusively into computer animation. The company did, however, distribute an extremely interesting stop-motion animated film in the summer of 2000 that at least kept them afloat as a player in the animation business. That film was *Chicken Run*, made by the British-based Aardman Animations, which had already gained considerable attention for its stop-motion clay animation shorts (especially those featuring the lovable everyman Wallace and his loyal, hyperintelligent dog Gromit).

The central trope of *Chicken Run* is an extended metaphorical comparison between chicken farms and Nazi prison camps, which seems rather unpromising as a premise, but which actually works out quite well in a film that ultimately goes beyond predecessors such as *Charlotte's Web* and *Babe* as a critique of the entire notion of keeping animals merely so they can be killed and eaten once they get large enough. In particular, here the critique becomes particularly specific in its identification of capitalist greed in the meatpacking industry as a key motivating force behind the raising of animals for slaughter. As the film begins, the chickens live on the concentration camp—like Tweedy chicken farm in Yorkshire, England, dreaming of escape. Then conditions become much worse when Mrs. Tweedy conceives a plan to generate more income by installing new machinery to convert the farm into a processing plant to produce chicken pies, using their own chickens as the main ingredient. With the chickens thus lined up for mass slaughter, the escape plans have to be speeded up, and the chickens finally do escape by constructing an elaborate flying machine that takes them over the farm's fences and away to freedom, setting up their own chicken utopia on a faraway island.

Chicken Run is a fascinating film with a distinctive look that sets it apart from anything seen before in children's films. It also manages to pull off the difficult task of being quite funny while dealing with serious issues without trivializing those issues. And, if paralleling the slaughter of chickens to mass extermination of Jews, communists, and gypsies in Nazi death camps at first seems rather offensive, the very outrageousness of the comparison might cause some viewers (mostly adults, probably) to at least stop to think about whether we should accept the mass killings of helpless animals in the unquestioning way that our society typically does. Benjamin and I don't eat meat at all, but Skylor does (having become addicted to eating the flesh of dead animals before I met him), and he announced his intention never again to eat chicken after he saw the film. That resolution lasted for about three days, but it was a start.

The killing of animals is also at the forefront of the next film Aardman produced for distribution by DreamWorks under a new distribution deal spurred by the success of *Chicken Run*. The first product of this new deal, *Wallace & Gromit: The Curse of the Were-Rabbit* (2005), brought the beloved British duo to the big screen in the U.S. Winner of the Academy Award for Best Animated Feature, *Wallace & Gromit* is a hilarious bit of British wit (entertaining to children and adults alike) that gains much of its energy from its parodic engagement with the entire legacy of the horror film genre, with nods toward science fiction and spy fiction thrown in as well. Here, Wallace (always a dedicated inventor and tinkerer) becomes a sort of mad scientist (though a good-hearted one), whose experiments accidentally transform him into a giant were-rabbit, which ravenously devours the vegetables in his unnamed British town whenever the moon is out. This development is made all the more serious by the fact that virtually all of the local citizens are frantically engaged in attempting to grow giant vegetables for entry in the upcoming annual Giant Vegetable Fete, which has been sponsored by the family of the local aristocrat Lady Tottington (Helena Bonham Carter) for more than five hundred years. What's worse, Wallace and Gromit, via their Anti-Pesto pest control business, have been charged by the locals with protecting their crops from the area's considerable bunny population, though of course the two employ only humane means of pest control. In fact, rather than kill the bunnies, they merely capture them, then keep them in their own basement, where they feed and care for them quite generously.

As usual, the always-sensible Gromit has to get his master out of trouble, and his stalwart attempts finally do save the day, but only after a healthy dose of comic destruction, much of it involving the attempts of the hunting-obsessed Lord Victor Quartermaine (Ralph Fiennes) to hunt down and blow away the were-rabbit, toward whom he holds a special grudge because both Quartermaine and Wallace are potential suitors to Lady Tottington. Neither wins her hand, but Quartermaine ends up in disgrace, while Wallace ends up a fast friend to Lady Tottington, who converts her vast estate into a bunny sanctuary with his help. In short, all's well that ends well, the film's various satirical jabs (at the aristocracy, at the clergy, at obsessed hobbyists) all being in the interest of lighthearted fun.

In *Flushed Away* (2006, also released by DreamWorks in the U.S.) Aardman went with the flow, so to speak, and switched to full computer animation, though still attempting to capture much of the style of their earlier stop-motion productions. Here, Roddy St. James (voiced by Hugh Jackman) is a spoiled pet rat from an upper-crust London home. While his human family is away, Roddy plans to live it up in their posh house, only to have the home invaded and taken over by Sid (Shane Richie), an uncouth but clever sewer rat, who subsequently flushes Roddy down the toilet to get him out of the way. Emerging in the London sewers, Roddy eventually discovers an entire underground alternative version of the city, populated mostly by rats, recalling the alternative London worlds of such recent works of British fantasy as Neil Gaiman's television series *Neverwhere* (1996) and China Miéville's novel *King Rat* (1998). In the alternative London, Roddy strikes up an uneasy alliance with the streetwise sewer rat Rita Malone (Kate Winslet), the differences between their respective backgrounds providing numerous opportunities for very British commentaries on class difference. The two, meanwhile, run afoul of the Toad (Ian McKellen), a sewer-based crime lord who seeks to recover from Rita a jewel that is supposedly a giant ruby that was accidentally washed down the drain in Buckingham Palace. Much comic mayhem ensues as the Toad's inept rat henchmen Whitey (Bill Nighy) and Spike (Andy Serkis) pursue Rita and Roddy through the London sewers. The jewel turns out to be a fake, but the Toad proceeds with his evil plans to destroy the underground rat city using the flood of waters produced by the massive toilet flushing that occurs during halftime of a televised World Cup soccer match featuring England (which loses on penalties). Roddy, having been safely returned to his original home, realizes the plot and returns to the sewers, warning Rita and saving the underground city and its inhabitants. Roddy then decides to stay in the sewers with Rita, while Sid stays up top, his expected easy life there disrupted when he learns that the family has just acquired a cat.

Flushed Away does a reasonably good job of capturing the earlier charm of Aardman's stop-motion animation, while allowing for a considerably broader range of action (including underwater scenes) than had the earlier technology. But computer animation isn't really Aardman's thing, and the making of this film led to creative differences that eventually ended their association with DreamWorks. Aardman subsequently entered into a distribution deal with Sony Pictures, though no products of this agreement have appeared as of this writing. Sony, meanwhile, itself entered the fray with the founding of Sony Pictures Animation in 2002. Feature-length theatrical films produced by Sony thus far include *Open Season* (2006), which revisits the anti-hunting territory of *Bambi* (but this time in a comic mode that makes hunting culture appear more ridiculous than sinister). *Surf's Up* (2007) is a spoof of surfing documentaries that features surfing penguins, penguins being the hot animated animals of the early twenty-first century.

DreamWorks, in the meantime, has produced some of the most interesting animated films of the new century, even apart from their distribution of Aardman products. The Oscar-winning computer-animated *Shrek* (2001) became a major milestone in the history of animated film. An irreverent romp through the world of fairy tales that takes direct parodic aim at the sentimental, simpleminded clichés of Disney's animated classics, *Shrek* was a huge hit that might well be the greatest animated children's film of all time. It also became the foundation of a major film franchise. As of this writing, two sequels have been released, and two more are already in the works.

Directed by Andrew Adamson and Vicky Jensen, *Shrek* lacks the eye-popping, gee-whiz, groundbreaking animation of the Pixar films, but it is very effectively animated. In particular, the animation style is actually quite appropriate to the tone and subject matter of the film, helping to create a medieval fairy-tale world that is somehow just a bit out of kilter. The lively soundtrack music is excellent as well, creating an anachronistic dissonance between its contemporary music and the medieval world of the film, something that was also done in the live-action film *A Knight's Tale*, released just a week earlier in a joint effort between Fox and Sony's Columbia Pictures unit. Consisting of a mixture of recent and vintage pop-rock hits, the music of *Shrek* not only provides effective accompaniment to the action but also helps to identify the film as brash, hip, and contemporary, virtually the opposite of the nostalgic tone that the classic Disney films seek to establish. It is, however, the action itself that most clearly sets *Shrek* apart from the Disney classics, a fact that is announced in rather startling fashion at the beginning of the film. The first scene features a beautifully illustrated fairy-tale book, the pages of which are turned to get the story started, as in *Snow White*. This pastiche, however, quickly turns to parodic commentary when a page is suddenly ripped from the book, followed by Shrek's emergence from the outhouse. The implication, of course, is that Shrek has wiped his ass with the torn-out page, providing some rather rude critical commentary on fairy tales in general, but especially on how fairy tales have been used by Disney.

Though based (very loosely) on the illustrated children's book by William Steig, the film version of *Shrek* goes well beyond the book in its all-out assault on fairy-tale clichés, employing a technique of inversion to make virtually every character into the opposite of what one would expect that character to be based on experience with Disney films. The title character (voiced by Mike Myers) is a hulking, uncouth, green-skinned ogre who nevertheless turns out not to be the monster of the piece, but the hero. A loner who resides in a remote swamp just so he will be left alone, Shrek begins his adventures in the film when his swamp is suddenly invaded by a horde of fairy-tale characters (including Pinocchio and Snow White and the Seven Dwarfs, among many others), exiled there by the diminutive Lord Farquaad (John Lithgow), ruler of the city-state of Duloc. In what amounts to a form of ethnic cleansing, Farquaad has decided to rid his land of this fairy-tale rabble as part of his effort to make Duloc his vision of a perfect society. But *Shrek* is a film that endorses messiness and champions respect for the other, so it is quite clear that Farquaad's Nazi-like quest for perfection has dystopian rather than utopian undertones. In any case, Shrek decides to travel to Duloc to try to convince Farquaad to remove the fairy-tale creatures from his swamp. In his travels he is accompanied by a talking donkey (Eddie

Murphy) who was among the exiles and who knows the way to Duloc.

Farquaad, meanwhile, has consulted a magic mirror (apparently lifted from *Snow White*) and has learned that, in order to become a true king, he must marry a princess. Then, in a riff on TV's *The Dating Game* that is typical of *Shrek*'s postmodern engagement with popular culture, Farquaad sifts through some potential mates and chooses one Princess Fiona (Cameron Diaz), who happens (in good fairy-tale fashion) to be imprisoned in a remote castle guarded by a fire-breathing dragon. Farquaad isn't about to undertake the dangerous task of rescuing Fiona on his own, so he decides to hold a tournament to choose a champion to do the job for him. About this time Shrek and Donkey stumble into Duloc. Shrek finds himself in the midst of the tournament and easily dispatches all of the participants; he is thus anointed the champion. He agrees to accept the role and promises to retrieve Fiona if Farquaad will remove the annoying fairy-tale characters from the swamp.

Shrek of course succeeds in rescuing the princess, laying waste to any number of fairy-tale clichés and wading through a sea of allusions to various forms of popular culture along the way. Then, in a virtual remake of the main plot line of the classic screwball comedy *It Happened One Night* (1934), he brings the princess back to Farquaad, finding that his initial assessment of her as dainty and spoiled needs to be revised.[14] In numerous ways (as when she matches him burp for burp or when she routs Robin Hood and his Merry Men in a riff on martial arts films), Fiona endears herself to Shrek, and their initially antagonistic relationship turns to love. The dragon, meanwhile, falls in love with the donkey, so all sorts of unlikely romance is in the air. Shrek nevertheless delivers Fiona to Farquaad, then returns to his swamp, only to have second thoughts and then rush back to her rescue, seconds before she is to be married to the despicable Farquaad (just as Clark Gable's Peter Warne rescues Claudette Colbert's Ellie Andrews from the altar in *It Happened One Night*). Shrek, with the aid of the formidable dragon (which, among other things, eats Farquaad), wins the ensuing battle. He wins Fiona as well, their love cemented when he discovers that, each night at sunset, she herself transforms into an ogre. Indeed, love's first kiss having the magic power that it does in fairy tales, Fiona permanently becomes an ogre once she and Shrek kiss for the first time, thereby reversing the familiar frog-turned-prince-via-a-kiss motif. Thus, despite having stood so many fairy-tale motifs on their heads (and having featured so many scenes, such as Farquaad's torture and interrogation of the Gingerbread Man, that would never appear in a Disney film), the film ends in typical fairy-tale fashion, with the two lovers set to live happily ever after—even if they are ogres.

Despite this ending, fairy-tale scholar Jack Zipes sees *Shrek* as a powerfully subversive film that "plays with all the conventions of the traditional folk and fairy tale to provoke readers to consider the relative nature of evil and beauty" (227). Of course, the principal target of the critique in *Shrek* is Disney, a fact that Zipes acknowledges. For example, Zipes sees the dystopian Duloc as a "sanitized Disney world," setting up a structural opposition in the film between the sterility of Duloc and the fertility of the swamp, "conformists versus outsiders, conventionality versus unconventionality, the tyranny of symmetry and homogenization versus the freedom of unsymmetry and heterogeneity" (229). Importantly, for Zipes, all of these oppositions represent real struggles within the American culture industry as a whole, but pose a particular challenge to Disney's hegemony in animated children's film, showing "through stunning digital animation how the world, art, and institutions can be depicted differently and be directed in a more humane manner" (230).

Shrek was a major success for DreamWorks, grossing more than $484 million in worldwide box-office receipts and drawing considerable critical praise, including the winning of the inaugural Academy Award for Best Animated Feature. Thus, even though part of the success of *Shrek* was due to the fact that it was so different from anything seen before, it was no surprise that the film was followed by a sequel, *Shrek 2* (2004). The narrative of *Shrek 2* is somewhat less interesting than that of *Shrek*, though the second film pushes the idea of reversing fairy-tale tropes even further than did the first. Here, Shrek and Fiona, now happily married, travel to the kingdom of Far, Far Away to meet with her parents, who happen to be the king (John Cleese) and queen (Julie Andrews)—and who are unaware that Shrek is an ogre or that Fiona has become one permanently as well. Not surprisingly, difficulties ensue, especially between Shrek and the king, leading Shrek to conclude that Fiona would be better off if she were to revert to human form and if he could become human as well. He thus seeks out a magic potion that does indeed return her to human form, while making him a handsome human. The donkey also gets into the act, becoming a beautiful white stallion.

Unfortunately, other forces are at work in the form of the Fairy Godmother (Jennifer Saunders) and her son Prince Charming (Rupert Everett), who connive to try to steal Fiona away from Shrek. These two conventional Disney heroes thus become the villains of the piece, though they are of course foiled by Shrek and Donkey, this time with a considerable assist from some other fairy-tale characters, especially Puss in Boots (Antonio Banderas), a swashbuckling, sword-wielding cat whose small size comically conflicts with his swaggering nature. Pinocchio (Cody Cameron) and the Gingerbread Man (Conrad Vernon) return from the first film to have increased roles in this film as well. In the end, Donkey (to his own disappointment) reverts to his original form, while Shrek and Fiona turn back into ogres. In a final twist, meanwhile, Fiona's father reverts to his true form as a frog, having formerly been made human via a spell supplied by the Fairy Godmother. Of course, in the light of all of these transformations, just what constitutes one's true form (or whether there is even such a thing) is seriously called into question. This motif resonates with the general destabilization of individual identity in postmodern culture, but here it is particularly interesting because of the challenge it poses to the long Disney tradition of defining success as the assumption of one's true identity.

Shrek 2 includes the same kind of pop-rock soundtrack as its predecessor, and is, if anything, even richer in its wealth of pop-cultural allusions, including lots of direct references to Disney and other children's films. Importantly, however, these allusions also include brief pastiches of several iconic scenes that would almost certainly not be recognized or appreciated by younger viewers, such as reproductions of the famous lapping-waves-on-the-beach love scene of *From Here to Eternity* (1953) or the bucket-of-water-dumped-on-the-dancer scene from *Flashdance* (1983). Such moments are clearly aimed at adult viewers and indicate the extent to which the makers of the *Shrek* sequence envisions such viewers as a key part of its audience. This appeal to adult audiences was apparently successful, as *Shrek 2* still ranks as the top-grossing animated film of all time in terms of both domestic ($441 million) and worldwide ($920 million) box-office receipts.

The *Shrek* franchise continued in 2007 with the release of *Shrek the Third*, which was slightly less successful, but still a megahit at $799 million in worldwide box office. This film also received somewhat less acclaim than its predecessors from critics, many of whom felt that the basic premise was getting a bit tired. Indeed, by the time of the third film, one could argue that the pastiche technique that is so central to the sequence had essentially doubled back on itself, so that *Shrek the Third* was partly a pastiche of the first two *Shrek* films. Among other things, Shrek himself is by the third film such a cultural icon that the energy gained in the earlier films from his struggles with his status as an outcast is essentially gone, which means that this third film also does much less to tackle such issues as class, race, and intolerance of difference of whatever kind. In fact, in this third film, Shrek is such an insider that he is openly embraced as the heir to the throne of Far, Far Away, though he himself doesn't really want the job. Most of the plot concerns Shrek's quest to locate and retrieve the one other person who is a qualified heir to the throne. This person is the young and seemingly unkinglike Arthur, who Shrek locates and extracts from the one environ more frightening and formidable than a dragon-guarded castle: high school.

This motif brings Arthurian legend into the mix of *Shrek*'s sources, just as Disney had used this source in *The Sword and the Stone* (1963). Moreover, in keeping with the free postmodern intermixture of cultural materials from different historical periods that is typical of the *Shrek* sequence as a whole, this motif also introduces high-school culture, especially as filtered through Hollywood films. Arthur, it turns out, is such a loser that he is not only shunned by the school's jocks and cheerleaders, but even picked on by the school nerds. Much of the story then involves his gradual ascension to kingly status, and he does indeed take the throne by the end of the film. Other sources of comedy in the film include Shrek's anxieties over his impending fatherhood, following Fiona's surprise announcement that she is pregnant. At one point Donkey and Puss in Boots swap bodies with comic results as well, though this motif is somewhat strained and adds little to the film. Indeed, these two characters in general have little to do in this third film, which might account for some of its relative lack of energy compared to the first two *Shrek* films.

The film becomes a sort of mock political thriller in which Prince Charming endeavors to take the throne by force, aided by an army of witches and other conventional fairy-tale (and Disney) villains, such as Rumpelstiltskin and Captain Hook. In the course of the coup,

Charming takes Fiona and her mother prisoner, along with a group of Disney princesses, including Cinderella, Snow White, and Beauty, who is presumably Belle from *Beauty and the Beast*. In a clear commentary on the treatment of gender in Disney films, these princesses assume an entirely passive stance, simply waiting for someone to rescue them. Fiona and her mother galvanize them into action, however, for which they announce their readiness in a high-energy sequence that includes such declarations of newfound strength and independence as burning their bras. Finally, in keeping with the general challenge to the usual good vs. evil scenarios of Disney films, the fairy-tale villains drop their support for Charming, who is then easily defeated, allowing Arthur to become king and allowing Shrek and Fiona to return to their swamp, where they are soon greeted by the birth of triplets.

That *Shrek the Third* was almost as big a hit at the box office as *Shrek 2* solidified the status of the *Shrek* franchise as one of the key phenomena in American popular culture of the early twenty-first century. With the exception of *Flushed Away*, DreamWorks' other computer-animated films have all been highly successful as well, all containing some of the same satirical edge and same engagement with the legacy of American popular culture. For example, *Shark Tale* (2004), released a few months after *Shrek 2*, basically rewrites the gangster film within the context of an animated children's underwater adventure. Here, a teeming reef (depicted as an underwater, piscine version of New York City) is plagued by attacks from sharks, who themselves are organized as a criminal mob under the leadership of Don Lino (voiced by none other than Robert De Niro, he of so many gangster roles, including that of the young Vito Corleone in 1974's *The Godfather: Part II*). One of Don Lino's henchmen, meanwhile, is the porcupinefish Sykes, voiced by Martin Scorsese, another key figure in the history of gangster films.

Shark Tale also features *Sopranos* stars Michael Imperioli and Vincent Pastore, further extending the film's dialogue with cultural representations of gangsters, though many have seen this dialogue as a negative, given that children would probably not appreciate the numerous references to gangster narratives. Other aspects of the film's engagement with popular culture are similarly problematic, as few young viewers are likely to appreciate the engagement with reggae/ Rasta culture that occurs through the characters of the jellyfish Ernie and Bernie, voiced by comedian Doug E. Doug and Ziggy Marley (a reggae star and the son of Bob Marley, the biggest reggae star of them all). Largely, though, the film is a vehicle for Will Smith (an actor kids tend to know and like), who provides the voice of the central character, a bluestreak named Oscar, who was also given many of Smith's mannerisms and facial characteristics by the film's animators.

Oscar is an underachiever who gets in trouble with Sykes over a bad debt, but then rises to stardom as the Shark Slayer after he takes credit for killing Don Lino's son Frankie (Imperioli), who actually died in an accident that Oscar had nothing to do with. Oscar cements his fortune and fame with the help of Lenny (Jack Black), Don Lino's other son, who happens to be a mild-mannered vegetarian, much to the displeasure of his father. Lenny agrees to pretend to be killed by Oscar as well, bringing the new Shark Slayer even more into the limelight—and drawing the attention not only of the media but of the sultry lion fish Lola (Angelina Jolie), who attempts to seduce Oscar so that she can share in his newfound wealth and stardom. Of course, Lola is a shameless gold digger who doesn't care about Oscar as a person (or fish); the woman who really cares about Oscar is his longtime friend, the angel fish Angie (Renee Zellweger), who gets pretty much pushed aside in all the frenzy over Oscar's new status. Of course, all is well by the end: Oscar confesses that he is not a shark killer and returns to his old job at the Whale Wash, though now as manager and co-owner (with Sykes). He and Angie also end up together, as do Lenny and Don Lino, who agrees to accept his son for what he is.

Shark Tale lacks the impressive underwater animation of *Finding Nemo*, which was released just over a year earlier. It also lacks the feel-good warmth of that film and suffers from the fact that, through most of the film, the main character Oscar is not very likeable, despite Smith's charm. Indeed, the most positive characters in the film are Angie and Lenny, the latter of whom homophobic groups such as the conservative Christian fringe group the American Family Association decoded as gay because of his peaceful nature, causing them to object to the fact that he was positively portrayed. However, if *Shark Tale* is gay friendly (which is debatable), that is hardly the main point of the film. If anything, the film is unusually conservative by DreamWorks standards, counseling, almost in the mode of Disney, despite the hip music and pop-cultural references, that one should learn to accept what one truly is, whether one be an ordinary whale washer or a vegetarian shark. Actually, there doesn't seem to be all that much of a point to this film other than entertainment, but far too many of the entertaining bits are probably above the heads of children. Even this aspect of the film, however, could be taken as a shot at Disney, whose long-term dedication to conveying positive values in its films seems condescending and pretentious in comparison.

Although *Shark Tale* is relatively forgettable, it was followed in 2005 by the release of *Madagascar*, the first film in what has also become a lucrative franchise and a major element of children's popular culture in the early twenty-first century. Another entry in the talking-animal subgenre, *Madagascar* focuses on a group of animals in the New York Zoo who long (some more than others) to experience life in the wilds of Africa. This is particularly true of the zebra Marty (Chris Rock), who has just turned ten years old as the film begins and regrets the fact that his life is half over without his having ever seen Africa. Marty's friends get caught up in the attempt as well, including the preening lion Alex (Ben Stiller), the hypochondriac giraffe Melman (David Schwimmer), and the sensible hippo Gloria (Jada Pinkett Smith).

The ill-fated attempt to escape to the wild ultimately lands Marty and his friends on a ship headed for Africa, animal rights groups having agitated for the return of the animals (apparently unhappy in the zoo) to the wild. To this point, then, one might think that *Madagascar* is going to follow the conventional Disneyesque arc of returning its animal characters to their proper natural state. One would be wrong. For one thing, the crates carrying the four central animal characters fall overboard (in the midst of the turmoil caused when a group of nefarious penguins hijacks the ship so that they can divert it to their natural home of Antarctica) and are washed ashore on the island of Madagascar, instead of nearby Africa. For another, these zoo animals are city slickers who are completely unprepared for life in the wild, quickly concluding that they were better off back in the zoo. The same, incidentally, goes for the penguins, who do, in fact, make it back to Antarctica, but are completely unable to deal with the weather there. They take one look, conclude that "this sucks," and head back north, eventually running out of fuel just off the coast of Madagascar again.

Meanwhile, the four central animal characters make their way into a friendly society of lemurs, led by the colorful King Julien (Sacha

Baron Cohen), and learn that the lemurs live in constant fear of the local predators, whom they refer to as "foosa," but who are actually fossa, a catlike species indigenous only to Madagascar. Drawn to look much like hyenas (and thus potentially drawing upon the negative reputation of hyenas from films such as *The Lion King*), these predators are ultimately routed by the newcomers, especially the formidable Alex, who is, after all, a lion. The zoo escapees become heroes among the grateful lemurs, but decide nevertheless to head back home to New York aboard the ship brought to the island by the penguins, who decide not to inform them that the ship is out of fuel.

The plot of *Madagascar* is, however, almost beside the point. The film is far more character driven than are most animated films, and the camaraderie among the four central characters is an unusually effective motif (without becoming overly sentimental). Moreover, this is a film that is about specific sequences, many of which are brilliant, often through their engagement with well-known images or motifs from previous films. As with the *Shrek* films, many of these intertextual dialogues seem designed for adult viewers, rather than children, as when a lemur, in the midst of a discussion of the threat posed by the dreaded fossa, holds up a book with the title *To Serve Lemur* and shouts "It's a cookbook!" The reference, of course, is to the classic 1962 *Twilight Zone* episode "To Serve Man," in which alien visitors arrive on earth bearing a book entitled *To Serve Man*, which turns out to be a cookbook, rather than a guidebook for helping humanity. But children could surely not be expected to catch the allusion. My favorite of these sorts of references in the film occurs when Alex constructs a rustic replica of the Statue of Liberty to use for signaling passing ships, only to have it accidentally burned down by Melman. The distraught lion then drops to the sand, crying in his distress, "You maniac! You burned it up! Darn you! Darn you all to heck!" The reference here to the famous ending of *Planet of the Apes* (1968) is again fairly obvious to those in the know, but probably inaccessible to most children. Meanwhile, the toning down of the original language ("Goddamn you all to hell!") makes the scene even funnier by calling attention both to our society's rather silly and Puritanical squeamishness over language and to the ironic disparity between the contexts of the scenes from the two films.

Many of the best intertextual sequences in *Madagascar* are those that surprise by violating (even mocking) the conventions of animated film as set forth in Disney films. Perhaps the most effective of these is the sequence in which Marty, Melman, and Gloria walk through the jungles of Madagascar, encountering a variety of cute, cuddly animals as they go, only to witness one after another of the tiny creatures being devoured by predators. Meanwhile, this sequence is intercut with one in which Alex takes himself into self-exile on the predator side of the island so that he will be prevented from eating his best friend Marty, who is looking more and more appetizing to him in his increasingly meat-deprived state (now that he lacks the food that had always been provided for him in the zoo). These two combined sequences thus deliver the message that life in the wild is not nearly so idyllic as depicted in Disney films from *Snow White* forward, nor is the relationship between predator and prey so amicable as in films such as *The Lion King*.

The point is made even more forcefully by the fact that this whole sequence plays out to the accompaniment of Louis Armstrong singing "What a Wonderful World," creating an ironic gap between the world described by the music and the fang-and-claw world depicted on the screen. Music, in fact, is often used to especially good effect in *Madagascar*, and often because of the dissonance between the background music and the action being depicted is particularly striking, as well as funny, as in the *Planet of the Apes* riff noted above. Thus, the film opens to the dulcet strains of the well-known "Born Free," as a zebra (whom we will eventually know as Marty) gallops happily through the wild—until the scene is interrupted by Alex, who snaps Marty (who is actually running on a treadmill in the zoo) out of the reverie in which he was fantasizing the previous scene. Much of the music of *Madagascar*, meanwhile, is taken from well-known pop hits or from earlier movies, though some is rerecorded for this film, as when Reel 2 Real's 1994 reggae hit "I Like to Move It, Move It" is spiced up with new vocals by Cohen as King Julien.

Madagascar is a highly entertaining film that conveys the importance of teamwork and friendship, but it lacks weighty messages; even its seeming assault on the clichés of Disney film seems more in good fun than genuinely subversive. Still, it combines with the more subversive *Shrek* films to provide a good indication of DreamWorks' strategy of assuming that its audiences are intelligent and culturally literate, whether they be adults or children. And the strategy seems to be a good one, given the commercial success of the two franchises.

Madagascar pulled in over $530 million in worldwide box office, while its sequel, *Madagascar: Escape 2 Africa* (aka *Madagascar 2, 2008*), took in over $580 million.

The sequel, incidentally, is pretty much more of the same, including allusions to *The Twilight Zone, Planet of the Apes*, and other works of popular culture over the past half century. The pop music soundtrack is similar as well, including a reprise of "I Like to Move It, Move It" that plays over the ending credits, this time with new vocals by rapper will.i.am, who also cowrote the film's score and provided the voice for a hippopotamus character called Moto Moto. The sequel does introduce some vague individual vs. the collective issues, as when Marty undergoes a sort of identity crisis when he realizes that he is virtually indistinguishable from all the other hundreds of zebras that he meets in Africa after he and the others crash in Africa while trying to fly back to New York on a plane salvaged from the jungles of Madagascar. (It turns out, of course, that Marty is distinguishable from the other zebras, in only because he still has a bite mark on his butt that was delivered to him by the hungry Alex in the first film.)

Probably the most obvious addition in *Madagascar 2* involves father-and-son material (apparently going for more family warmth) related to Alex's discovery of his family on the preserve on which they crash in Africa. In one of the film's many numerous echoes of *The Lion King*, Alex learns that his father, Zuba (Bernie Mac), is king of the preserve, but that his rule is threatened by an evil usurper, Makunga (Alec Baldwin). Meanwhile, the water supply to the preserve is cut off when a gang of tourists stranded in Africa dam up the river that feeds the preserve. Alex and Marty then set off on a journey to restore the water supply (somewhat like Mumble's quest in *Happy Feet*). Of course they succeed, after which the four central animals decide to remain on the animal preserve, where Alex will share the throne with his father, despite the fact that he fails to meet the conventional expectations of a lion king, preferring to dance (with choreography inspired by Bob Fosse and Jerome Robbins) rather than fight.

Madagascar: Escape 2 Africa goes much lighter, though, than *The Lion King* in its emphasis on the rightful order of things, including kingly succession. It does, however, add one potentially problematic political dimension in its treatment of the culture of the animals in Africa as a cobbled-together batch of stereotypes derived from popular Western depictions of so-called primitive cultures around the world. Thus, Alex at one point is expected to fight another lion for the right to succeed Zuba in a ritualistic battle that might have been derived from the actual dominance rituals of lions but is here dramatized in a way reminiscent of Native American ritual combats as presented in any number of films. Similarly, while Alex and Marty go to investigate the loss of water, King Julien comes up with the idea of tossing a sacrificial victim into a nearby volcano, thus appeasing the gods and restoring the water supply. This idea then triggers a whole subplot that mirrors any number of earlier films, such as *Joe Versus the Volcano* (1990),[15] that build on a similar motif (usually attributing the practice to various South Pacific cultures, rather than African ones). Indeed, *Ice Age: The Meltdown* had used the same motif (though only in passing) only two years earlier.

Granted, these colonialist motifs are treated as jokes in *Madagascar 2*, but, given the legacy of racial and cultural stereotyping in American film, they could still be problematic. On the other hand, the most savage behavior in the film is attributed to the American tourists (apparently all New Yorkers) who find themselves stranded in Africa because the penguin gang from the first film has hijacked their vehicles to use them for parts in rebuilding the crashed plane (which they ultimately do, constructing a craft reminiscent of the escape plane in *Chicken Run*). Not only do these tourists selfishly dam up the river that feeds the animal preserve (thus potentially providing a commentary on the exploitation of local resources by American interests around the world), but they also capture Alex at one point and attempt to cook him on a spit. All in all, though, *Madagascar 2* is very much like the first film in its emphasis on entertainment and lack of any real interest in political commentary, though this motif could of course itself be taken as a subtle critique of the moralizing didacticism of so many Disney films.

By the time of *Over the Hedge* (2006), the next release from DreamWorks Animation, it was becoming increasingly clear that DreamWorks' animation strategy is fundamentally different from that of Pixar. Thus, where Pixar seeks to produce animation that startles and amazes, DreamWorks goes for extremely good animation that is less spectacular and thus less intrusive and less likely to steal the show from the characters and the story. In this sense, then, DreamWorks animation is much more in line with the conventional

Hollywood style, in which technique is supposed to remain invisible, leaving audiences to concentrate on stories and characters. *Over the Hedge* is a big-budget production with big-name voiceover stars that nevertheless includes a significant amount of social satire, especially in its skewering of the fast-food-fueled consumerist mentality that drives suburban life in America and that has brought humanity to the brink of destroying the planet. On the other hand, this is a fun film that treats such issues with a very light touch, dealing less extensively with weighty political issues (especially environmentalist ones) than does the comic strip of the same title on which it is based. The basic premise driving the plot of *Over the Hedge* is that RJ the raccoon (Bruce Willis) steals then accidentally destroys the stash of food that had been set aside for the winter by the imposing bear, Vincent (Nick Nolte). Vincent gives RJ one week to replace the food or be killed, and RJ quickly realizes that his only hope for gathering so much food so quickly is to steal it from the new suburban community, El Rancho Camelot, that has suddenly sprung up (apparently during the winter hibernation) next to the woods where all the film's animal characters live, set off by a large and seemingly endless hedge (that the smaller animals can move through with ease).

RJ manages (with a little deception) to recruit a group of the other forest animals, led by the box turtle Verne (Garry Shandling) and the squirrel Hammy (Steve Carell), to help him raid the suburb for food. These main characters are supported by an ensemble cast of other animals—including the theatrical opossum Ozzie (William Shatner) and the skunk Stella (Wanda Sykes)—that provides the film with some of its best comic highlights. Meanwhile, the animals learn important lessons about cooperation and working together, presumably conveying these same lessons to the children who watch the film. In addition, wandering into the world of humans for the first time, the animals provide an astonished point of view that helps to highlight the unnatural affluence of suburban life, which so many take for granted. As in the case of many Disney films, human characters provide the film with its principal villains, including the murderous exterminator Dwayne "The Verminator" LaFontant (Thomas Haden Church) and Gladys Sharp (Allison Janney), a control freak who takes her position as president of the local homeowners' association way too seriously.

However, as opposed to the presentation in *Bambi* of "Man" as a vague, almost metaphysical evil, *Over the Hedge* provides a detailed presentation of the competitive and consumerist mentalities that drive LaFontant and Sharp. LaFontant is more sinister but less gross than exterminator Stan Beals in *The Ant Bully* (released two months later), and the figures of both over-the-top pest-killers provide some vague commentary on the cavalier way in which humans wipe out animals who become inconvenient—though neither is as effective in the satirical treatment of this motif as *Wallace & Gromit* had been. In any case, the real focus of the satire of *Over the Hedge* is not LaFontant, but the entire suburban consumerist culture that he is hired (by Sharp) to protect—by any means necessary, including the use of illegal devices. This satire is focused mostly on the self-centered, status-obsessed, gas-guzzler-driving suburbanite Sharp, a shrill harpy who runs the suburb almost like a military camp and who serves as a sort of dramatization of the drive for domination and control that lies at the center of consumerist culture. Still, the satire is relatively light (focusing mostly on the excessive food consumption of humans), and there is virtually no exploration of the fact that the building of the suburb is destroying the natural habitats of the animals. One is tempted to read the film as a sort of allegory of contemporary global politics and economics, with the humans representing the United States, consuming far more than its share of resources while blissfully ignoring the plight of the rest of the world (represented by the animals), which is forced to get by on the leftovers. Unfortunately, while the film does nothing to contradict such allegorical readings, it does little to encourage them, either, and children are unlikely to make such a connection unless an alert parent makes it for them. Still, the film does at least provide such a parent with material for making such points. The main lesson actually built into the film, however, is the one about the importance of collective action, though this message is here coded safely in terms of family togetherness, the various forest animals learning to work together because they are a family, which is fine as far as it goes, especially given the extended and unconventional nature of the family. Thus, the previously individualist RJ finally learns to trust the other animals and to consider himself as one of them, ultimately escaping Vincent with their help. Still, this message has the potential downside of suggesting to children that they need not cooperate with anyone outside their own family—or even that anyone outside the family, like Sharp or the bear, represents the "Them," to which the "Us" of the family is inevitably opposed.

The next DreamWorks animated film, *Bee Movie* (2007), returns, via its focus on bee society, to the individual vs. the collective themes of *Antz*, though much less effectively. Here, comedian and TV sitcom superstar Jerry Seinfeld is cast in the role of Barry Benson, a bee who seeks more individual meaning in life than is offered by his conformist society. In particular, Barry graduates from college only to discover that he is now expected to choose a job (from a very limited range of available opportunities) and then will be expected to stay in that job for the rest of his life. But Barry finds that he doesn't know what he wants to do for the rest of his life, thus triggering a personal crisis. This sequence, incidentally, includes a clever riff on *The Graduate* (1967) tossed in for adult viewers, which potentially helps to reinforce the obvious connection between Barry's plight and the plight of young humans entering the workplace, but it's done mostly in fun, with little satirical punch.

This crisis causes Barry to go out into the world beyond the hive, where he makes many discoveries about humans and human society, including the fact that humans operate huge honey farms where captive bees exploitatively are used to produce honey for the consumption of humans. One is tempted to read this highly regimented bee farm as a version of the American suburb, with the treatment of the bees becoming a satirical commentary on the Taylorist routinization and exploitation of labor by capitalism. But the movie does little to encourage such readings, and few children are likely to make the connection, if, indeed, did the filmmakers themselves. A more obvious interpretation is the environmentalist one that humans are constantly using nature for their own benefit, often in exploitative and destructive ways.

Here, however, is where the real trouble with *Bee Movie* begins. What follows Barry's revelations concerning the honey industry, in fact, seems completely confused in a political sense. Barry decides to take humanity to court in order to try to ban the further use of bee labor to make honey for humans. He wins an unlikely victory (already sending one misleading message to children), freeing bees of the necessity to work constantly in order to produce more and more honey, most of which is stolen by humans. But when the bees stop working, the delicate ecological balance of the world collapses. Flowers and other plants begin to die out en masse, threatening the survival of animals and, ultimately, of humans. This motif is a highly promising one (especially given the fact that the declining bee population does appear to be at risk worldwide), and it is certainly valuable to teach children the importance of even seemingly small elements of the ecology to the health of the whole. The problem, however, is in the presentation of this particular scenario as a willful decision by the bees to stop working when not forced to do so, which seems to be informed by particularly antilabor sentiments, as well as effacing the reality that the threat to bees (and thus the ecology) in our own world comes from without (due to the environmental destruction wrought by humans) rather than from within. Moreover, as with so many other environmentally themed films, the solution to the problem is all too easy: Barry figures out what is going on, rallies the bees to pollinate the few remaining flowers, and almost instantaneously rejuvenates the plant population of the earth, to the accompaniment of Sheryl Crow's rendition of the Beatles' "Here Comes the Sun." Environmental problems, especially those involving delicate shifts in the ecological balance, are notoriously difficult to solve, requiring a great deal of long-range resolution and sacrifice. Here, however, humans need do nothing, and the problem essentially solves itself, which is probably the last thing children need to believe about the destruction of the environment. DreamWorks, like Disney, seems to feel that happy endings are a requirement for children's films.

With *Kung Fu Panda* (2008), DreamWorks moved into the realm of Chinese culture, somewhat as Disney had done with *Mulan*, though here the characters are talking animals rather than humans. Moreover, this film picks up an extra intertextual dimension by filtering its presentation of Chinese culture through martial arts films such as Ang Lee's *Crouching Tiger, Hidden Dragon* (2000), probably the one aspect of Chinese popular culture best known in the West.[16] This engagement with martial arts culture is largely successful, and the film was a big box-office success (including in China), bringing in approximately $632 million, thus making it DreamWorks' most commercially successful non-*Shrek* film—and a great follow-up to *Bee Movie*, which was their least successful, especially internationally.

Though a very funny film, *Kung Fu Panda* treats its materials reasonably respectfully, including the use of its Chinese setting to produce a look that stands apart from the typical animated film. Still, despite its setting and subject matter, the central premise of the film is a quintessentially Western one, a version of the "Chosen One" narrative that has proven so popular with young audiences, especially in the U.S.[17] The central character, Po (Jack Black), feels completely out of place working in his father's noodle restaurant, his lonely outsider status dramatized by the fact that Po is a giant panda, while the other members of his family are geese. Po feels that he is fated for something greater than serving noodles, which, of course, he turns out indeed to be. In fact, Po, a big fan of the martial arts, is fated to become the Dragon Warrior and to save his homeland, the Valley of Peace, from destruction by the super-villain Tai Lung (Ian McShane). Thus, the intertextual mix that makes up the film also includes that very Western form (and one that is likely to be familiar with most young viewers in the U.S.), the superhero movie.

Much of the narrative of *Kung Fu Panda* consists of the story of Po's unlikely transformation from an obese, overeating dreamer into the actual Dragon Warrior, beginning with his initial designation as the Chosen One, despite the expectations of all that this legendary figure would arise from among the Furious Five, a group of martial arts stars who have been training with the legendary Master Shifu (Dustin Hoffman). Po is as surprised as anyone at the designation, yet he surprisingly perseveres through the difficult training administered to him by Master Shifu and the Five, who include Tigress (Angelina Jolie), Mantis (Seth Rogen), Viper (Lucy Liu), Monkey (Jackie Chan), and Crane (David Cross), all of whom are themselves skeptical of Po's suitability for the role.

Indeed, Po does not really emerge as the Dragon Warrior until his final confrontation with Tai Lung, who escapes from a seemingly inescapable prison, then defeats Shifu and the Furious Five, leaving only Po to protect the valley. But, fate being what it is, Po defeats and destroys Tai Lung in the spectacular extended battle sequence that provides the climax of the film, though there is also an extended denouement in which the Furious Five acknowledge Po as the Dragon Warrior and as their superior as a martial-arts master. Meanwhile, the exact nature of the film's individualist message becomes clear from the fact that Po's final transformation into the Dragon Warrior is triggered not by his training or other arcana that he expects to be revealed to him via the legendary Dragon Scroll (which turns out to be blank), but simply by the fact that he learns to believe in himself and to trust that he can, indeed, become the Dragon Warrior, despite seeming to be such an unlikely candidate and despite the skepticism of others.

The message here seems very congruent with the problematic "anyone can cook" message of Pixar's *Ratatouille*, released a year earlier. After all, Po is the Chosen One, fated to be the Dragon Warrior, and no amount of self-confidence could make him the Dragon Warrior otherwise. In *Ratatouille* it turns out that the real message is that, while not literally anyone can cook, a great cook might come from anywhere. Here, not just anyone can be the Dragon Warrior, but the Dragon Warrior might emerge from anywhere. Put differently (and in a way that oddly echoes the Calvinist doctrine of predestination), the film implies that there's no way of predicting who might be special if he or she were fated to be so in the first place; but most people have no hope of being special at all, no matter how hard they try.

In *Monsters vs. Aliens* (2009), DreamWorks extends this focus on special people with an ambitious animated science fiction film based on the premise that the earth is invaded by aliens who seem completely immune to all conventional earth weapons. The earth, however, turns out to have a stock of unconventional weapons in the form of a group of monsters that the U.S. government has been rounding up for secret internment in the notorious Area 51. The government then decides to unleash these monsters against the invading aliens, offering the monsters their subsequent freedom in return for their cooperation. The monsters succeed, of course, and this premise offers numerous possibilities for spectacular action scenes and the animation of these scenes is indeed impressive (including the use of Tru3D, the new DreamWorks effects technology, analogous to Disney's Digital 3-D, a version of the RealD Cinema technology). The scenario of *Monsters vs. Aliens* also offers numerous opportunities to engage in dialogue with the whole legacy of monster and science fiction movies; allusions to earlier films are there in abundance. For example, some of the monsters seem derived from specific classic science fiction/ monster films. Thus, the central character in the film is Susan Murphy (aka Ginormica, voiced by Reese Witherspoon), an ordinary young woman who suddenly grows to nearly fifty feet in height after exposure to a strange meteorite, thus echoing the title character of *Attack of the 50 Foot Woman* (1958), while another central monster, B.O.B. the Blob (Seth Rogen), seems derived from *The Blob* (1959). All in all, though, this aspect of the film is ultimately a bit disappointing, and the dialogue with previous films (despite occasional clever nods, especially to the films of DreamWorks principal Steven Spielberg) doesn't add as much to the film as it might have. Indeed, *Monsters vs. Aliens* is a disappointing film in general that sacrifices heart for big explosions and that fails to explore a number of important political themes that seem central to the film's basic scenario.

For one thing, there is no real questioning of the legality or morality of the Area 51 monster internment program, even though the monsters seem almost entirely benevolent. They may inadvertently be dangerous, but in general their only crime is in being radically different from the general population. The film presents the monsters from a sympathetic point of view and presents the U.S. government and military as bungling incompetents. (The U.S. president, voiced by political satirist Stephen Colbert, seems particularly ludicrous, perhaps as a jab at President George W. Bush, in office during the making of the film.) But there is no real interrogation of the ominous implications of the monster internment program or of the way in which, for example, it echoes the internment, without trial, of suspected terrorists by the U.S. government during the years of the recent Bush administration. Indeed, the film plays the internment of the monsters for laughs, which is especially troubling.

Granted, the film's basic sympathy for the monsters suggests tolerance for their difference, even if the film fails to take the U.S. government adequately to task for its official intolerance. Moreover, the film's chief point-of-view character is Susan, the most human of the monsters, while the other monsters do not have well-developed personalities but are simply manifestations of their particular form of monstrosity. Still, as with *Monsters, Inc.*, the fact that each monster is monstrous in an entirely different way can be taken as a vague statement in favor of individualism. Indeed, the most important difference between the monsters and the aliens (for whose difference the film has no tolerance at all) is that the monsters are highly individualistic (though they work well together as a team), while the aliens serve as images of conformity and communality. Indeed, the aliens of the film are all either mass-produced robots or mass-produced clones of the chief alien, one Gallaxhar (Rainn Wilson). Thus, perhaps in keeping with its roots in 1950s science fiction, the film constructs its good vs. evil opposition in the classic Cold War terms of individualism vs. communalism, which is probably not the most valuable lesson children in 2009 need to learn, if it ever was.

Monsters vs. Aliens is vaguely progressive in its use of a female protagonist (Susan), especially in the way her experiences in the film cause her to evolve from a fairly conventional young woman (dreaming of marriage to a successful man) to a strong and independent figure who finally realizes that her self-centered fiancé is a jerk and sends him packing. Of course, female protagonists were hardly unusual by the time of this film, even those with superpowers. Indeed, the very fact that Susan's most heroic deeds are accomplished via her superhuman size and strength probably weakens the film's status as a statement in favor of feminine capability, because ordinary women do not have such superior abilities.

All in all, the collected DreamWorks animated films are informed by a political ideology that is definitely less coherent than the one that has long informed Disney films, though the Disney ideology has been less coherent since the death of Walt Disney himself. It is also fairly safe to say that the ideology of the DreamWorks films is somewhat to the left of that which drives the Disney films. However, this is not to say that the DreamWorks films are particularly subversive; indeed, the DreamWorks films are pretty much in line with the official mainstream ideology of American democracy and capitalism (if not with actual day-to-day practice in American society), while the Disney films (especially in their lingering fascination with medieval monarchism) are generally situated to the right of the official American mainstream by the standards of the early twenty-first century, despite their careful effort to present themselves as the cinematic embodiment of Americanism. The DreamWorks films thus collectively mount a challenge not only to Disney's hegemony in children's animated film, but to the whole process through which Disney established and maintained that hegemony. This challenge itself, meanwhile, has ramifications that go well beyond the world of children's film, posing questions not only about the culture industry as a whole, but about the role of that industry in American society.

Conclusion:
The Politics of Children's Film:
What Hollywood Is Really Teaching
Our Children

Leonard S. Marcus notes that, during the 1950s, when American cultural production occurred in the shadow of repressive anticommunist purges, American children's literature flew to some extent under the radar and was sometimes able to address more progressive political themes than more mainstream American literature. According to Marcus, "the people responsible for creating the children's books that librarians purchased with public funds and that parents and grandparents gave as gifts to the children they loved were viewed by the new government overlords of ideological purity as of too little consequence to be worthy even of investigation" (194).[1] Given the special attention paid to the high-profile Hollywood film industry by Senator McCarthy and his ilk, these overlords might have considered children's film to be worthy of more scrutiny than children's literature, except that the children's film industry already had its own built-in overlord in the person of Walt Disney, himself a key collaborator in the government's attempt to purge Hollywood of leftist influences.

Nevertheless, the lack of official concern about the political content of children's books (except comic books) in the 1950s, despite the fact that such literature might be expected to have a formative effect on impressionable young minds, is indicative of the way in which children's culture has often been regarded as inherently apolitical by the American culture industry. On the other hand, many on the Left have long regarded children's literature as an important medium for the expression of progressive political ideas.[2] There has never been a mechanism for the production of leftist children's films (or leftist films in general, despite occasional independent efforts such as 1954's *Salt of the Earth*). Thus, the very lack of attention to the political content of children's film (even on the part of filmmakers themselves) opens certain opportunities for political readings of children's films. These unanticipated political readings need not be progressive, of course, but the vaguely liberal leanings of children's films, at least in the last couple of decades, at least makes left-of-center readings possible in many cases.

Such readings are particularly available with regard to specific issues, especially in recent decades, when certain politically correct points of view on some issues have become sacrosanct. In some cases, the treatment of these issues seems obligatory and disingenuous, as when recent children's films frequently critique consumerism while serving themselves as major consumer products. Even in these cases, however, the films potentially offer entry points that parents can use to discuss such issues with their children. Other children's films convey positive political messages that can function a bit more directly. At least as far back as *Dumbo*, for example, American children's films have consistently counseled respect for those who are different from the norm. Granted, Disney's films in particular have sometimes descended into troubling racist stereotyping, but that is mostly a matter of insensitivity and inattentiveness, and it would certainly be unfair to argue that Disney's films intentionally promote racism, even in the early years of the company. While Disney has had its slips even in recent years (*Aladdin* is the most notable example), since the beginnings of the renaissance of the 1990s the company has been devoted to the politically correct promotion of multiculturalism. Even so, Douglas Brode's determined claim that Disney virtually invented multiculturalism (and created the counterculture of the 1960s) doesn't quite ring true.[3]

Children's films at least since the Disney renaissance have consistently attempted to present more enlightened views of gender, even though certain problematic images (such as that of the Disney princess) have proved stubbornly resistant to updating. To an extent, in fact, one might say that racism and sexism are no longer issues in children's film, in the sense of representing contested terrain. Children's film, like American society as a whole, is officially opposed to both sexism and racism; the question that remains is not whether to oppose sexism and racism, but simply how successful a given film might be in proving its opposition to these now discredited attitudes, absolutely unsupportable in principle, if not necessarily in practice. Yet racism and sexism linger in the cracks and crevices of American life, so children's films that support equality in matters of race and gender are still valuable.

Because such films at this point do little more than support what has already been accepted as the consensus view of American society, race and gender as issues have been of relatively little concern to me in this volume. However, there are other topics on which children's film has also achieved essential unanimity, even if these topics remain to some extent contested issues in American political life. One thinks, for example, of the hotly debated issue of gun control, an issue that has in recent years (after events such as the April 1999 school shootings in Columbine, Colorado, as well as other highly publicized school shootings) become particularly prominent in discussions of American children's culture. It would be hard to think of a children's film that openly supports gun culture, even though there is much support in American public life (especially among powerful organizations such as the National Rifle Association) for the widespread availability of guns, even to children. Indeed, children's film as a rule is strongly anti-gun, with Disney classics such as *Bambi* leading the way in portraying guns as destructive devices with little or no positive function. Among other things, the sheer unthinkability of a pro-gun children's film (though guns certainly figure prominently in Hollywood film as a whole) serves as an acknowledgement that guns cannot seriously be regarded as good for children, suggesting the hypocrisy of the forces that would promote gun ownership and use in America, even among children. Hunting, a particularly sacred activity to the gun lobbies, has been portrayed in an especially negative light in Disney and other films (the killing of the deer in *The Iron Giant* is a good example); it is presented largely as an offense against nature.

Disney's consistent championing of nature (often in opposition to human intrusions or abuses) over the years has provided one of the company's proudest traditions, even if some would see its presentation of nature as at times so distorted as to represent an abuse of its own kind. Meanwhile, the pro-nature stance of so many children's films leads directly and logically into the important topic of environmentalism, another issue that, like gun control, is hotly contested in American political life. No one can seriously dispute that it is a good idea to protect the environment and to preserve the planet for this and future generations. Moreover, there seems to be very little disagreement in the scientific community that we have reached a time of environmental crisis in which urgent action is required in order to prevent irreversible, possibly fatal damage to earth and its ecosystems. Yet there is still widespread support in the political realm for the notion that the situation is not all that bad and that we need not do anything inconvenient or expensive to combat the problem of environmental decay. Indeed, during the eight years of the recent Bush administration it was official U.S. government policy that the environmental crisis was no crisis at all and should not be allowed to inhibit the unrestrained pursuit of profit by corporate interests.

Thus, there seems to be a genuine need for any sort of cultural production that might call attention to the urgency of our current environmental crisis. Moreover, as there is a long tradition of environmentally friendly (or at least nature-friendly) children's films, this particular area would seem to be one in which children's films might make an especially valuable contribution. In fact, it would be very difficult to imagine a children's film at this juncture that would promote industrialization and development, even if at the expense of the environment, though that attitude was official U.S. government policy from the beginning of 2001 to the beginning of 2009. And children's films are indeed making inroads in the direction of promoting environmental responsibility, although the industry seems to be proceeding slowly and cautiously, presumably due to a desire not to alienate parents who might not approve of such messages. Thus, the most effective environmentalist children's film to date, Pixar's *WALL-E*, almost seems designed to deflect attention from its own political message. Moreover, none of the environmentally themed children's films to have appeared in recent years, from the Fox-distributed *FernGully: The Last Rainforest* (1992) and *Once upon a Forest* (1993) to *WALL-E* (2008), are as effective or as insistent in pursuing their messages (complete with a critique of the corporate sources of the ecological problems they address) as *The Lorax* was in a brief animated television special way back in 1972.

Such considerations aside, it is almost certainly the case that children's films do not have their most powerful and important impact at the level of promoting specific attitudes toward particular issues. Especially for young viewers, the details of such issues can be hazy at best. Children's films can, however, have a profound impact at the level of promoting certain fundamental attitudes and basic expectations concerning what the world is like and how one should live in it. These basic attitudes and expectations are the stuff of what we intellectuals call "ideology," itself a vexed category with numerous different implications for different theorists over the years. In this volume, I have surveyed a wide variety of children's films, noting, where appropriate, some of the ideological messages that can potentially be derived from those films. These messages vary widely from one film to another, of course, though I think that some consistency can be found within the films produced by a particular studio,[4] especially in the case of Disney films during the reign of Walt Disney, though later Disney and Pixar films still have a more consistent ideological content than do the films of most other studios. In addition, some overall observations can be made about the politics of American children's film as a whole, which I would like to do in the remainder of this concluding chapter.

First, it is safe to say that the most consistent ideological message embedded in American children's film has to do with the promotion of an individualist mind-set. Almost every film I have discussed actively promotes individualism in one way or another, which is not particularly surprising, given that individualism is probably the central constitutive component of the official ideology of the United States as a nation and of capitalism as a system. Of course, individualism itself is an inherently versatile concept that plays out differently in different films, and the very notion of what it means to be an individual is open to debate and contestation.

To a surprisingly great extent, Disney's films are consistently informed by a conception of individualism that sees each individual as endowed by nature, from birth, with particular built-in characteristics that make that individual suited to play certain specific roles in society. As I have noted, this particular form of individualism is highly problematic, perhaps best suited to a medieval worldview ruled by rigid concepts of inheritance that historically predate the rise of modern individualism. By contrast, the Disney notion that individuals are defined by their innate characteristics is virtually identical to the attitude that recent feminist and other social theorists have referred to as "essentialism," which has been seen as quite central to modern conceptions of race, class, and gender. According to this view, individuals of certain races, classes, and genders have a number of natural inclinations and abilities by virtue of belonging to these groups. However, careful examinations of these essentialist conceptions have shown that they typically have little or no basis in physical reality and consist instead largely of constellations of stereotypes designed to further existing power structures. Perhaps the quintessential example of such examinations of essentialism is Edward Said's demonstration, in *Orientalism* (1978), that Western descriptions of non-Western peoples have tended to emanate more from the Western imagination than from actual reality. This led to the development of a highly consistent discursive structure through which characteristics valued in the official ideology of the West are associated with white Europeans and North Americans, while characteristics considered negative in the West are projected onto the nonwhite peoples outside the dominant sphere of Europe and North America. Such discursive movements led to hierarchical notions of race and served as a key ideological justification for nineteenth-century European colonialism, while continuing to further Western economic and cultural imperialism in the postcolonial era. In the same vein, any number of feminist theorists, dating back to Simon de Beauvoir's *The Second Sex* (1949), have similarly argued that the patriarchal power of men has been furthered through the development of essentialist stereotypes about women.

That essentialism has been a central mode of stereotyping in terms of both race and gender is not particularly surprising, given that both of these forms of social categorization have at least some apparent biological basis, even if the characteristics associated with race and gender via essentialist stereotyping are not actually products of biology. From this point of view, it may not be coincidental that one of the most frequent criticisms of Disney's classic films has involved their stereotypical depiction of race and gender. After all, given that the ideology of these films is so thoroughly shot through with essentialism, then it only stands to reason that they would have difficulty getting outside the discourses of race and gender that essentialism has underwritten in the West for hundreds of years.

Essentialism has not been as obviously related to ideas about class in the U.S., partly because of the odd double movement through which Americans like to believe that theirs is a classless society. At the same time they believe in a rhetoric of upward mobility through which some citizens may enjoy a higher status and more privileges than others, but all have an equal opportunity to succeed, regardless of their origins. However, though the notion of upward mobility might seem to imply the reality of class, as practiced in the U.S. it actually participates in the denial of class by making unequal status a matter of differential individual achievement rather than collective inequalities. In addition, the glorification of upward mobility that constitutes such a central part of the American national narrative has an insidious flipside: it implies that those who do not enjoy social and economic success owe their failure not to inferior class standing (and thus diminished opportunities) but to their own personal shortcomings, whether those involve lack of ability, lack of effort, or even lack of moral fiber. When combined with a belief in essentialism, this phenomenon is particularly damaging because it implies that those who do not succeed in our society fail to do so because of innate, unchangeable flaws in their own character. One might expect, meanwhile, that this kind of attitude would be particularly harmful to children, who are more likely than adults to internalize the stereotypes with which others describe them. Up to a certain age, at least, children have little or no opportunity to improve the social and economic status into which they have been born. Thus, children who are poor are in danger of interpreting that situation as a sign of their own personal inferiority. In fact, children who in any way differ from the images of normality that are conveyed in popular culture (which usually means white and male, as well as affluent) are similarly in danger of concluding that they are somehow personally at fault, somehow abnormal in fundamental ways.

The essentialist individualism of the classic Disney films, then, far from encouraging children to be all they can be in the pursuit of the American dream, threatens to marginalize disadvantaged children and to lead them to conclude that, through their own personal shortcomings, they do not deserve to partake of that dream. This problem, of course, is at least partly a matter of genres and sources: Disney's classic films tend to be fantasies based (however loosely) on fairy tales, and one could obviously argue that the ideology embedded in fairy tales is simply inconsistent with the official ideology of the United States.

On the other hand, Disney's more recent films, including the Pixar films, tend to adhere with surprising consistency to the same essentialist notions of individualism as do the older, classic films, even when the newer films (as in the case of *all* Pixar films thus far) are not based on fairy tales. Granted, characters in the Pixar films are more likely to be able to grow and change based on the experiences they undergo in the course of the film (Nemo's father becomes less cautious after a transoceanic adventure; Lightning McQueen becomes less self-centered after experiencing true friendship), but these changes remain rather limited and, in their own way, stereotypical. Meanwhile, most of the characters even in these newer films adhere strictly to type and find it difficult or inadvisable to go against their basic natures.

Outside the world of Disney, however, there are numerous children's films that convey a more typically American version of anyone-can-be-president individualism in which children are, in fact, encouraged to seek their own identities unconstrained by the identities that were thrust upon them by the accident of birth. As I noted in the previous chapter, Warner's *The Iron Giant* is particularly clear in its delivery of this message, as both Hogarth Hughes and the huge robot of the title are urged at different points in the film to believe that they can make their own choices about what sort of person—or machine—they will become. And, as a group, one of the clearest ways in which the animated films produced by DreamWorks can be differentiated from the films of Disney and Pixar is in their different portrayal of individualism as a matter of individual choice, rather than individual destiny.

While all DreamWorks films convey individualist messages of one sort or another, the clearest case in which the nature of DreamWorks individualism differs from the essentialist messages of the classic Disney films probably occurs in the *Shrek* sequence, in which the title character is by nature a vile and dangerous ogre, but turns out to be a virtuous hero because he ultimately chooses to pursue that course. Time and again, especially in the first two *Shrek* films, Shrek is expected to behave in a certain fashion merely because he is an ogre. Indeed, numerous characters in these films have the same experience, as when Fiona is expected to be dainty and proper because she is a princess. Yet Fiona turns out to be as much an ogre as a princess, while Shrek turns out to be heroic and good-hearted. Indeed, one way of describing the overt critical engagement of the *Shrek* sequence with the classic Disney films would be as an extended critique of essentialist stereotyping of precisely the kind that is typical of the Disney films.

Moreover, numerous characters in other DreamWorks films participate in much the same critique. Z in *Antz* is slotted from birth to be a worker; Lenny in *Shark Tale* is expected to be ruthless and predatory simply because he is a shark; Po in *Kung Fu Panda* is seen as an unlikely candidate for heroism merely because he doesn't look the part. Such characters then refute the stereotypes that have been thrust upon them, as Z refuses merely to live out his life in his seemingly fated role, Lenny refuses to eat other fish simply because he was born a shark, and Po becomes the Dragon Warrior seemingly against all odds.

Importantly, though, the refusal to adhere to type is very much part of what makes each of the above characters special representatives of individualism. If Disney and Pixar protagonists are expected to learn their fated roles and then to occupy them, DreamWorks protagonists are, as a rule, expected to question the roles that are thrust upon them by the expectations of others and to fashion new identities for themselves based on their own sense of what is appropriate for them to be and do. This version of individualism tends to give the DreamWorks films a vaguely antiauthoritarian air, especially given that these films so frequently present challenges to the conventions of Disney's films, the ultimate authority in the world of animated children's film.

Of course, this subversive aspect of the DreamWorks films is actually much more in line with the official ideology of American capitalism than is the vaguely medieval orientation of Disney's individualism. Disney's is in many ways a form of anti-individualism, looking back to the premodern origins of the romance/fairy-tale genre within which so many of the films are formulated. In point of fact, though, the opposed versions of individualism that can be found in the Disney and DreamWorks films both represent different aspects of American individualism, to a great extent separated simply by time: Disney individualism largely congealed by the 1950s (and, with minor variations, has stayed pretty much in place ever since),[5] while the ideology of the DreamWorks films arose in the 1990s.

The 1950s, of course, are widely remembered as both a Golden Age and a repressive time of conformist terror, a combination that perhaps helps to explain the twofold essence of so many Disney films, which often want to have it both ways on so many issues. Thus, despite the strong strain of nostalgia for the purity and simplicity of the 1950s that runs through so much American popular culture from the 1970s forward, there was already, in the 1950s, a powerful sense that something very troubling was afoot that was changing our basic conception of what it meant to be a modern individual. Perhaps the single best-known work of contemporary cultural criticism from the 1950s, for example, is William Whyte's *The Organization Man* (1956), described by Jackson Lears as the "locus classicus of the 1950s critique of conformity" (44). Writing in the midst of the 1950s, Whyte argues that the growing regimentation of corporate culture in the decade is producing a population of corporate clones, virtually bereft of any genuine individual identity. However, far from attributing this phenomenon to capitalism as a system, Whyte essentially suggests that the enforced conformism of the 1950s represents a betrayal of the true individualistic values of capitalism in favor of an emphasis on the group—which (in the terms of the 1950s) is code for creeping communism.

Disney's emphasis on a world of magic and imagination would seem the very antithesis of Whyte's description of the corporate culture of the 1950s, with the corporate conformism (a new manifestation of the drive toward routinization and rationalization earlier associated with capitalism by Weber) described by Whyte thus appearing as an unnatural imposition to which Disney's glorification of the natural might seem the perfect antidote. Read through Whyte, though, Disney's critique of American corporate culture is not a critique of capitalism so much as an attempt to rescue some romantic version of "real" capitalism (thus defined as the "natural" way for a society to be organized) from the corrupting influence of a communistic conformism; this attitude is not evidence of countercultural attitudes (as Brode might have it), but is instead perfectly in line with Walt Disney's own well-known red-baiting.[6] It is certainly the case that parents in the 1950s were much concerned with the possibilities of creeping conformism, whether they associated it with capitalism or not, and this fact is clearly reflected both in the decade's fascination with natural child-rearing techniques that focused on the development of the individual imagination (epitomized by the popularity of Dr. Benjamin Spock as a child-rearing guru) and in the growing stature of Disney in the decade as a force that might help to develop this imagination.[7]

On the other hand, Disney's version of essentialist individualism seems highly problematic as an antidote to the corporate conformism of the decade, since it still suggests that the successful individual is one who ultimately does what is expected of him or her by others. In this sense, the cultural critic from the 1950s whose work sheds the most light on the particular Disney conception of individualism is probably David Riesman, who argues in *The Lonely Crowd* (1950) that changes in American society in the years after World War II are beginning to bring about the development of new "personality types" among Americans. For Riesman, these personality types cause individuals to act in certain predefined ways and thus contribute to the inability of individual Americans to develop any genuine sense of personal identity. He sees America, at the beginning of the 1950s, as being in the process of a fundamental shift from the dominance of "inner-directed" personality types (who act out of a sense that what they are doing is right) to the dominance of "other-directed" personality types (who act primarily out of the hope that others will approve their action), especially among the affluent middle classes. *The Lonely Crowd* thus becomes an extended warning against creeping conformism, a warning that, in the course of the coming decade, would be echoed again and again by social scientists. At the same time, as his title indicates, Riesman warns that this shift to an emphasis on approval by the Other is fraught with a number of inherent difficulties, including a tendency for individuals to feel inauthentic and inadequate in their quest for approval and to feel alienated from others, who serve not as their fellows but as their judges.

Disney's protagonists, so concerned with fulfilling the roles that are expected of them from birth, would seem to be the ultimate examples of the other-directed personality type. Meanwhile, the authoritarian potential of the spread of other-directed personality types described by Riesman is obvious and can easily be seen as one of the central targets of the rebellious 1960s, with their powerful emphasis on an individualism that would allow each individual to do his or her "own thing," without worrying about approval from authority figures or from the society at large. The decline of Disney in the 1960s thus makes perfect historical sense: clinging to a 1950s version of individualism, Disney's films were simply out of step with a decade that was reacting in so many ways against the 1950s. Then again, Thomas Frank has convincingly argued that we need to be highly suspicious

of the individualist and countercultural impulses of the 1960s, noting
that these impulses served the purposes of American corporate capitalism only too well, opening up lucrative new markets and leading
more to an explosive growth in consumerism than to genuinely subversive political change. Frank demonstrates that American capitalism, largely through images disseminated in television (and other)
advertising, helped to create the widely accepted notions that the
1960s were a time of liberation from the conformist routinization of
the 1950s and that the presumably hip 1960s counterculture was a
"life-affirming opponent of mass society" (14). For Frank, in fact, the
complicity between 1960s consumer capitalism and the counterculture goes far beyond the mere appropriation of the latter by the former. Instead, he argues that the counterculture of the 1960s was
largely *produced* by capitalism, creating new products and new marketing opportunities more than genuinely new social and political
ideas.

Importantly, Frank also notes the extent to which so many ideas of
the 1990s seem to be reinscriptions of the same ideas from the 1960s,
so that it should come as no surprise that the 1960s version of American individualism should also be current in the 1990s. Frank, for
example, argues that the whole notion of "Generation X," so prevalent in the 1990s, was essentially a Madison Avenue creation
designed to link the youth of the 1990s to the youth of the 1960s for
marketing purposes (Frank 233–34). This analysis provides a context
for the particular form of individualism that is central to the Dream-
Works films as a whole, which can then be seen as rooted not only in
the 1990s, but also in the 1960s. From this point of view, Dream-
Works is a reaction against Disney in very much the same way that
the 1960s were a reaction against the 1950s. In any case, Frank's suggestion that the 1960s actually extended the penetration of capitalism
into every aspect of American life helps to indicate the way in which,
from the 1950s to the end of the twentieth century, individual lives
were controlled more and more firmly by capitalism, rather than the
reverse, so that the hip new individualism espoused by the Dream-
Works films needs to be viewed with considerable suspicion that they
are a source not of oppositional ideas but of perfectly mainstream
ones.

This view would also align the DreamWorks films much more
directly with the countercultural ideas of the 1960s than the Disney

films align, despite Brode's arguments that Disney was a crucial component in the historical rise of the 1960s counterculture. In any case,
Frank's argument would suggest that, even if Disney were to be
thought of as ideologically aligned with the counterculture, that would
in no way contradict the widespread notion that Disney's films are
steeped in white middle-class American capitalist values, with a hint
of medieval nostalgia thrown in as a sort of smoke screen. Indeed,
building on the work of Frank, Joseph Heath and Andrew Potter have
convincingly argued that the whole idea of "counterculture" is perfectly consistent with and supportive of consumer capitalism. Heath
and Potter describe the counterculture in ways that seem much more
suggestive of the DreamWorks films than of the classic films of Disney. For example, they note that "coolness" (a phenomenon one
would certainly associate more with DreamWorks films such as *Shrek*
than with the classic Disney films) is a key component of most conceptions of counterculture, which for them means that cool is a thoroughly consumerist notion, with the nonconformist emphasis of
coolness simply meaning that, in order to be cool, one must attempt
to do "whatever other people are *not* doing," which in modern consumer society usually means staying just ahead of the curve by pur-
chasing the newest and most innovative products (or seeing the
newest films), which of course then immediately become the most
popular products.

However, Heath and Potter differ from those who would see the
promotion of coolness simply as a Madison Avenue marketing strategy that manipulates the population into incessant consuming in the
never-ending quest to be cool. For them, cool is "the central status hi-
erarchy in contemporary urban society," essentially playing the role
in late capitalism that class had played in capitalism's earlier classic
phase (191). Further, they note that cool operates according to a
strictly binary logic: either something (or someone) is cool, or it isn't.
Thus, "the rise of cool as the central status system of the counterculture represents nothing short of the society-wide triumph of the logic
of high school" (192).

This last comment reminds us that the concept of cool (as it functions in the early twenty-first century) emanates far more from recent
youth culture than from, say, the beat culture of the 1950s, which is
so often associated with the concept. I have been concerned in this
volume primarily with the film-viewing experience of children

roughly in the age range three to ten, and thus of children who are younger than the teenagers who are generally associated with youth culture in this sense. Still, there is no firm and fixed boundary between children's culture and youth culture; each influences the other and both surely make a contribution to what our culture defines as cool, even as our accepted definition of cool makes a major contribution to the kinds of children's culture that our society produces. Children's film is thus both a reflection of the mainstream values of our society and constitutive of those values, which are to an extent constantly in flux, continual change and innovation being a basic and inviolable tenet of consumer capitalism.

Of course, the sorts of changes that might be worked by children's films are largely superficial, matters of style, while the basic substance of capitalism remains unchallenged. If, in the early twenty-first century, Disney's children's films still largely reflect the individualist ideology of the 1950s, while DreamWorks's children's films still largely reflect the individualist ideology of the 1960s, then it is clear that certain fundamental attitudes change, at best, very slowly over time. That it took thirty years for children's film to catch up with the 1960s, reflecting the attitudes of that decade only in their reinscribed version in the 1990s, only serves to show just how slowly things often move in that risk-averse industry.

In addition, while the representation of individualism in American children's films might have changed slowly over time, it is still the case that such films continue to promote individualism as a central and unchallenged value, presenting it as a sort of commonsense virtue that surely no one could possibly dispute—except, of course, for some of the villains in the films. Moreover, while children's films present any number of images of illegitimate authority figures who should not be obeyed simply because they are in authority (think all those evil stepparents in Disney, General Mandible in *Antz*, or Farquaad in the first *Shrek* film), American children's films as a whole counsel obedience to authority in the abstract, especially if legitimate figures of authority are put in place. Even in the recent *Monsters vs. Aliens*, in which all authority figures are represented as buffoons, the heroic monsters of the title obey the basic dictates of an authority that had earlier unjustly imprisoned them. They triumph by doing so—even if it might have made more sense for them to make common cause with the aliens as the enemies of earthly (or at least American) authority.

Very seldom do children's films present images of collective action that might be interpreted as even remotely political. Such images are, in fact, so rare that, when *The Ant Bully* presented motifs that could be interpreted in this way, it brought forth nearly hysterical cries that it was purveying communist sympathies, even as late as 2006, when anticommunist hysteria had largely subsided as a crucial element of American political rhetoric. While children's films frequently tout the importance of working together with others, they tend to do so in very personal terms, such as helping out one's friends (e.g., *Madagascar* or *Cars*) or banding together with one's family (e.g., *Ratatouille* or *Over the Hedge*), however unconventional that family might be.

Partly because of the political potency of the idea of "family values" in recent American public life and partly because families are envisioned as the chief audiences for the films, the promotion of such values has become one of the central projects of American children's films in recent years. Thus, even an outsider like Shrek can become acceptable as long as he settles down, marries, and has children. But the modern nuclear family is actually more an individualist institution than a group one; it is the place where children learn to think of the social world as a matter of "us" (the family) vs. "them" (everyone else), not to mention the fact that it is the principal carrier of patriarchal ideas and the chief source of ideological indoctrination (Althusser views it as a key "Ideological State Apparatus") and class identity ("we," our family, are this kind of people with this kind of expectations). There is certainly some virtue in the way recent films (including and maybe even especially Disney films) have suggested that viable family units need not necessarily include two parents of opposite sexes, together with their mutual biological offspring. But the basic notion of family (as a collection of individuals comprising some parent-child combination) remains not only unchallenged but actively promoted. Even when groups not consisting of parents and children are represented as functioning well together, they are nevertheless typically reinscribed in terms of family. Thus, the traveling group of animals in the *Ice Age* films works because it operates *like* a family, even if it isn't literally one. Even Pixar's WALL-E, a robot with no family per se, finds true love and seems poised to begin a new family unit with his EVE, while the decay of the family unit seems to be a key sign of the dehumanization of the passengers aboard the *Axiom* in that film.

The promotion of family values is about the most uncontroversial move possible in contemporary American culture, and the centrality of such values to the messages embedded in American children's films is indicative of the way such films attempt to avoid any potentially controversial material, even if children's culture is such a sensitive realm that controversy sometimes arises nonetheless. This sensitivity places a severe limitation on the kinds of political messages that children's films can deliver, even if the attitudes conveyed by children's films, partly as a result of this fear of controversy, do tend to be a bit more liberal, humane, and tolerant than is our society as a whole. In general, I think it is safe to say that parents who wish their children to adopt the mainstream values of American society (with a slight dash of extra tolerance and humanity) can feel confident that pretty much any major American children's film will serve the purpose of conveying these values, though newer films are of course likely to convey more up-to-date versions of these values than are older ones. For parents who wish their children to question the mainstream values of American capitalist society, the very fact that children's films are central repositories of these values can make them useful as well, simply because they provide examples of the sorts of ideas that children need to learn to challenge in order to become creative and independently thinking individuals. In this case, though, the onus is on parents who must watch and think through the films with their younger children, asking the kinds of questions that children eventually need to learn to ask for themselves as they grow older. Thus, learning to resist the messages inherent in children's films can potentially provide children with some of the tools they will need to become resistant readers of the cultural messages with which they will be bombarded the rest of their lives. Children's films themselves seldom promote this kind of critical viewing, even if they routinely pay lip service to the value of independence and imagination. There are cases (such as the challenge to Disney in the *Shrek* films) in which children's films present examples of overt challenges to cultural authority. Even in these cases, though, a certain amount of parental support is needed in order for younger children to understand just what is being challenged and why.

Of course, teaching children in the U.S. to be resistant readers of children's films is no mean task, partly because most of the signals they will receive from society around them reinforce, rather than challenge, the views embedded in the films. Also, many American children's films can be quite effective as works of art, aesthetically fascinating and potentially enthralling to young viewers. They are thus difficult to resist, both because they are themselves so powerful and because most parents (myself included) would not want to deny their children the experience of interesting works of art. I *want* my children to enjoy and appreciate works of art such as *Dumbo, The Nightmare before Christmas, Shrek*, and *WALL-E*, even if I don't want them to accept without question the messages conveyed in these films. This dilemma, of course, adheres in American popular culture as a whole, often carrying insidious messages but also often extremely well-made and aesthetically interesting. Children's films can thus prepare children to be consumers of a wider range of American popular culture as they get older. However, whether these films prepare children to be ideal consumers or whether they prepare them to be resistant readers will be decided on a case-by-case basis, with parents playing a crucial role in the outcome.

Notes

PERSONAL PROLOGUE

1. For an excellent discussion of some of the political motivations (mostly from the right, but sometimes from the left as well) behind recent antiyouth rhetoric in American culture, see Grossberg.

2. If one is interested in precise definitions, American "children's films" are probably almost all best viewed as "family films" because they are so concerned with commercial appeal, which generally requires an ability to entertain adult audiences, as well as children. See Bazalgette and Staples for a discussion of the distinction between American family films and European films that are more properly considered as children's films.

3. See my book *Postmodern Hollywood* for a fuller discussion of those tendencies.

CHAPTER 1

1. See my book *Red, White, and Spooked* for an extended discussion of the way this rationalization of existence has contributed to the prominence of supernatural motifs in modern American culture.

2. The Oz story has remained popular fodder for Hollywood film through the decades, including a 1978 screen adaptation (with an all-African-American cast) of the Broadway musical version of the original book. Follow-up films for children include the animated sequel *Journey Back to Oz* (1974, featuring Judy Garland's daughter Liza Minelli as the voice of Dorothy) and the live-action sequel *Return to Oz* (1985).

3. Interestingly, *Toy Story* only comes in sixth in the AFI's recent list of the ten greatest animated films of all time, ranking behind not only *Snow White*, but also *Pinocchio, Bambi, The Lion King*, and *Fantasia*, in that order. All of the top five films, significantly, are Disney films, and nine of the ten on the list (*Shrek* comes in at eighth) are either Disney or Pixar films.

4. Note that Baum's book had earlier been adapted (very loosely) to screen via the silent film of the same title in 1925, though that version seems less aimed at children than is the 1939 version.

5. *The Blue Bird* resembles *The Wizard of Oz* in numerous ways: seeking the Blue Bird of happiness, Temple's Mytyl has sometimes-perilous adventures in full-color magical lands after an opening domestic sequence in black and white; she then returns, having learned that home is the best place to seek happiness. It's a dull and dated film, perhaps interesting mostly because of the retrospective oddity of its German setting and anti-war theme, given that the film was produced while World War II was already underway in Europe but while the U.S. had yet to enter the conflict. Still, the dullness of *The Blue Bird* helps to show just how special a film *The Wizard of Oz* really is.

6. Matt Roth sees a more ominous political message in the film, arguing that it is shot through with fascist imagery and ideas. Noting that Walt Disney himself regularly attended meetings of the American Nazi Party while the film was in production, Roth concludes that *Pinocchio* could "very well have served as a Hitler Youth training film" (17). See also Marc Eliot's *Walt Disney: Hollywood's Dark Prince* for a particularly critical examination of Disney's right-wing inclinations.

7. For an excellent discussion of this strike and of the Disney company's determined efforts to break the union that instituted it, see Denning (403–22).

8. In *Bambi II*, the 2006 direct-to-video sequel, the Great Prince plays a more prominent role, learning to overcome his initial awkwardness and to become an effective father to the young Bambi. The film thus reflects changing views of the roles of fathers in child rearing between 1942 and 2006.

9. *Saludos Amigos* (1942) and *The Three Caballeros* (1943), the two films about South American culture that Disney produced during the war at the request of the U.S. government (which hoped to further wartime solidarity between South America and the U.S.), also interwove animated scenes with live-action scenes, though they did not involve technically complex combinations of the two.

10. Disney's lack of respect for the original source might perhaps be seen in the opening title card that acknowledges the source but misspells the original author's name as "Lewis Carrol."

11. Byrne and McQuillan also argue that this wolfhound is portrayed as Jewish; Jews and communists were often linked in the Cold War discourse of the 1950s (99).

12. See my extensive discussion of bourgeois sentimentality in *Ulysses, Capitalism, and Colonialism* (147–68).

13. See Pietz for a discussion of the use, during the Cold War, of Orientalist stereotypes to characterize Soviets and other communists.

14. Granted, this king is voiced by Italian American bandleader Louis Prima, but he sounds black, especially in conjunction with the monkeys. Prima, meanwhile, was closely associated with the black-dominated New Orleans jazz scene and was often compared with Louis Armstrong.

15. It might be noted that this aspect of *Mary Poppins* is well within the mainstream of Disneyfied treatment of the condition of the working class. Recall, for example, the "happy-hearted roustabouts" of *Dumbo* or (even more directly) the happy, singing miners of *Snow White and the Seven Dwarfs*. We know, of course, that mining is traditionally one of the most dangerous, grueling, and underpaid of all professions, yet the dwarfs (who seem to enjoy their work immensely) assure us in one of their songs that "It ain't no trick to get rich quick / If you dig dig dig with a shovel or a pick." Considering the labor activism of the 1930s, that line should have caused widespread outrage even then, but apparently it didn't.

16. In addition to the films, there is no better example of capitalist routinization than the impressive crowd control that reigns in the Disney theme parks, in which the behavior of hordes of visitors, many of them small children, is orchestrated with almost frightening efficiency and precision. Little wonder, then, that the theme parks have received substantial attention from cultural critics. See, for example, the collection edited by Klugman, et al.

CHAPTER 2

1. *The Computer Wore Tennis Shoes* was successful enough that it spawned two sequels, both also featuring Russell: *Now You See Him, Now You Don't* (1972) and *The Strongest Man in the World* (1975).

2. Magically animated objects appear in many Disney films, a motif that is acknowledged particularly directly in the mostly live-action *Bedknobs and Broomsticks* (1971), in which the lead character is an apprentice witch who is trying to learn the technique of "substitutiary locomotion," that is, the animation of inanimate objects.

3. This theme is also central to *The Brave Little Toaster Goes to Mars* (1998), the second of two largely unremarkable straight-to-video sequels of the original *The Brave Little Toaster*. Here, the intrepid appliances travel to

Mars to save the infant son of the now grown-up-and-married Master, who has (accidentally, it turns out) been whisked away there. On Mars, they encounter a society of rogue appliances who have escaped from earth to avoid the planned obsolescence that was part of their original design.

4. Among other things, the popular Reese, a white Southerner, was one of the chief supporters of Jackie Robinson when the latter broke in with the Dodgers as the first African American to play Major League baseball. But Reese was also a fine shortstop and, later, a popular announcer.

5. There is, of course, a double entendre here, suggesting that the wagon can be used not only for transportation, but as a setting for sexual trysts.

6. *The Lion King* has since been surpassed at the domestic box office by *Shrek 2* (2004) and *Finding Nemo* (2003) and at the worldwide box office by *Shrek the Third* (2007) as well. But *The Lion King* remains (and perhaps always will remain) the highest-grossing hand-drawn animated film in history.

7. On the other hand, llamas are described as "haughty" and "aristocratic" in Disney's *Saludos Amigos* (1943), so the transformation might not be all that dramatic.

CHAPTER 3

1. Barbie and G.I. Joe were to have been featured characters as well, but, in an unusually shortsighted move on the part of toymakers Mattel and Hasbro, Pixar was unable to secure the rights to use their images.

2. *Howdy Doody* was canceled in 1960, after a thirteen-year run. The Western genre was itself in decline at that time, though the demise of *Howdy Doody* was also related to the rise of more sophisticated children's entertainment television and not simply to the decline of the Western.

3. Joseph Zornado finds a long legacy of fascistic ideas in Disney films, dating back to what Zornado sees as Walt Disney's own sympathy for Hitler and his Nazi regime (135–69).

4. See, however, Audrey Anton for an argument that *The Incredibles* does not go far enough in denouncing conformity and mediocrity and that, by having the Parrs return to normal at the end, the film fails to endorse the superiority of supers.

5. Ironically, Ranft was killed in a car crash while the film was still in production, providing a stark reminder of one element of car culture that *Cars* omits entirely. *Cars* also chooses not to address the environmental problems to which automobiles have made such a central contribution.

6. From 1971 through 2003, the key seasonal NASCAR trophy was known as the Winston Cup, though the name was changed to the NEXTEL Cup in 2004, as a nod toward corporate sponsorship of the prize.

7. Larry the Cable Guy (real name Daniel Whitney) starred in his own feature film *Larry the Cable Guy: Health Inspector* in 2006. He is one of several comedians (Bill Ingvall and Jeff Foxworthy are the best-known others) who have recently made careers out of lampooning Southern redneck culture, though from a presumably sympathetic point of view. Whitney performs with an affected Southern accent, but is actually from Nebraska.

8. The fire engine Red (Joe Ranft) and the forklift Guido might be considered working vehicles as well, and both are indeed represented as less intelligent than the bulk of the film's characters. Meanwhile, the vehicles who serve most clearly as workers, the cow-tractors and the paving machine Bessie, are both coded as subhuman.

9. The Rust-Eze ads thus echo the Be-Like-Mike ads employed during the 1990s to suggest to impressionable youth that wearing their sneakers would somehow make them resemble basketball superstar Michael Jordan. Tellingly, McQueen sticks out his tongue in moments of extra exertion on the track, just as a protruding tongue while driving to the basket for a soaring slam dunk was one of Jordan's trademarks on the basketball court.

10. The documentary was accompanied by the release of a companion book, Karen Paik's *To Infinity and Beyond!: The Story of Pixar Animation Studios*. See also David Price's *The Pixar Touch* for another example of slick Pixar self-promotion in book form.

11. Compare the near contemporaneous (but little seen) *City of Ember* (2008), in which the remnants of humanity take up residence in an underground city after the surface is decimated, with the plan of returning after 200 years—a plan that is nearly forgotten.

12. One might compare here the minor French/Canadian/Spanish production *Pinocchio 3000* (2004), in which a robot eventually attains humanity in a science fiction rewrite of the Pinocchio story. Interestingly, this film also involves a strong focus on environmental themes, with its basic human versus machine opposition reinforced by an opposition between nature and a dehumanizing drive toward progress and development that threatens to wipe out nature and to make all humans robotic.

13. There are potential complications, however. Though the film ends with an optimistic shot of the countryside around the city, showing it covered with greenery, it is also the case that the returning humans are extremely ill-prepared to start life anew on earth. Captain McCrea, for example, is excited about the prospect of growing pizza plants to provide food for the new settlers.

14. These scenes involve humans, including BNL CEO Shelby Forthright (Fred Willard), from the time before the 700-year sojourn in space, thus providing a contrast that emphasizes the change in the species during that time.

15. WALL-E hardly speaks at all, though he does make a number of expressive noises that are reminiscent of R2-D2. Significantly, the electronic voice effects for both movie robots were designed by the same person, Ben Burtt.

CHAPTER 4

1. Wojcik-Andrews argues that *The Land Before Time* is an overt Christian allegory and that the trip to the Great Valley represents a return to the Garden of Eden. However, the film's presentation of its dinosaur protagonists and their milieu openly endorses the theory of evolution, and the utopian basis of the Great Valley (the availability of plentiful food for all) is primarily economic, rather than religious. If anything, the Great Valley is a sort of socialist utopia where universal affluence allows all of the dinosaurs to share equally in the valley's bounty.

2. White, incidentally, had spurned Disney's attempt to gain the rights to make a film adaptation of his book, apparently fearing that they would do considerable damage to his original.

3. For more on Burton's films within the context of postmodernism, see my *Postmodern Hollywood*.

4. Selick also directed *Coraline* (2009), a film adaptation of Neil Gaiman's novel of the same title, this time with no involvement by Burton. Though it features some interesting 3-D effects, *Coraline* is reminiscent of *The Nightmare before Christmas* in its visual style, but without the energy added by Elfman's music. Here, incidentally, the title character struggles (successfully) to return to her original home after being lured into an alternative spirit world, thus restoring the natural order.

5. Animal experimentation is also crucial to *The Secret of NIMH*, which features hyperintelligent rats made so as a result of equally gruesome lab experiments, conducted at NIMH, which stands for the National Institute of Mental Health, potentially announcing a critique of government-sponsored research programs. Again, however, this motif is essentially dropped in to motivate the plot; a critique of animal experimentation is not a major point of the film.

6. This theme is treated more prominently in Disney's *The Shaggy Dog,* the 2006 remake of Disney's live-action film of the same name from 1959 (with liberal elements from the original's 1976 sequel, *The Shaggy D.A.,* thrown in as well). In the original, a human took the form of a dog via ancient Egyptian magic; in the remake it's illicit genetic experimentation that causes the transformation. The 2006 film is certainly critical of the illegal animal experiments that it portrays, but it also seems to suggest that they are a special case of unusual evil, thus coming up short of a condemnation of animal experimentation in general.

7. For a much more cogent critique that clearly attributes environmental destruction to the effects of excessive capitalist exploitation of the natural environment, see *The Lorax* (1972), an animated musical television adaptation of the 1971 book of the same title by Dr. Seuss.

8. There is no evidence that such an animal ever existed, but of course *Ice Age* is unconcerned with such details, just as it is perfectly happy to introduce a band of ultrastupid dodo birds for comic effect, even though dodos never existed anywhere where they might come into contact with mammoths or saber-toothed cats.

9. Moreover, Scrat had by this time become such a star that the DVD release of *Ice Age: The Meltdown* includes a short film, "No Time for Nuts," devoted to Scrat and his antics. Scrat also appeared in the Fox television series *Family Guy*, promoting *Ice Age: The Meltdown* the week before it opened.

10. The entertaining 1997 Warner animated feature *Cats Don't Dance* suffered a vaguely similar fate, living on via DVD after poor corporate marketing caused it to tank at the box office.

11. The boy here echoes advice given him earlier by McCoppin, who had earlier urged Hogarth not to let himself be defined by others but to be the person he chooses to be.

12. This seemingly incongruous link between the frigid world of Antarctic penguins and the sunny world of surfing culture subsequently became the premise for an entire feature film in the Sony Animation release *Surf's Up* (2007).

13. Actually, the DreamWorks story seems to have had more legs than Kimmel realized. The deal with Paramount expired in 2008, and Dream-Works elected to go its separate way, largely via an influx of cash from Indian conglomerate Reliance ADA Group. Meanwhile, the new company, almost weirdly, entered into an extensive deal to have its films distributed by, of all companies, Disney. However, DreamWorks Animation was not part of the distribution deal and remains essentially an independent entity, though many of the same principals are involved.

14. Zipes suggests that the main plot of the film is derived from one of the Grimm Brothers' fairy tales, "The Young Man Who Went Out in Search of Fear" (227).

15. In *Joe Versus the Volcano*, the title character (played by Tom Hanks) nearly sacrifices himself in a volcano because he believes he is dying anyway; in *Madagascar 2*, Melman retraces the same steps.

16. Stephen Chow's *Kung Fu Hustle* (2004), a martial-arts comedy from Hong Kong, has been noted as a particularly important predecessor to the film, though the engagement with martial-arts film in *Kung Fu Panda* is aimed more at the genre as a whole than at specific examples of it.

17. This type of narrative, of course, appears in cultures worldwide, including in China. Thus, martial arts films such as *Hero* (2002) feature the motif. The particular emphasis on Po as a sort of alienated adolescent, though, seems especially Western.

CONCLUSION

1. Julia Mickenberg makes a similar point, noting that "children's books . . . for the most part, operated below the radar of red-hunters" (*Learning* 4).

2. See Mickenberg's *Learning from the Left* for a survey of radical children's literature in the U.S., especially during the Cold War years. See also the anthology edited by Mickenberg and Philip Nel for some key examples of such literature.

3. Among other things, Brode's claim completely disregards (perhaps out of ignorance) a long and rich legacy of cultural production on the American Left, much of which has, at least since the 1930s, focused on the presentation of multicultural perspectives. As Mickenberg emphasizes throughout her study of American leftist children's literature, much of this production has included children's books designed to critique racism and to promote tolerance for alternative cultural perspectives. My guess is that these leftist cultural traditions have done far more than Disney to establish a climate in which multiculturalism could flourish.

4. The same, to an extent, could be said of Hollywood film in general. See, for example, Thomas Schatz's argument in *The Genius of the System* that, at least during the great studio era from the 1920s to the 1950s, films from given studios tended to have a distinctive style and content that made the studio, more than the director, the most important authorial force for each film. In the 1960s and beyond, the prevalence of such studio styles diminished greatly for mainstream films, but children's films retained more consistency, partly due to the ongoing dominance of Disney.

5. Thus, while one might expect the ideology of the Pixar films to be rooted in the 1990s, Disney's own ideological structure was so firmly in place by this time that it has exercised a lasting influence, becoming the basic ideology of the Pixar films as well, with just a few minor adjustments.

6. The most extensive documentation of Disney's anticommunist activities (including his long association with the FBI as an informant against others in the film industry) can be found in Eliot.

7. See Sammond for an extended historical account of the points of contact between Disney's cultural productions and American child-rearing practices, each of which has influenced the other.

Bibliography

Althusser, Louis. "Ideology and Ideological State Apparatuses." *Lenin and Philosophy and Other Essays*. Trans. Ben Brewster. London: Monthly Review P, 1971. 170–83.

Anton, Audrey. "The Nietzschean Influence in *The Incredibles* and the Sidekick Revolt." *The Amazing Transforming Superhero: Essays on the Revision of Characters in Comic Books, Film, and Television*. Ed. Terrence R. Wandtke. Jefferson, NC: McFarland, 2007. 209–29.

Bazalgette, Cary, and Terry Staples. "Unshrinking the Kids: Children's Cinema and the Family Film." *In Front of the Children: Screen Entertainment and Young Audiences*. Ed. Cary Bazalgette and David Buckingham. London: British Film Institute, 1995. 92–108.

Beauvoir, Simone de. *The Second Sex*. 1949. Trans and ed. H. M. Parshley. New York: Bantam, 1961.

Booker, M. Keith. *Alternate Americas: Science Fiction Film and American Culture*. Westport, CT: Praeger, 2006.

———. *Postmodern Hollywood: What's New in Film and Why It Makes Us Feel So Strange*. Westport, CT: Praeger, 2007.

———. *Red, White, and Spooked: The Supernatural in American Culture*. Westport, CT: Praeger, 2008.

———. *Science Fiction Television*. Westport, CT: Praeger, 2004.

———. Ulysses, *Capitalism, and Colonialism: Reading Joyce after the Cold War*. Westport, CT: Greenwood, 2001.

Brode, Douglas. *From Walt to Woodstock: How Disney Created the Counterculture*. Austin: U of Texas P, 2004.

———. *Multiculturalism and the Mouse: Race and Sex in Disney Entertainment*. Austin: U of Texas P, 2006.

Byrne, Eleanor, and Martin McQuillan. *Deconstructing Disney*. London: Pluto P, 1999.

Dale, Edgar. *How to Appreciate Motion Pictures: A Manual of Motion-Picture Criticism Prepared for High-School Students*. New York: Macmillan, 1938.

Davis, Amy M. *Good Girls and Wicked Witches: Women in Disney's Feature Animation*. Bloomington: Indiana UP, 2007.

Denning, Michael. *The Cultural Front: The Laboring of American Culture in the Twentieth Century*. London: Verso, 1996.

Eliot, Marc. *Walt Disney: Hollywood's Dark Prince*. New York: Carol Communications, 1993.

Forman, Henry James. *Our Movie Made Children*. New York: Macmillan, 1934.

Frank, Thomas. *The Conquest of Cool: Business Culture, Counterculture, and the Rise of Hip Consumerism*. Chicago: U of Chicago P, 1997.

Goad, Jim. *The Redneck Manifesto: How Hillbillies, Hicks, and White Trash Became America's Scapegoats*. New York: Simon and Schuster, 1997.

Grossberg, Larry. *Caught in the Crossfire: Kids, Politics, and America's Future*. Boulder, CO: Paradigm, 2005.

Heath, Joseph, and Andrew Potter. *Nation of Rebels: Why Counterculture Became Consumer Culture*. New York: HarperBusiness, 2004.

Hiaasen, Carl. *Team Rodent: How Disney Devours the World*. New York: Ballantine, 1998.

Jameson, Fredric. *Postmodernism, or, The Cultural Logic of Late Capitalism*. Durham, NC: Duke UP, 1991.

Kimmel, Daniel M. *The Dream Team. The Rise and Fall of Dream-Works: Lessons from the New Hollywood*. Chicago: Ivan R. Dee, 2006.

Klugman, Karen, Jane Kuenz, Shelton Waldrop, and Susan Willis, eds. *Inside the Mouse: Work and Play at Disney World*. Durham, NC: Duke UP, 1995.

Leach, William. *Land of Desire: Merchants, Power, and the Rise of a New American Culture*. New York: Vintage-Random House, 1994.

Lears, Jackson. "A Matter of Taste: Corporate Cultural Hegemony in a Mass-Consumption Society." *Recasting America: Culture and Politics in the Age of Cold War*. Ed. Lary May. Chicago: U of Chicago P, 1989. 38–57.

Mickenberg, Julia. *Learning from the Left: Children's Literature, the Cold War, and Radical Politics in the United States*. New York: Oxford UP, 2006.

Mickenberg, Julia, and Philip Nel, eds. *Tales for Little Rebels: A Collection of Radical Children's Literature*. New York: New York UP, 2008.

Murphy, Patrick D. "The Whole Wide World Was Scrubbed Clean: The Androcentric Animation of Denatured Disney." *From Mouse to Mermaid: The Politics of Film, Gender, and Culture*. Ed. Elizabeth Bell, Lynda Haas, and Laura Sells. Bloomington: Indiana UP, 1995. 125–36.

Nadel, Alan. *Containment Culture: American Narratives, Postmodernism, and the Atomic Age*. Durham, NC: Duke UP, 1995.

Paik, Karen. *To Infinity and Beyond!: The Story of Pixar Animation Studios*. San Francisco: Chronicle Books, 2007.

Pietz, William. "The 'Post-Colonialism' of Cold War Discourse." *Social Text* 19–20 (Fall 1988): 55–75.

Price, David A. *The Pixar Touch: The Making of a Company*. New York: Knopf, 2008.

Riesman, David, with Reuel Denney and Nathan Glazer. *The Lonely Crowd: A Study of the Changing American Character*. New Haven, CT: Yale UP, 1950.

Roth, Matt. "A Short History of Disney-Fascism: *The Lion King*." *Jump Cut* 40 (1996): 15–20.

Said, Edward. *Orientalism*. New York: Vintage-Random House, 1979.

Sammond, Nicholas. *Babes in Tomorrowland: Walt Disney and the Making of the American Child, 1930–1960*. Durham, NC: Duke UP, 2005.

Schatz, Thomas. *The Genius of the System: Hollywood Filmmaking in the Studio Era.* New York: Henry Holt, 1988.

Schickel, Richard. *The Disney Version: The Life, Times, and Art of Walt Disney.* 3rd ed. Chicago: Ivan R. Dee, 2007.

Sklar, Robert. *Movie-Made America: A Cultural History of American Movies.* Rev. ed. New York: Vintage-Random House, 1994.

Weber, Max. *The Protestant Ethic and the Spirit of Capitalism.* 1904–1905. Trans. Talcott Parsons. 1930. London: Routledge, 1995.

Whyte, William. *The Organization Man.* New York: Simon and Schuster, 1956.

Wojcik-Andrews, Ian. *Children's Films: History, Ideology, Pedagogy, Theory.* New York: Garland, 2000.

Zipes, Jack. *Breaking the Magic Spell: Radical Theories of Folk and Fairy Tales.* Revised and expanded edition. Lexington: UP of Kentucky, 2002.

Zornado, Joseph L. *Inventing the Child: Culture, Ideology, and the Story of Childhood.* New York: Routledge, 2006.

Films Cited

The Absent-Minded Professor (Dir. Robert Stevenson, 1961)

A.I. Artificial Intelligence (Dir. Steven Spielberg, 2001)

Aladdin (Dir. Ron Clements and John Musker, 1992)

Alice in Wonderland (Dir. Clyde Geronimi, Wilfred Jackson, and Hamilton Luske, 1951)

Alice in Wonderland (Dir. Tim Burton, 2010)

Alien (Dir. Ridley Scott, 1979)

Anastasia (Dir. Don Bluth and Gary Goldman, 1997)

The Ant Bully (Dir. John A. Davis, 2006)

Antz (Dir. Eric Darnell and Tim Johnson, 1998)

Atlantis: The Lost Empire (Dir. Gary Trousdale and Kirk Wise, 2001)

Attack of the 50 Foot Woman (Dir. Nathan Juran, 1958)

Babe (Dir. Chris Noonan, 1995)

Back to the Future (Dir. Robert Zemeckis, 1985)

Bambi (Dir. David Hand, 1942)

Bambi II (Dir. Brian Pimental, 2006)

Batman (Dir. Tim Burton, 1989)

Batman Returns (Dir. Tim Burton, 1991)

Bedknobs and Broomsticks (Dir. Robert Stevenson, 1971)

Bee Movie (Dir. Steve Hickner and Simon J. Smith, 2007)

Beetlejuice (Dir. Tim Burton, 1988)

Big Trouble in Little China (Dir. John Carpenter, 1986)

The Black Cauldron (Dir. Ted Berman and Richard Rich, 1985)

The Black Hole (Dir. Gary Nelson, 1979)

Blade Runner (Dir. Ridley Scott, 1982)

The Blob (Dir. Irvin S. Yeaworth, Jr., 1959)

The Blue Bird (Dir. Walter Lang, 1940)

Bolt (Dir. Byron Howard and Chris Williams, 2008)

The Brave Little Toaster (Dir. Jerry Rees, 1986)

The Brave Little Toaster Goes to Mars (Dir. Robert C. Ramirez, 1998)

Brother Bear (Dir. Aaron Blaise and Robert Walker, 2003)

Bugs Bunny's Third Movie: 1001 Rabbit Tales (Dir. Friz Freleng, Chuck Jones, and Robert McKimson, 1982)

A Bug's Life (Dir. John Lasseter and Andrew Stanton, 1998)

Cars (Dir. John Lasseter and Joe Ranft, 2006)

The Cat from Outer Space (Dir. Norman Tokar, 1978)

Cats Don't Dance (Dir. Mark Dindal, 1997)

Charlie and the Chocolate Factory (Dir. Tim Burton, 2005)

Charlotte's Web (Dir. Charles A. Nichols and Iwao Takamoto, 1973)

Charlotte's Web (Dir. Gary Winick, 2006)

Chicken Little (Dir. Mark Dindal, 2005)

Chicken Run (Dir. Peter Lord and Nick Park, 2000)

Chitty Chitty Bang Bang (Dir. Ken Hughes, 1968)

Cinderella (Dir. Clyde Geronimi, Wilfred Jackson, and Hamilton Luske, 1950)

Close Encounters of the Third Kind (Dir. Steven Spielberg, 1977).

Commando (Dir. Mark L. Lester, 1985)

The Computer Wore Tennis Shoes (Dir. Robert Butler, 1969)

Coraline (Dir. Henry Selick, 2009)

The Corpse Bride (Dir. Tim Burton, 2005)

Crouching Tiger, Hidden Dragon (Dir. Ang Lee, 2000)

Davy Crockett, King of the Wild Frontier (Dir. Norman Foster, 1955).

Davy Crockett and the River Pirates (Dir. Norman Foster, 1956).

The Day the Earth Stood Still (Dir. Robert Wise, 1951)

Dinosaur (Dir. Eric Leighton and Robert Zondag, 2000)

Doc Hollywood (Dir. Michael Caton-Jones, 1991)

La Dolce Vita (Dir. Federico Fellini, 1960)

Dr. Seuss' Horton Hears a Who! (Dir. Jimmy Hayward and Steve Martino, 2008)

Dr. Seuss' How the Grinch Stole Christmas (Dir. Ron Howard, 2000)

Dumbo (Dir. Ben Sharpsteen, 1941)

Edward Scissorhands (Dir. Tim Burton, 1990)

8 1/2 (Dir. Federico Fellini, 1963)

The Emperor's New Groove (Dir. Mark Dindal, 2000)

Enemy Mine (Dir. Wolfgang Petersen, 1985)

E.T. the Extra-Terrestrial (Dir. Steven Spielberg, 1982).

Fantasia (Dir. James Algar, et al., 1940)

FernGully: The Last Rainforest (Dir. Bill Kroyer, 1992)

Finding Nemo (Dir. Andrew Stanton and Lee Unkrich, 2003)

Flashdance (Dir. Adrian Lyne, 1983)

Flushed Away (Dir. David Bowers and Sam Fell, 2006)

The Fox and the Hound (Dir. Ted Berman, Richard Rich, and Art Stevens, 1981)

Frankenweenie (Dir. Tim Burton, 1984)

From Here to Eternity (Dir. Fred Zinnemann, 1953)

Gerald McBoing-Boing (Dir. Robert Cannon, 1951)

Ghidora, the Three-Headed Monster (Dir. Ishiro Honda, 1965)

The Gnome-Mobile (Dir. Francis Ford Coppola, 1967)

The Godfather: Part II (Dir. Francis Ford Coppola, 1974)

The Goonies (Dir. Richard Donner, 1985)

The Graduate (Dir. Mike Nichols, 1967)

The Great Mouse Detective (Dir. Ron Clements, Burny Mattinson, David Michener, and John Musker, 1986)

Gremlins (Dir. Joe Dante, 1984)

Happy Feet (Dir. George Miller, Warren Coleman, and Judy Morris, 2006)

Harriet the Spy (Dir. Bronwen Hughes, 1996)

Harry and the Hendersons (Dir. William Dear, 1987)

Heaven's Gate (Dir. Michael Cimino, 1980)

Hellboy (Dir. Guillermo del Toro, 2004)

Hello, Dolly! (Dir. Gene Kelly, 1969)

Herbie: Fully Loaded (Dir. Angela Robinson, 2005)

Hercules (Dir. Ron Clements and John Musker, 1997)

Hero (Dir. Yimou Zhang, 2002)

Honey, I Shrunk the Kids (Dir. Joe Johnston, 1989)

Hook (Dir. Steven Spielberg, 1991)

Hotel for Dogs (Dir. Thor Freudenthal, 2009)

The Hunchback of Notre Dame (Dir. Gary Trousdale and Kirk Wise, 1996)
Ice Age (Dir. Chris Wedge and Carlos Saldanha, 2002)
Ice Age: The Meltdown (Dir. Carlos Saldanha, 2006)
The Incredible Shrinking Man (Dir. Jack Arnold, 1957)
The Incredibles (Dir. Brad Bird, 2004)
Invaders from Mars (Dir. William Cameron Menzies, 1953)
The Iron Giant (Dir. Brad Bird, 1999)
It Happened One Night (Dir. Frank Capra, 1934)
James and the Giant Peach (Dir. Henry Selick, 1996)
Jaws (Dir. Steven Spielberg, 1975)
Joe Versus the Volcano (Dir. John Patrick Shanley, 1990)
Joseph: King of Dreams (Dir. Robert LaDuca and Robert C. Ramirez, 2000)
Journey Back to Oz (Dir. Hal Sutherland, 1974)
The Jungle Book (Dir. Wolfgang Reitherman, 1967)
The Karate Kid (Dir. John G. Avildsen, 1984)
A Knight's Tale (Dir. Brian Helgeland, 2001)
Kung Fu Hustle (Dir. Stephen Chow, 2004)
Kung Fu Panda (Dir. Mark Osborne and John Stevenson, 2008)
Lady and the Tramp (Dir. Clyde Geronimi, Wilfred Jackson, and Hamilton Luske, 1955)
The Land Before Time (Dir. Don Bluth, 1988)
Larry the Cable Guy: Health Inspector (Dir. Trent Cooper, 2006)
Lemony Snicket's A Series of Unfortunate Events (Dir. Brad Silberling, 2004)
Lilo & Stitch (Dir. Dean DeBlois and Chris Sanders, 2002)
The Lion King (Dir. Roger Allers and Rob Minkoff, 1994)
The Lion King II: Simba's Pride (Dir. Darrell Rooney and Rob LaDuca, 1998)
The Little Mermaid (Dir. Ron Clements and John Musker, 1989)
Looney Tunes: Back in Action (Dir. Joe Dante, 2003)
The Lorax (Dir. Hawley Pratt, 1972)
The Love Bug (Dir. Robert Stevenson, 1968)
Madagascar (Dir. Eric Darnell and Tom McGrath, 2005)
Madagascar: Escape 2 Africa (Dir. Eric Darnell and Tom McGrath, 2008)
Mary Poppins (Dir. Robert Stevenson, 1964)
McCabe and Mrs. Miller (Dir. Robert Altman, 1971)

Meet the Robinsons (Dir. Stephen J. Anderson, 2007)

Monsters, Inc. (Dir. Pete Docter, David Silverman, and Lee Unkrich, 2001)

Monsters vs. Aliens (Dir. Rob Letterman and Conrad Vernon, 2009)

Mulan (Dir. Tony Bancroft and Barry Cook, 1998)

NeverEnding Story (Dir. Wolfgang Petersen, 1984)

The Nightmare before Christmas (Dir. Henry Selick, 1993)

North by Northwest (Dir. Alfred Hitchcock, 1959)

Now You See Him, Now You Don't (Dir. Robert Butler, 1972)

Old Yeller (Dir. Robert Stevenson, 1957)

Oliver and Company (Dir. George Scribner, 1988)

Once Upon a Forest (Dir. Charles Grosvenor, 1993)

One Hundred and One Dalmatians (Dir. Clyde Geronimi, Hamilton Luske, and Wolfgang Reitherman, 1961)

Open Season (Dir. Roger Allers, Jill Culton, and Anthony Stacchi, 2006)

Over the Hedge (Dir. Tom Johnson and Karey Kirkpatrick, 2006)

Pee-wee's Big Adventure (Dir. Tim Burton, 1985)

Peter Pan (Dir. Clyde Geronimi, Wilfred Jackson, and Hamilton Luske, 1953)

Pinocchio (Dir. Hamilton Luske and Ben Sharpsteen, 1940)

Pinocchio 3000 (Dir. Daniel Robichaud, 2004)

Pinocchio in Outer Space (Dir. Ray Goosens, 1965)

Planet of the Apes (Dir. Franklin J. Schaffner, 1968)

Pocahontas (Dir. Mike Gabriel and Eric Goldberg, 1995)

The Prince of Egypt (Dir. Brenda Chapman, Steve Hickner, and Simon Wells, 1998)

Queen of Outer Space (Dir. Edward Bernds, 1958)

Raiders of the Lost Ark (Dir. Steven Spielberg, 1981)

Ratatouille (Dir. Brad Bird and Jan Pinkava, 2007)

Return to Oz (Dir. Walter Murch, 1985)

The Road to El Dorado (Dir. Eric "Bilbo" Bergeron, et al., 2000)

Robots (Dir. Chris Wedge and Carlos Saldanha, 2005)

The Rocky Horror Picture Show (Dir. Jim Sharman, 1975)

The Running Man (Dir. Paul Michael Glaser, 1987)

Salt of the Earth (Dir. Herbert J. Biberman, 1954)

Saludos Amigos (Dir. Anon., 1942)

The Secret of NIMH (Dir. Don Bluth, 1982)

The Shaggy D.A. (Dir. Robert Stevenson, 1976)

The Shaggy Dog (Dir. Charles Barton, 1959)

The Shaggy Dog (Dir. Brian Robbins, 2006)

Shark Tale (Dir. Bilbo Bergeron, Vicky Jensen, and Rob Letterman, 2004)

Short Circuit (Dir. John Badham, 1986)

Shrek (Dir. Andrew Adamson and Vicky Jensen, 2001)

Shrek 2 (Dir. Andrew Adamson, Kelly Asbury, and Conrad Vernon, 2004)

Shrek the Third (Dir. Chris Miller and Raman Hui, 2007)

Sinbad: Legend of the Seven Seas (Dir. Patrick Gilmore and Tim Johnson, 2003)

Sleeping Beauty (Dir. Clyde Geronimi, 1959)

Snow White and the Seven Dwarfs (Dir. David Hand, 1937)

Son of Flubber (Dir. Robert Stevenson, 1963)

Song of the South (Dir. Harve Foster and Wilfred Jackson, 1946)

Space Jam (Dir. Joe Pytka, 1996)

Spirit: Stallion of the Cimarron (Dir. Kelly Asbury and Lorna Cook, 2002)

Star Trek: The Motion Picture (Dir. Robert Wise, 1979)

Star Wars (Dir. George Lucas, 1977)

The Strongest Man in the World (Dir. Vincent McEveety, 1975)

Surf's Up (Dir. Ash Brannon and Chris Buck, 2007)

Susie, the Little Blue Coupe (Dir. Clyde Geronimi, 1952)

Sweeney Todd: The Demon Barber of Fleet Street (Dir. Tim Burton, 2007)

Swiss Family Robinson (Dir. Ken Annakin, 1960)

The Sword in the Stone (Dir. Wolfgang Reitherman, 1963)

Tarzan (Dir. Chris Buck and Kevin Lima, 1999)

The Terminator (Dir. James Cameron, 1984)

The Thief of Baghdad (Dir. Ludwig Berger, et al., 1940)

The Three Caballeros (Dir. Norman Ferguson, 1943)

Titan A.E. (Dir. Don Bluth and Gary Goldman, 2000)

Tobor the Great (Dir. Lee Sholem, 1954)

Total Recall (Dir. Paul Verhoeven, 1990)

Toy Story (Dir. John Lasseter, 1995)

Toy Story 2 (Dir. John Lasseter, Ash Brannon, and Lee Unkrich, 1999)

Treasure Island (Dir. Byron Haskin, 1950)

Treasure Planet (Dir. Ron Clements and John Musker, 2002)

Tron (Dir. Steven Lisberger, 1982)

20,000 Leagues Under the Sea (Dir. Richard Fleischer, 1954)

2001: A Space Odyssey (Dir. Stanley Kubrick, 1968)

Up (Dir. Pete Docter, 2009)

Vincent (Dir. Tim Burton, 1982)

Wallace and Gromit: The Curse of the Were-Rabbit (Dir. Steve Box and Nick Park, 2005)

WALL-E (Dir. Andrew Stanton, 2008)

Who Framed Roger Rabbit (Dir. Robert Zemeckis, 1988)

The Wild (Dir. Steve Williams, 2006)

Willy Wonka and the Chocolate Factory (Dir. Mel Stuart, 1971)

The Wiz (Dir. Sidney Lumet, 1978)

The Wizard of Oz (Dir. Victor Fleming, 1939)

Young Sherlock Holmes (Dir. Barry Levinson, 1985)

Index

About the Author

M. Keith Booker is the James E. and Ellen Wadley Roper Professor of English and Director of the Program in Comparative Literature and Cultural Studies at the University of Arkansas, Fayetteville. He is the author of numerous books on literature and popular culture.